SUPERVEG

For Amy and Beth

I love you to the old tomato.

Celia Brooks

SuperVeg

OVER 100 RECIPES CELEBRATING THE JOY AND POWER OF THE 25 HEALTHIEST VEGETABLES ON THE PLANET

Photography by Jean Cazals

MURDOCH BOOKS

SYDNEY · LONDON

Contents

The Joy and Power of SuperVeg

Hello reader. I'm so glad you're here. You'll find my unbridled passion for vegetables vibrating through every page of this book, and you are the reason for it. It's laid bare here in words and pictures for you, to inspire you, to enchant you into the kitchen and, most importantly, to feed you and those you love. It will nourish you and enhance your life force with the natural power of the nutrients of vegetables, the elixir of life. Which all adds up to joy.

The Joy

The joy starts here, I hope, with the reading: absorbing my thoughts, experience and passion. It then extends to motivating you to source the vegetables and appreciate their beauty and value in the flesh. Next you'll be engaging with them in the kitchen, and enjoying producing delicious food to share with those you love. The added joyful bonus is that this food has the power to make you feel good and enhance your health.

The Power

Health crazes come and go; scientific research proves and then contradicts; but one truth that is indisputable is this: *plants should make up the bulk of our diet to sustain a healthy life.* Eating plants protects us from the dangers of the environment, as well as the potential for disease already within us, and supports every essential bodily function on a molecular level. The 25 SuperVeg in this volume are the most powerful of all (see more on page 13).

I forged a career in food by accident. All of a sudden, for the first time around age 20, I discovered what a creative process cooking was and I didn't want to do anything else. Vegetables were the first ingredients I fell in love with and have always been at the heart of my obsession. Vegetables are natural, beautiful, creative materials that are fun to transform into delicious food that makes people happy. So, that's what I've been doing for a living for nearly 30 years: cooking, teaching, writing, creating recipes and waxing lyrical about food, mostly vegetables. In the last 12 years I've been growing my own vegetables on a small rented patch of urban land in London, which has extended my vegetable love to a new dimension. My whole experience has been driven and cultivated through authentic passion, and this volume conveys the summation of my vegetable wisdom to date. Long live the SuperVeg, and long may you live too!

Celia Brooks

Vegetables – the elixir of life

Each of us is a miraculously complex and unique bundle of trillions of cells. Each cell is on a coded mission to live, doing its allocated job in harmony with the others. Certain brain cells have the essential job of triggering the excretion of hormones that drive our consciousness towards food. Once we figure out how to breathe air first thing out of the womb, our mother's breast milk is the very next fundamental. We need the nourishment as well as the nurture.

Over time, as we grow, our unique composition develops partly by code, and partly by responding to the environment, to survive. Just as we build our lives and character in relationships with the people who nurture us and who we nurture, we build a relationship with food because it nurtures us daily. We are irrepressibly driven to it and, if we are fortunate, we are able to make choices that satiate our hunger according to our desires. Ideally, we develop a loving relationship with food, just as ideally we boundlessly love our nearest and dearest, but relationships are complicated.

STRENGTH + PROTECTION = FITNESS FOR SURVIVAL

Winning the battle of biological survival depends on being the fittest, based on two core strengths: A) the ability to fight and B) good protection. Fulfilling our cells' demands so that we function enables the warrior within. Our protective armour works against outside factors to defeat the enemy – disease. We are constantly bombarded with toxins, bacteria and viruses that threaten us, and we must keep on the right side of vulnerable every day of our lives, until we finally and inevitably succumb.

What we eat is the crucial essence of both core strengths, and makes us either well adapted or at risk. A core maintained mostly on plant foods gives us an advantage. Plants provide inner strength and balance in the form of carbohydrates, vitamins, minerals, fats, fibre and even protein. While it is possible to attain all the necessary protein for a healthy diet from plant foods alone (nuts, seeds, beans and legumes), non-vegans will supplement their protein intake with animal products such as dairy, eggs, fish and meat. For the defensive armour, plants are the best food source of all, providing phytonutrients (phyto = plant). These nutrients are not essential for us to function, but they are essential for defence. They endow us with the power to fight off disease. Plants produce phytochemicals to fight off predators and pathogens from themselves. When we eat the plants, the chemicals become powerful defensive nutrients for us. Thanks plants!

There are over 25,000 different types of phytonutrients, with many different benefits, including repairing damage inflicted by toxic environmental factors and boosting our immune system, heart health and eyesight. Some are antioxidants, which repair cell damage from free radicals, others are anti-inflammatories, reducing inflammation – the root of most disease, including cancer and heart disease.

Plant foods of course include grains, beans and legumes, but here we are celebrating vegetables, and some fruits that we think of as vegetables. SuperVeg are the 25 greatest vegetables of all for the power of their nutrition, but also for the joy of their flavour and the act of cooking them. See page 13 for the reasons why I selected these 25 SuperVeg.

SUPERVEG SUPERPOWERS

At the beginning of each chapter, there is a nutritional excellence section, highlighting each SuperVeg's most potent power – its superpower – and also which nutrients it has high levels of, both for essential function and for disease prevention. There are many more nutrients provided by each vegetable at good, moderate or trace levels, I have not listed all of these, but they are still wonderful and beneficial.

RAW VS. COOKED

Contrary to popular belief, raw isn't always better when it comes to veg. Some nutrients can be destroyed in cooking, but others become more available through heat exposure. Many vegetables contain both types of nutrients. Just eat vegetables! If they taste really good, we are more likely to eat them, so how they are prepared is somewhat irrelevant.

FIBRE

Fibre is not listed in the nutritional excellence sections because every SuperVeg in this book is a great source of fibre, an essential part of a healthy diet. But guess what? Fibre is not a nutrient – we don't digest it! It moves right through us. It's like a cleaning team for our digestive tract, sweeping out residues that can cause disease. As it makes progress through the system, it regulates our blood sugar levels, which contributes to heart health, prevents diabetes and makes us feel fuller for longer, which can help prevent deadly obesity. Fibre also provides fuel for beneficial gut bacteria, which support our immune defence and are linked to good mental health via the enteric nervous system.

FAITH AND TRUST

Once you grasp the reality of how these SuperVeg can really help you live a longer and better life, I hope you will be inspired to eat more of them, experiencing their joy and power every day.

I have enlisted a qualified nutritionist, Alli Godbold Dip ION mBANT CNHC, to fact-check all the nutritional information in this book so it can be trusted. The recipes have all been thoroughly tested, so they can be relied upon to work for you too.

ADDITIONAL HIGH-PERFORMANCE VEGETABLES FOR NUTRITION

The following vegetables are either primarily used as supplements and garnishes in dishes or were outdone by another vegetable on some other front in selecting the 25 finalists, but they are certainly super for nutrients. Many are included throughout the book, playing supporting roles. By all means include these vegetables in your diet whenever possible too:

SPROUTED BEANS Such as chickpeas, lentils, adzuki and mung beans.

ALFALFA SPROUTS AND OTHER SPROUTED SEEDS Such as radish, broccoli, sunflower, mustard and cress.

Note: These are easy to sprout at home – all you need is a large jar and some paper towels – try it!

BEAN SPROUTS (LONG-SPROUTED MUNG BEANS)

LEAFY HERBS Especially parsley.

MICRO LEAVES Such as chard, pea shoots and kale.

MICRO HERBS Such as basil, coriander (cilantro) and amaranth.

SEAWEED

WILD FORAGED SEASONAL LEAVES Such as sorrel, nettles, dandelion leaves, chickweed and ground elder – get yourself an identification manual for your local area.

RADISHES, SWEDE (RUTABAGA), TURNIPS AND ROCKET (ARUGULA) Plus any other member of the highly esteemed brassica (cabbage) family.

GREEN BEANS AND ALL POD BEANS Such as snow peas (mangetout) and sugar snaps.

Note: Most beans and legumes I left out of the SuperVeg selection process completely, as they are a special category unto themselves – but they feature prominently in my recipes. The one exception I made is for peas. Peas belong in the realm of SuperVeg. Read why in *Peas* on page 230.

The SuperVeg kitchen – tools and ingredients

There are a few tools and cupboard ingredients I highly recommend that are used regularly in this book. Obviously I love cooking so much that I have devoted my entire life to it, but I still like to take it easy. I love shortcuts and time-saving tricks. Certain pure, high-quality 'convenience foods' in tins and packets are a godsend. I also adore efficient tools that make cooking joyful and stress-free. I love it when cooking a dish delivers a result that exceeds the effort I put in. It's domestic magic.

ESSENTIAL TOOLS

CHEF'S KNIFE Your BFF, in tandem with an easy-to-use sharpener.

PARING KNIFE For small fiddly jobs.

CHOPPING BOARDS I use a set of cheap, thin, plastic cutting mats that go in the dishwasher. They're convenient, hygienic and easy to store. I replace them every 6 months.

PEELERS Not just for peeling, both a swivel peeler with a vertical blade and a Y-peeler with a horizontal blade are good to have. The latter can also be used for making thin, flat ribbons of carrots, cucumbers, etc. A julienne tool is handy for making elegant thin ribbons.

GRATERS A sturdy box grater for vegetables along with a fine microplane for zesting lemons and grating nutmeg and hard cheese such as Parmesan.

SPIRALIZER I use a small handheld one for making spaghetti strands of raw zucchini (courgette), summer squash and carrots.

SCISSORS Sometimes scissor snipping is easier than knife chopping, especially for watercress, English spinach and chives.

MORTAR AND PESTLE I can't live without my large, heavy-duty granite one from Thailand, which I got in a Chinese grocery shop. Heft is key for crushing power. This is going with me to my desert island, even if it does sink the ship!

CITRUS SQUEEZER An ingenious gadget with two hinged cups that forces maximum juice out of half a lemon/lime with no seeds.

MIXING BOWLS Plastic and stainless steel; lots of different stackable sizes.

DIGITAL SCALES A good-quality set of digital scales are compact, and reliable when it comes to accuracy.

GOOD-QUALITY NON-STICK FRYING PANS One 24 cm (9½ inches) and one 28 cm (11¼ inches).

CASSEROLE DISHES Several of the recipes are baked in a rectangular oven-to-table casserole dish measuring approx. 20 x 30 cm (8 x 12 inches). I also use a ceramic oval dish with a similar capacity, and a round dish about 25–28 cm (10–11¼ inches) in diameter.

BAKING TRAYS A couple of large and a couple of small – flat with a shallow edge.

NON-STICK FOIL/BAKING PAPER The advent of non-stick foil has been a blessing – I use it to line just about every oven tray, mostly to save on washing up. I love how it moulds to the pan and stays put. If you can't find it, use non-stick baking paper instead.

ZIP-SEAL PLASTIC STORAGE BAGS Both large and small are super handy, not just for storing veg and leftovers in the fridge and freezer, but also for coating veg in various ways (as noted in recipes) and smashing things without making a mess.

DISPOSABLE PLASTIC OR LATEX GLOVES Mostly useful for handling chillies and beetroots (beets).

BLENDER
A hand blender or immersion blender is an inexpensive and indispensable tool, especially for puréeing soups directly in the cooking pot. A standing blender or a high-powered, bullet-type blender is also useful. A food processor is also used occasionally in this book, but is not essential. That said, it can make very quick work of

roughly chopping or grating vegetables. If you fall in love with vegetables the way I have, it can be very handy to have.

MICROWAVE I believe the microwave to be a valuable tool for certain jobs, especially for quickly steaming vegetables, for heating pre-cooked grains and reheating leftovers. It's a machine that vibrates water molecules in food to create heat. Most vegetables have a high water content and respond well to microwave cooking when properly calculated. Specific instructions are given in the book where appropriate.

REAL CONVENIENCE FOODS

TINNED BEANS I always stock chickpeas, butter beans, black beans and kidney beans. Soaking dried beans overnight and then boiling them is something I rarely do anymore.

PRE-COOKED LENTILS AND GRAINS Modern technology has finally delivered us perfectly good, ready-to-eat, healthy wholegrains and lentils that are widely available in long-life sealed packets. Avoid fancy flavourings and go for the basic, naked types that can save you time and effort. I stock quinoa and wholegrain rice, plus puy lentils and black 'beluga' lentils. Unused portions can be frozen, then thawed or reheated in a microwave.

QUICK-COOK POLENTA I don't recommend ready-cooked polenta, but the dry cornmeal labelled 'instant' or 'quick-cook' is ready in less than 5 minutes, as opposed to the traditional type, which requires about 30–40 minutes of perpetual stirring.

COUSCOUS The quickest carb to cook from dry. Definitely seek out wholegrain or barley couscous for nutrient value, as white couscous is basically just refined pasta.

BURGHUL (BULGUR) WHEAT The next quickest wholegrain – boil with a 2:1 salted water : burghul ratio for 10 minutes or until absorbed.

CHESTNUTS Cooked and peeled, from a tin or vacuum pack.

VEG STOCK I buy stock powder, which is easier to use than cubes. Often I will make a fresh stock, or save vegetable cooking or steaming water in a plastic bag and freeze it. Otherwise the stock powder comes in very handy.

MISO This nutritious Japanese soya bean paste functions as an instant stock or flavour foundation for so many things. I also use it as a salty spread for buttered toast, like Marmite. I buy both white sweet miso and dark and they keep in the fridge for several weeks after opening.

RUNNY HONEY AND PURE MAPLE SYRUP I mostly use these in place of granulated sugar for balancing sweetness in savoury dishes – they are easy to blend and have rich flavour notes, plus they are the healthiest option. I always opt for squeezy bottle packaging for both, which minimises sticky messes.

PEPPERMINT TEABAGS For occasions when dried mint is required as a herb, it tastes best from tea bags – just snip one open and empty the contents.

The 25 SuperVeg

Why I selected these 25 SuperVeg

WHAT DID IT TAKE TO MAKE THE CUT? IT WAS A SERIOUSLY TOUGH COMPETITION!

First, I had to narrow down the competition by actually defining a *vegetable* – it's rather ambiguous once you start getting technical. Like determining which sports should participate in the Olympics – is water ballet a sport or an art? After some chin scratching, I went with plants that we perceive as vegetables, rather than their technical status. (Fruits stayed, legumes did not – see opposite and page 9.)

The next round involved evaluating all these vegetables on the POWER of their nutrition – if they generally had a high nutrient density or contained particular health-boosting nutrients in abundance, they were up for the next round. (This stage didn't eliminate very many to be honest! Veg are awesome!)

Next, I evaluated them for the JOY of their versatility, deliciousness and accessibility. Every SuperVeg had to be able to play a central role in a dish. Seaweed, for example, scores top marks for nutrient density, but it's rare you would want it to be the main ingredient in a dish, plus it's not that easy to acquire (unless you are an expert coast-dwelling forager). Ordinary potatoes did not make the cut either, but they are still used in this book – you can read more on that under *Sweet Potato* (page 76).

Kohlrabi is the most esoteric of all the SuperVeg finalists. I'm on a mission to snare it from obscurity! It may not be as widely available as the other SuperVeg, but it should be. Seek it out, and find out why under *Kohlrabi* (page 66).

The 25 SuperVeg are not rated in order.

They are equally super, for different reasons. They are categorised by general botanical type (again not strictly technical, but perceived): *Roots and Bulbs*, *Shoots and Leaves* and *Veggie Fruits*. Most people know that tomatoes and avocados are fruits, not vegetables, but some of the veggies that are technically fruits might come as a surprise. By definition, a fruit is a seed-bearing structure made by a flowering plant. So, pumpkins (winter squashes), eggplants (aubergines) and even pea pods are indeed fruits. Mushrooms are not even plants – but they behave like shoots, so even though they have a 'fruiting body', I put them with the shoots.

Finally, having selected the 25 SuperVeg and positioned them into three balanced categories, I set out to open my mind and create easy, delicious and healthy recipes and ideas for each SuperVeg that make the most of their best assets and prove their brilliance. This is a cookbook, but also my heartfelt homage to the greatest vegetables on earth.

I would need a thousand-page tome (and a couple more years time) to include all the recipes I wanted. At first, I included some desserts. Certain vegetables lend themselves beautifully to sweet dishes. Carrots, zucchini (courgettes) and beetroots (beets) make deliciously moist cakes; avocados make luscious creamy puddings; eggplants can be floured and fried and layered up with melted dark chocolate and raspberry jam into an unbelievably decadent chocolate torte! Seriously! In the end, I felt these recipes were taking space away from healthier everyday dishes, so this collection is the rather brutally harvested cream of the crop.

Roots and Bulbs

Beetroot
Carrot
Celeriac
Fennel
Onion and Garlic
Kohlrabi
Sweet Potato

Beetroot

... its distinctive earthy, sweet flavour
sings the solo in every chorus of flavours.

Beetroot

Beetroot (beet) divides people. I don't think I've ever met a person who is ambivalent about beetroot – it's love it or hate it. Hardly surprising for a food with such an alpha personality: as soon as you cut it, it truly bleeds and wreaks havoc on your hands, tools and work area; its colour dominates any other ingredients that come in contact with it; and its distinctive earthy, sweet flavour sings the solo in every chorus of flavours. Its irrepressibility makes it both irresistible and irritating. Such is the fate of a total prima donna. Who'd have thought a grubby little root could scrub up to be so polarising?

Opinions aside, the beet is a hugely significant food source worldwide for humans and animals, for both its root and greenery. In the mid 1700s a German scientist discovered that a certain white beet contained high levels of sucrose, at a time when world domination was based on trade between empires, and sugar was gold, along with slavery. This led to the breeding of a new plant – a high-sucrose 'Frankenveg': the white sugar beet – specifically for sugar extraction, which could be grown in temperate climates to rival tropical sugar cane, previously the only source of sugar. This was a game-changer. Sugar beet is still a major global cash cow, providing up to 30 percent of the world's refined sugar.

THE NUTRITIONAL SUPERPOWER

Betalains – powerful antioxidants, excellent for heart health, detoxifying the body and protecting from cancer.

OTHER HIGH LEVELS OF NUTRITIONAL EXCELLENCE

- Folate, for cell vitality.
- B-complex vitamins, for converting food into fuel and giving us energy.
- Iron, for blood health.
- Copper, for bone and tissue health.
- Magnesium, for bone health (especially the greens).
- Several other antioxidants (especially the greens) including vitamin A/beta-carotene – anti-cancer, anti-inflammatory and protecting you from toxins.

SEASON

Early summer through winter.

VARIETIES

A chemical compound called geosmin is responsible for the earthy flavour of beetroot – it's also responsible for that lovely smell after a rainfall. There are hundreds of beetroot varieties and some have been bred to minimise geosmin and also to eliminate the magenta assault. Chioggia and Candy beetroot have pink and white stripes, and there are also golden and white varieties.

CHOOSE AND STORE

If the roots have the fresh and lively leaves intact, so much the better as it's a bonus vegetable (see *Ultimate Baked Beetroot and Its Greens*, page 24), and it also means they are very fresh. Freshness is not as crucial for roots as other veg, unless you are able to eat them on the same day they are harvested, which is a supreme flavour experience. Roots by nature store well. Baby beetroots – large cherry size – are rare to find, but beets are best on the small side, anything from golf ball to tennis ball size. If raw, they should always feel hard as a rock. Store in a sealed plastic bag in the fridge in the crisper drawer.

PROCESSED AND PRESERVED

Pre-cooked beets are fine to use, but may have a slightly shallower flavour than fresh. If sold ready baked or roasted, they should still be firm and smell fresh. Vacuum-packed boiled beets are handy and taste fine. Pickled beets are versatile and convenient (being preserved, they keep for ages) when you want that vinegar punch with it (see *Beetroot and Blue Cheese in Witlof Leaves*, page 21, and *Pink Baby Corn Blossoms*, page 163). Beetroot powder is a phenomenal natural colouring agent for desserts such as meringues if you want a hot pink hue.

PREP

- Fresh beetroot should first be scrubbed before trimming. If greens are attached, cut them off just above where the stems meet the root. (See tips on washing greens: *Ultimate Baked Beetroot and Its Greens*, page 24). Before you get a knife near the root you might want to put on plastic gloves to stop your hands getting stained, and choose a non-absorbent chopping board, such as a plastic one.

- It's not essential to peel the roots. If boiling whole, it's important not to cut the roots at all so the colour doesn't leach into the water. Boil until tender, then drain and, when cool enough to handle, the skins will slip off easily (again, wearing gloves for this is advised).

- If roasting beetroots, you can pare off any spindly roots first, then slice, halve or quarter, or leave whole and roast with a slick of oil and some seasoning.

- If using raw, first cut away any spindly roots and shave off the scruff where the leaves were attached, then slice or grate. Again, no need to peel as long as it's well scrubbed.

Beetroot's best mates

Orange | Pineapple | Coconut | Apple | Avocado | Lemon, lime |
Any good-quality vinegar | Honey | Horseradish | Mustard | Chocolate |
Thyme, rosemary, sage | Dill, basil, tarragon | Cumin, coriander seed, clove |
Cream, crème fraîche, yoghurt | Goat's cheese | Blue cheese | Walnuts |
Toasted sesame seeds | White potatoes | Watercress, rocket

Cook and eat

Roasted balsamic beetroot

Toss the prepared roots (see previous page) with olive oil, sea salt and black pepper in a lined baking dish. Drizzle with balsamic vinegar and add a few thyme sprigs, if desired. Bake at 200°C (400°F) until tender throughout.

Smashed fried beetroot

Boil small fresh beetroots in well-salted water with a little vinegar until completely tender, then cool and trim the tops and the root spindles. Place the beetroots one at a time between two sheets of baking paper and crush them until fairly flat but still intact, then gently fry in a little olive oil until crisp on both sides, turning once.

Beetroot and coconut soup

Use pre-cooked beetroot or boil and skin fresh beetroots. Chop and simmer in half veg stock, half coconut milk to cover, and season with lemon juice and zest, ground cumin and crushed garlic, then purée.

PICKLED BEETROOT (BEET) IS A VINTAGE STAPLE, and it's a perfect convenience when all you need is a little beetroot in something for that unique colour, a hint of earthiness and a sweet vinegar tang.

This is a fun little number for guests: a finger salad, all done in a snap. This makes a fairly small quantity, so multiply as necessary. Sans witlof (chicory), the beetroot-cheese mixture makes a lovely spread for bread or crackers, or you could coat a tortilla with a thick layer, roll it up and slice it like sushi for another bit of fun with pink food.

Beetroot and blue cheese in witlof leaves

MAKES 8 NIBBLES | **PREP** 15 MINS | **COOK** 0 MINS

30 MINUTES OR LESS | FEAST DISH | GOOD SOURCE OF PROTEIN | GLUTEN FREE

50 g ($1^3/4$ oz) pickled beetroot (beet), ideally in sweet vinegar, drained and roughly chopped

30 g (1 oz) walnuts, roughly chopped

75 g ($2^1/2$ oz) semi-hard blue cheese, such as Stilton, at room temperature

1 tablespoon Greek-style yoghurt

few twists of freshly ground black pepper

8 white or red witlof (chicory) leaves, roughly the same size

OPTIONS
Serve as a nibble with cocktails or as a side salad as part of a spread of sharing dishes.

SPECIAL EQUIPMENT
None

1 Combine everything except the witlof in a small bowl and mash together with the back of a spoon until evenly combined, though not totally smooth. The cheese should still have some small chunks.

2 Use a heaped teaspoon to place a bite-sized amount of the beetroot-cheese mixture inside the witlof leaves, then serve.

A SIMPLE SALAD OF THREE RAW INGREDIENTS and a dressing here, adding up to more than the sum of its parts. Beetroot (beet) is hard to compete with in a salad – it's such a diva, upstaging everything else on the plate as soon as it shifts, releasing its tyranny of pigment and earthy sweetness. Fresh pineapple is one ingredient that actually takes it on, making it even more colourful and bright against its yellow canvas, and supporting the beetroot's flavour with its own tangy dominance. It's a surprise, kept secret here until the two make contact on the diners' plates, but you could mix them on the serving platter at the last minute too. Sugar snaps add a bright green colour swatch and a fresh crunch. Shelled, cooked and cooled edamame would be another good choice.

Beetroot, pineapple and sugar snap salad

SERVES 4–6 AS A SIDE | **PREP** 30 MINS | **COOK** 0 MINS

30 MINUTES OR LESS | FEAST DISH | LOW CALORIE | GLUTEN FREE | DAIRY FREE | VEGAN

1 x sesame balsamic dressing from *Roasted Asparagus and Egg with Sesame Balsamic* (page 95)

300 g (10^1/$_2$ oz) prepared fresh pineapple or 1 ripe pineapple (see NOTES)

100 g (3^1/$_2$ oz) sugar snap peas

2 raw beetroots (beets), about 150–200 g (5^1/$_2$–7 oz), leaves removed

OPTIONS
Serve as the foundation of a Buddha bowl, adding grains and boiled eggs or tofu to balance nutrition.

SPECIAL EQUIPMENT
Latex or rubber gloves for handling beetroot if desired, box grater and a large flat or shallow serving plate or dish.

1   Make the dressing and set aside.

2   If using a whole pineapple, cut off the stem end and a thin slice from the bottom. Cut into four or five thick slices across, then place each slice flat on the chopping board and, cutting downwards, cut the skin off, along with any prickles under it, trying to maintain as much flesh as possible. Cut the tender flesh away from the core, then weigh about 300 g (10^1/$_2$ oz), which should be about two-thirds of a medium pineapple (refrigerate or freeze the remainder).

3   Cut the pineapple into 1 cm (^{1}/$_2$ inch) dice and set aside.

4   Slice the sugar snaps quite thinly on the diagonal and set aside.

5   Scrub the beetroots and drain. (Now you may wish to put on some gloves to stop your hands getting stained.) Do not peel, but cut off the spindly root and any scraggles. Pare the rough bits at the top. Grate the beetroots coarsely into a bowl, discarding any tough bits of skin.

6   Presentation is key, and half the fun. Prepare the veg in circles on a serving dish, placing the beetroot on top of the pineapple and scattering over the sugar snap peas and some dressing. Alternatively, on a flat serving platter, make three equal blocks or stripes of purple beetroot, yellow pineapple and green sugar snaps. Serve with separate dessertspoons for each, and one for the dressing, in a bowl alongside.

NOTES
An alternative serving suggestion would be to toss half the pineapple with half the beetroot just before serving and arrange on the platter on top of the remaining beetroot, topping with the reserved pineapple and arranging the sugar snaps around it or alongside. The tossed beetroot will dye the pineapple bright pink.

To tell if a pineapple is ripe, smell its bottom! It should be pleasantly fragrant. If you can pull a leaf out from the centre of its stem, that may be an indicator too, though some say that's an old wives' tale.

FANS OF BEETROOT (BEET) WILL SWOON at every stage of creating this homage to the crimson root – especially the eating part – and also engaging with its botanical beauty and watching it do its thing with its unfathomable and savage colour. It's one of a kind.

This is my ultimate treatment for a lovely bunch of relatively freshly dug beetroots, fresh enough that their delicious greens are still shiny and lively, their pink stems still taut and crisp. If the greengrocer has removed this precious cargo from the roots, it is probably because the leaves are past their best – the roots keep much longer than the greens, and it may be late in the season. You can substitute chard or English spinach.

Ultimate baked beetroot and its greens

SERVES 4–6 | **PREP** 35 MINS | **COOK** 1 HOUR

FEAST DISH | GLUTEN FREE | DAIRY FREE | VEGAN

500 g (1 lb 2 oz) beetroots (beets), about 6 small–medium (untrimmed weight minus weight of greens)

1 tablespoon extra virgin olive oil

2 teaspoons good balsamic vinegar

sea salt and freshly ground black pepper

300 g (10^1/$_2$ oz) beetroot (beet) greens (total bunch weight about 800 g/1 lb 12 oz) or chard or English spinach

300 ml (10^1/$_2$ fl oz) coconut milk

60 g (2^1/$_4$ oz) shelled pistachio nuts, pounded or chopped with a large pinch of sea salt

OPTIONS

Substitute flaked almonds or hazelnuts if pistachios are not available.

Serve with cooked grains or crusty bread and a watercress and avocado salad.

SPECIAL EQUIPMENT

Casserole dish suitable for serving at table – oval or rectangular and approx. 20 x 30 cm (8 x 12 inches), latex or rubber gloves for handling beetroot, if desired, and foil.

1 Preheat the oven to 180°C (350°F) and brush the dish generously with oil. Bring the dish near your chopping board.

2 Scrub the beetroots and drain. (Now you may wish to put on some gloves to stop your hands getting stained.) Do not peel, but cut off the spindly root and any scraggles. Pare the rough bits at the top. Slice quite thinly and toss into the dish as you go.

3 Add the oil and balsamic to the beetroot slices along with salt and pepper. Toss with your hands to coat evenly and spread out to cover the bottom of the dish. Cover with foil, place in the oven and bake for 30 minutes.

4 Meanwhile, prepare the greens. They tend to harbour a lot of dirt. Rinse both leaves and stems first under cold running water and drain the sink thoroughly. Discard any limp or yellowing leaves. Fill the sink to submerge the greens and jostle them about. Leave them while the remaining grit settles. After about 5–10 minutes, lift them out into a colander.

5 Grab a lidded pan that will accommodate the greens. Chop the leaves and stems roughly and place in the pan as you go. Place the pan over a medium heat with just a pinch of salt (no need to add water unless they have dried off completely). Stir, then cover and cook for about 5–7 minutes, stirring occasionally, until the leaves have collapsed. Drain and set aside.

6 When 30 minutes is up on the roots, remove the dish from the oven and distribute the cooked greens over the top. Pour over the coconut milk. Return to the oven for 20 minutes, by which time the roots and greens should be gently bubbling in a thick magenta emulsion.

7 Scatter the crushed pistachios over the top. Return to the oven for 5–7 minutes, until the nuts are light golden. Serve right away, or at room temperature.

NOTE

Tinned coconut milk may solidify if cool. If you open a tin and find lumps and watery juice, empty into a microwave-safe bowl and nuke for 30 seconds–1 minute, then whisk until smooth.

Carrot

... it sports excellent team colours with its leggy orange root and verdant frilly tops.

Carrot

If there had to be a mascot for the entire vegetable kingdom, the carrot would probably be elected to fill that role. It's been a staple vegetable worldwide since records began, and it's universally recognised and appreciated by most (though not all – my partner is one of the few staunch carrot haters I have ever met). It sports excellent team colours with its leggy orange root and verdant frilly tops. It's the ultimate vegetable icon. Here are two wonderful legends about carrots, which are rooted in truth, as all good myths are.

Carrot legend one: Carrots are not naturally orange. In the seventeenth century, the Dutch bred an orange carrot in an early hybridisation experiment by crossing a naturally purple one with a yellow one in honour of their King William of Orange. As it turned out, it wasn't just a cosmetic success, but it spawned an exceptionally sweet carrot, which ultimately achieved world domination.

Carrot legend two: In World War Two, the British RAF cooked up a delicious piece of propaganda that their pilots were eating copious amounts of carrots to improve their night vision during missions to repel the German air raids as the enemy attacked the UK. This was a ruse to hide the fact that they were using a new technology: radar. This proved to be both successfully deceptive and great PR for carrots!

THE NUTRITIONAL SUPERPOWER

Beta-carotene in high concentration – anti-cancer, anti-inflammatory, amazing for heart and eye health.

OTHER HIGH LEVELS OF NUTRITIONAL EXCELLENCE

- Falcarinol, an antioxidant for heart and tissue health; also cancer-protective.

- B-complex vitamins, for converting food into fuel and giving us energy.

- Copper and calcium, for bone and tissue health.

SEASON

Year-round; baby carrots in spring and early summer.

VARIETIES

Seek out varieties grown for flavour such as Nantes and Chantenay. Older heritage varieties ranging in colour from white to yellow to purple are making a comeback in farmers' markets. Purple carrots taste earthy and beet-like. Yellow carrots have a slight citrus tang. White carrots can be a little on the bland side. Beware of prepared bags labelled 'baby carrots', which are ready-peeled pinkie-sized rods in plastic bags – they are probably not babies at all but large carrots mechanically carved into small pieces. They smell and taste like they are already starting to rot.

CHOOSE AND STORE

Immature carrots usually taste the sweetest. Buy real baby carrots with a little of the tops still attached, to use raw for crudités or for a steamed side veg. (Never buy ready-peeled carrots – see above.) Carrots with the greens attached will be fresher. Jumbo carrots are handy for grating and spiralizing. Store your carrots in a sealed plastic bag in the crisper drawer of the fridge.

PROCESSED AND PRESERVED

Fresh is always best with carrots. Frozen can have a woody texture; tinned are usually treated with a chemical to keep them firm and they taste sour – avoid.

PREP

- Store-bought carrots usually arrive in your kitchen fairly clean, but they should still be scrubbed. If they are not organic, then pesticide residues will be concentrated in the skin. The skin also naturally contains a concentration of nutrients, so avoid peeling if you can. Organic carrots do taste noticeably better than non, so my rule of thumb with carrots and most root veg is, if possible, buy organic and never peel.

- Cut carrots in discs or strips or sticks, or stubby segments, before steaming, boiling or roasting. Carrots to be eaten raw, unless they are sticks or thin ovals for crudités, are best broken down to make it easier on the jaw – finely sliced, shredded, grated, put through a spiralizer or cut with a julienne tool. You can also use a peeler to shave long paper-thin strips, curls or ribbons – soaking these in iced water makes them extra crunchy and curly.

Carrot's best mates

Apple | Orange | Orange flower essence | Cumin, coriander seed, cinnamon, anise, cardamom, nutmeg | Fresh coriander (cilantro), parsley, dill | Garlic | Ginger | Honey | Toasted sesame seeds | Tahini | Peanuts, walnuts | Sherry, Madeira | Red wine

Cook and eat

Carrot tops

These have a very strong flavour, like pungent parsley (they are related), so you wouldn't want to eat them in the same quantity you'd eat beet greens, but they can be treated as a herb or as a garnish. Always wash and dry thoroughly as they tend to harbour grit. They can be used in small amounts, either raw as a decorative salad leaf or garnish, or steamed. Use raw in cleaned bunches as a pretty backdrop to line a dish.

Carrot juice

Fresh carrots make the most delicious juice of all veg – sweet and almost milk-like in flavour. Whether fresh or bottled, carrot juice makes an exceptional vegetable stock – see *Tagine of Carrots, Butter Beans and Apricots* (opposite).

Madeira-braised carrots

Simmer thick rounds of carrots in equal amounts of Madeira wine (or sherry) and vegetable stock to cover, with a knob of butter, until the carrots are very soft and the liquid is reduced to a light gravy.

Parmesan-roasted carrots

Toss carrot sticks in olive oil and sea salt and roast in a 200°C (400°F) oven until almost tender. Sprinkle generously with finely grated Parmesan cheese (or vegetarian alternative) and toss to coat, then cook until golden and crusty.

THE OVERRIDING ELEMENT IS SWEETNESS, from carrots, dried apricots and sweet spices – typical of Moroccan tagines. The sweet is anchored in the realm of the savoury with umami from the red wine, shiitake mushrooms, tomatoes, onions and garlic, and all the notes are absorbed and encapsulated by the infused beans.

I want to point to one perhaps surprise element, which is using carrot juice as the main stock. It is an amazing ingredient. Try it in place of vegetable stock anywhere you could use a hint of sweetness and creaminess and don't mind the colour. Freshly pressed is sublime, but even pasteurised is fine to use – seek it out in the juice aisle at your grocer.

Tagine of carrots, butter beans and apricots

SERVES 4–6 | **PREP** 15 MINS | **COOK** 1 HOUR 5 MINUTES

GOOD SOURCE OF PROTEIN | GLUTEN FREE (IF SERVED WITH GLUTEN-FREE COUSCOUS OR GRAINS) |
DAIRY FREE (IF OPTIONAL GARNISH IS OMITTED OR DAIRY-FREE YOGHURT USED) |
VEGAN (IF OPTIONAL GARNISH IS OMITTED OR DAIRY-FREE YOGHURT USED)

$1^1/_2$ tablespoons extra virgin olive oil

300 g ($10^1/_2$ oz) slender carrots, trimmed, unpeeled, sliced

1 large red onion, roughly chopped

100 g ($3^1/_2$ oz) fresh shiitake mushrooms, stems removed (trimmed weight), sliced

sea salt and freshly ground black pepper

1 teaspoon coriander seeds

3 garlic cloves, chopped

5 cm (2 inch) cinnamon stick

$^1/_4$ teaspoon nutmeg, ideally freshly grated

400 g (14 oz) tin butter beans, drained

150 g ($5^1/_2$ oz) cherry tomatoes

10 dried apricots (about 80 g/$2^3/_4$ oz), thickly sliced

250 ml (9 fl oz/1 cup) full-bodied red wine

500 ml (17 fl oz/2 cups) carrot juice

To serve
Greek-style yoghurt (optional)

chopped parsley

OPTIONS
Serve with couscous, giant couscous, quinoa or burghul (bulgur) wheat.

SPECIAL EQUIPMENT
Wide, lidded, heavy-based soup pan.

1   Heat the pan over a medium heat and add the oil, then the carrots, onion and shiitakes with a little salt. Stir and cook, covered, for 15 minutes, stirring occasionally.

2   Crush the coriander seeds with a mortar and pestle. Alternatively, place in a small zip-seal plastic bag and crush with the back of a dessertspoon.

3   Add the garlic and spices and cook, stirring, for 2 minutes until fragrant, then add the remaining ingredients. Stir well, bring to the boil, then lower the heat to a simmer and cook for 45 minutes, stirring occasionally.

4   Serve in warm bowls, ladled over couscous or your chosen grain. Alternatively, serve alone as a chunky soup. Top each bowl with a spoonful of yoghurt (if using) and chopped parsley.

TRADITIONALLY, 'CONFIT' REFERS TO THE SLOW COOKING AND PRESERVATION of meat in its own fat, but the term has come to be applied to anything that is cooked slowly to the utmost tenderness in oil, especially garlic and tomatoes. Here carrots are rendered to melting and super sweet in a low oven with garlic and spices in a silky robe of olive oil. The concentrated sweetness of the carrots is offset with tangy lemon-infused beans.

Seek out the heritage carrot varieties that are making a comeback in farmers' markets. Yellow, purple and white – they each have individual flavour nuances and look gorgeous too. Otherwise good old orange carrots will, of course, respond well to this treatment.

Confit carrots with white bean salsa

SERVES 4 | **PREP** 15 MINS | **COOK** 2 HOURS 5 MINS

FEAST DISH | GOOD SOURCE OF PROTEIN | GLUTEN FREE | DAIRY FREE | VEGAN

60 ml (2 fl oz/$1/4$ cup) extra virgin olive oil

$1/2$ teaspoon cumin seeds

$1/2$ teaspoon fennel seeds

6 large garlic cloves, peeled, left whole

500–600 g (1 lb 2 oz–1 lb 5 oz) carrots (a mixture of coloured heritage varieties if available, and common – small or large), baby carrots can be left unpeeled; larger carrots can be peeled and cut into 7.5 cm (3 inch) lengths on the diagonal, then halved or quartered

sea salt and freshly ground black pepper

For the bean salsa

400 g (14 oz) tin white beans, such as cannellini beans, drained and rinsed

1 tablespoon lemon juice

handful of parsley, finely chopped

OPTIONS
Serve with a green salad and crusty bread.

SPECIAL EQUIPMENT
Casserole dish approx. 20 x 30 cm (8 x 12 inches) and foil.

1   Preheat the oven to 150°C (300°F). Place the casserole dish in the oven to heat up.

2   Heat a frying pan over a medium heat and add the oil, cumin seeds, fennel seeds and garlic cloves and stir. Once they start to sizzle, take the pan off the heat. Carefully remove the empty dish from the oven and place the carrots in it. Pour the entire contents of the frying pan over the carrots. Season with salt and pepper, stir to coat evenly, and spread out the carrots in one layer. Cover the dish with foil, place it back in the oven and bake for 2 hours, without stirring.

3   Make the bean salsa now so it has time to marinate. Combine all the ingredients in a bowl with a healthy dose of salt and pepper and stir. Cover the bowl and set aside, stirring from time to time while the carrots cook.

4   Once the carrots are done, they should offer little or no resistance when prodded with a fork. Remove from the oven and leave to stand for 10 minutes with the foil still attached.

5   Transfer the carrots and garlic to a serving platter, leaving behind as much of the oily pan juices as possible. Pour the juices into the bowl of beans and stir well. (If not much juice remains, stir a splash of olive oil into the beans instead.)

6   Serve the carrots with the bean salsa spooned over or on the side.

NOTE
This keeps well and can be served warm or cold.

GOT A SPIRALIZER? Here's an opportunity to make good use of it to create crisp and attractive tendrils of raw carrot for this bright and refreshing salad. No spiralizer? No problem – just grate the carrots coarsely, or even shave into ribbons with a veg peeler. This delicately composed salad makes a tasty light lunch, and it's also pretty and delicious enough for entertaining as part of a feast.

Raw carrot and orange salad with tahini dressing

SERVES 4 AS A SIDE | **PREP** 20 MINS | **COOK** 0 MINS

30 MINUTES OR LESS | FEAST DISH | LOW CALORIE | GOOD SOURCE OF PROTEIN | GLUTEN FREE | DAIRY FREE | VEGAN

For the tahini dressing

$1^1/_2$ tablespoons tahini

1 tablespoon lemon juice

sea salt

For the salad

300 g ($10^1/_2$ oz) large, fat carrots, peeled

1 large seedless orange

1 punnet of growing cress, cut from base, or 2 handfuls of sprouting beans or seeds (such as mung beans, sunflower sprouts or alfalfa sprouts or a mixture)

25 g (1 oz) shelled pistachio nuts, toasted and roughly chopped, or flaked almonds, toasted

few coriander (cilantro) leaves (optional)

SPECIAL EQUIPMENT

Spiralizer, grater or veg peeler for preparing the carrots.

1 To make the dressing, first boil a small amount of water in the kettle. Place the tahini in a small bowl (a layer of oil often separates at the top of the tahini jar, just dig your spoon in under it). Pour 60 ml (2 fl oz/$^1/_4$ cup) boiling water over the tahini and use a fork to stir until smooth. Add the lemon juice and a large pinch of salt and stir well. Don't worry if the mixture curdles – just keep stirring until smooth. Set aside.

2 Process the carrots into strands, using either a spiralizer, grater, peeler, food processor or mandoline (you may have some chunks left over to use elsewhere). Place the strands in a bowl and chill until serving.

3 Take the whole orange, unpeeled, and cut off the top and bottom. Cut equatorially into three or four thick slices, then lay each slice on the chopping board and cut downwards to remove all the skin and white pith. Cut the flesh into bite-sized chunks, paring away any pithy or tough bits from the core or elsewhere. Be sure to remove any seeds. Chill until ready to assemble the salad.

4 Assemble the salad just before serving. First, mix the cress or sprouts through the carrot strands in the bowl then, on a large serving plate or in individual shallow bowls or plates, make a bed of the carrot-sprout mix as loose and tall as possible. Add the orange chunks. Spoon over the dressing next, or keep separate for each person to add, but do not toss. Scatter over the nuts and coriander leaves, if using, and eat right away.

Celeriac

... it's all warts and scraggles on the outside, but beneath its less than glamorous exterior is a covetable, creamy white globe with endless possibilities.

Celeriac

Celeriac, AKA celery root, has a mysterious PR problem. Why is it not better known and loved in the English-speaking world? People at the supermarket checkout have seen me load a large, knobbly, whitish-green orb onto the conveyor belt and asked me 'What IS that thing?', launching me into a diatribe about its many delicious uses – and they are probably sorry they asked…

Its tall and slender cousin celery gets all the attention, and yet celery is not nearly as versatile, nutritious or even as interesting. Don't get me wrong, I love celery, but for me celeriac is the real star. Celeriac is the root base of a plant closely related to celery, and only the root is eaten as the stems are tough and dark green so they are always cut off (normal celery plants don't form a root bulb). Some food writers describe celeriac as 'ugly', and while it is a bit of a beast of a vegetable, weighing up to a kilo and about the size of a small child's head, all I can see is its beauty. It's all warts and scraggles on the outside, but beneath its less than glamorous exterior is a covetable, creamy white globe with endless possibilities.

Celeriac is low in calories and low in carbs, but it performs like a starchy vegetable and can be puréed, roasted and fried. It imparts a wonderful rich dimension to vegetable broth. It can also be eaten raw. Anything you can do with a carrot, you can do with celeriac. Celeriac has a unique flavour, similar to celery but with a pronounced sweetness. Coming in such a prolific size, it's economical too. It certainly ticks all the SuperVeg boxes and I think it deserves more love in everyone's kitchen and diet.

THE NUTRITIONAL SUPERPOWER

Vitamin K, for bone and brain health.

OTHER HIGH LEVELS OF NUTRITIONAL EXCELLENCE

- Falcarinol and other cancer-fighting antioxidants.
- Phosphorus, for healthy cell metabolism.
- B-complex vitamins, for converting food into fuel and giving us energy.

SEASON

Autumn through winter.

VARIETIES

You may be lucky enough to find some heirloom celeriac varieties in a farmers' market, but usually there's just one basic celeriac.

CHOOSE AND STORE

Celeriac may still have roots and fresh stem stubble attached, and if they do and also appear damp, this is a sign of freshness, and these will have the most flavour. They do have a good shelf life, so usually a good deal of the roots and top spindles will have been cut off and sometimes they will be wrapped in plastic. This is fine – just make sure it feels heavy and firm all over. The larger the celeriac, the more chance there is that there will be a hollow, woolly patch right at the centre, so choose medium size rather than enormous, for better flavour and less waste. Store in the fridge in a sealed plastic bag, or unwrapped in a cool larder (as you would store potatoes).

PROCESSED AND PRESERVED

These are a rarity. Only in France have I seen brined shredded celeriac in jars. Celeriac responds well to pickling and fermenting, so you may be lucky enough to find some.

PREP

- Arm yourself with a large sharp knife. The root side of the celeriac will most likely be harbouring dirt. Sometimes the entire root base has already been cut away, other times there are a few knobbles enclosing pockets of soil, so be sure to carve that section entirely off. The rest of the globe, the pale green, round majority of the vegetable, should be peeled – place cut-side down (if you've cut the root end off) on the chopping board, then shave off just the outer greenish skin to reveal the creamy flesh underneath. Then cut into the desired slices, chunks or wedges. If you find a woolly hollow inside, just cut around it. If using celeriac raw, grate or julienne it. A food processor is very handy for finely slicing or grating celeriac – feed long, fat wedges into the appropriate rotary blade. (See also *Celeriac Grits*, page 40.)

- Most cooks insist on plunging cut celeriac straight into acidulated water, but I don't bother – the discolouration is minor and hardly worth the extra fuss, unless it is sitting out exposed to the air for a long time.

Celeriac's best mates

Tomatoes, tomato sauce, tomato paste | Orange | Apple | Lemon |
Saffron | Parsley | White potatoes | Coconut milk | Cream, crème fraîche,
yoghurt | Parmesan | Blue cheese | Capers | Mustard | Butter |
Almonds, walnuts | Chestnuts | Tarragon | Truffle | Eggs any style

Cook and eat

Celeriac grits

Cubes of celeriac can be processed exactly the same way as for
Cauliflower Couscous (page 122) and the grits can be eaten raw or cooked.
They are so called because the result is not loose like couscous; it has a
denser consistency similar to grits or cooked polenta. Once cooked, stir in
a little butter and ground black pepper and serve as a side dish or in place
of a grain base.

Celeriac mash

The best mash is made using equal parts celeriac and floury potatoes,
both cut into chunks boiled together in well-salted water, drained
thoroughly and mashed with milk and butter. Celeriac is also superb with
sweet potatoes as a mash.

Celeriac fries

Cut into 1 cm (^{1}/2 inch) diameter sticks, and toss with olive oil, sea salt
and black pepper. Spread out in a single layer on a lined baking tray and
cook at 220°C (425°F) for 20–30 minutes, until soft and tinged with gold.
Eat warm with a fork (they remain a little floppy, unlike potatoes). They even
taste good cold. A tiny drizzle of sweet chilli sauce is a nice enhancement.

Celeriac latkes

Use equal parts grated celeriac and grated potatoes in your traditional
latke recipe for a surprisingly delicate variation.

UNLIKE A TRADITIONAL PAN-FRIED POTATO RÖSTI, this one is baked, so it can be left to its own devices in the oven while it transforms into an astoundingly rich and flavourful dish that hardly resembles celeriac, but still capitalises on this wonderful vegetable's naturally sweet and creamy merits. Garlic and toasted sesame seeds add nutrition and depth of flavour, but they can be omitted for a more neutral effect if desired.

Celeriac and coconut rösti

SERVES 4 | **PREP** 20 MINS | **COOK** 50 MINS

GLUTEN FREE | DAIRY FREE | VEGAN

30 g (1 oz) raw sesame seeds

1 large celeriac (approx. 750 g/1 lb 10 oz unpeeled weight)

3 garlic cloves

coarse sea salt

300 ml ($10\frac{1}{2}$ fl oz) coconut milk

1 tablespoon coconut oil, melted + more for greasing the casserole dish

OPTIONS
Substitute olive oil for coconut oil if desired.

Serve as a carb side dish in place of grains or potatoes.

SPECIAL EQUIPMENT
Casserole dish approx. 20 x 30 cm (8 x 12 inches), a food processor with a grater attachment or a box grater and a mortar and pestle (optional).

1   Preheat the oven to 200°C (400°F) and grease the casserole dish well with coconut oil.

2   Heat a small frying pan without oil over a medium heat and add the sesame seeds. Toast, stirring frequently, until golden and popping. Remove from the pan and transfer to a plate to cool.

3   Peel the celeriac using a sharp knife and cut away the roots and any muddy deposits, then rinse and pat dry. Cut into manageable segments, then grate using either a food processor with the rotary grating blade attachment or by hand on a box grater. Place the grated celeriac in a large bowl.

4   Crush the garlic with a large pinch of sea salt using a mortar and pestle until smooth, then add to the celeriac. (Alternatively use a garlic press and add the salt to the bowl.)

5   Add the toasted sesame seeds and coconut milk to the bowl and stir everything together until evenly mixed.

6   Transfer the mixture to the casserole dish and spread out evenly, smoothing the top. Dribble the melted coconut oil over the top and use a pastry brush to gently distribute the oil all over the surface.

7   Bake for 40–50 minutes, until deep golden, firm and crisp. Serve hot.

THE FINISHED ARTICLE IS REMINISCENT OF VEGGIE LASAGNE, but the only aspect it shares with the original is the tomato sauce. I have been seduced into an obsession with blended cashew nuts as a substitute for dairy cream, so I reworked a celeriac gratin of mine, using the cashew cream in place of cream and Parmesan. I was thrilled with the results. It's not a diet dish – it's rich and moreish and it is packed with protein as well as being 100 percent plant based.

Celeriac and cashew cream lasagne

SERVES 4 | **PREP** 30 MINS + 1 HOUR SOAKING | **COOK** 1 HOUR

FEAST DISH | GOOD SOURCE OF PROTEIN | GLUTEN FREE (IF TAMARI IS USED) | DAIRY FREE | VEGAN (IF MAPLE SYRUP IS USED)

For the cashew cream

200 g (7 oz/1¼ cups) raw cashew nuts

150 ml (5 fl oz) water

2 teaspoons lemon juice

1 tablespoon light soy sauce or tamari

For the tomato sauce

2 tablespoons extra virgin olive oil + more for drizzling

1 onion, finely chopped

2 garlic cloves, finely chopped

2 tablespoons tomato paste (concentrated purée)

400 g (14 oz) tin chopped tomatoes

1 teaspoon red or white wine vinegar

1 teaspoon maple syrup or honey

sea salt and freshly ground black pepper

1 large celeriac (approx. 750 g/1 lb 10 oz unpeeled weight)

2 handfuls of basil leaves

OPTIONS

Serve with a leafy green salad dressed in a balsamic vinaigrette.

SPECIAL EQUIPMENT

Blender and a casserole dish approx. 20 x 30 cm (8 x 12 inches) or an oval dish.

1   Boil the kettle. Place the cashews in a bowl and pour boiling water over them to cover. Leave to cool and keep them submerged until ready to use.

2   Preheat the oven to 200°C (400°F). Brush the casserole dish generously with oil.

3   Prepare the celeriac. Peel it using a sharp knife and cut away the roots and any muddy deposits, then rinse and pat dry. Cut into about six pieces and slice as thinly as possible. (Alternatively use a food processor with a slicing blade or a mandoline – the thinner the better.)

4   Make the tomato sauce. Heat a large saucepan (large enough to stir the celeriac into it) over a medium heat and add the olive oil, then the onion, and cook until it is translucent. Add the garlic and fry for about 2 minutes until fragrant. Add the tomato paste and cook for about 3 minutes, stirring constantly, until sticky. Add the remaining ingredients and stir well. Bring to the boil, lower to a simmer and cook for about 5 minutes, until slightly thickened. Taste for seasoning.

5   Stir the celeriac into the sauce. Cover the pan and simmer for about 10 minutes, stirring occasionally, until the celeriac starts to tenderise.

6   To make the cashew cream, drain the soaked cashews and place in a blender with the rest of the ingredients. Blend at high speed until completely smooth.

7   Stir half the cashew cream into the tomato-celeriac mixture. Tear in a handful of basil leaves and stir. Transfer to the casserole dish. Pour the remaining cashew cream over the top and smooth the surface. Decorate with whole basil leaves and finish with a light drizzle of olive oil.

8   Bake for 30–40 minutes until golden and bubbling. Serve right away.

NOTE

The cashew nuts can be soaked up to 24 hours in advance. The lasagne keeps well, portioned and refrigerated, for up to 3 days.

THIS HAS BEEN TRENDING ON LONDON RESTAURANT MENUS for a while now, and I thought it was just a gimmicky flash in the pan until I tried it at home. I thought, well, why go to all the trouble of making a throw-away dough to bake a celeriac in if it doesn't really improve the vegetable? I guess I tried eating it at the wrong restaurants, because once I did it myself, it was a totally worthwhile effort. The salt dough only takes a few minutes to throw together and what you end up with is a transformation to a whole new level of sublime – an uberceleriac.

Once baked, you have quite a large quantity of ready-to-eat celeriac, which keeps well – up to 5 days in the fridge. It can be sliced into thin or thick-ish steak-like slabs (and fried, if desired, though not essential – reheating in the oven or microwave is fine too) and served as a base for a topping such as a poached egg, sautéed mushrooms or legumes. Think of it as a substitute for grains or potatoes – lots of the recipes in this book go well with this. It can also be cut in wedges or chunks, mashed or shredded for a variety of textures, though the slab is the easiest and most effective on the plate, in my opinion.

Salt-baked celeriac

SERVES 6 | **PREP** 25 MINS | **COOK** 1 HOUR + COOLING

LOW CALORIE | DAIRY FREE | VEGAN

1 large celeriac (approx. 750 g/1 lb 10 oz unpeeled weight)

250 g (9 oz) rock salt

500 g (1 lb 2 oz/3^1/$_3$ cups) plain (all-purpose) flour

OPTIONS
Serve as a carb side dish in place of grains or potatoes.

SPECIAL EQUIPMENT
Large baking tray, non-stick baking paper, rolling pin and a skewer.

1 Preheat the oven to 180°C (350°F) and line a large baking tray.

2 Peel the celeriac using a sharp knife and cut away the roots and any muddy deposits, then rinse and pat dry.

3 Make the salt dough. In a large bowl, mix the salt and flour, then mix in 300 ml (10^1/$_2$ fl oz) water using a wooden spoon. Get your hands in and start kneading against the side of the bowl until it draws together into a hard dough. (Add a little more flour if it is sticky.)

4 Place a large sheet of baking paper on your work surface and pop the dough on it, then place another sheet on top and press the dough down. Roll out the dough between the sheets into a circle with a thickness of about 5 mm (^{1}/$_4$ inch).

5 Place the celeriac directly on the dough in the middle and wrap the dough around it, completely enclosing it and making sure there are no holes.

6 Transfer to the baking tray and bake for 1 hour, or until the celeriac offers no resistance when pierced through to the middle with a skewer.

7 Allow to cool completely. Remove the crust and discard it. The celeriac is now ready to be sliced and fried or reheated to your liking (see suggestions above).

Fennel

... a tight, multi-layered capsule, like a closed flower bud of petals that are crisp and toothsome, pale and elegant, subtle and divisive.

Fennel

Fennel as a vegetable is also known as bulb fennel or Florence fennel. This is a different fennel from the feathery dill-like herb that also produces fennel seeds, one of my favourite spices, and fennel pollen, a rare delicacy favoured by chefs, but does not produce a vegetable mass. Fennel the vegetable is a tight, multi-layered capsule, like a closed flower bud of petals that are crisp and toothsome, pale and elegant, subtle and divisive. Some people cannot abide the liquorice flavour, which is most pronounced when eaten raw, but tempered to barely detectable once cooked.

Fennel is a bit of a fancy-pants vegetable, and can be expensive. Different treatments of it deliver such different results, from raw, fragrant, crisp shavings to a soft and melting braised slab. So while it might not be an everyday staple, it adds a little adventure and luxury to the plate, by nature of its beautiful shape and perfume.

THE NUTRITIONAL SUPERPOWER

Anethole, which gives fennel its aniseed taste, is anti-inflammatory and cancer-protective.

OTHER HIGH LEVELS OF NUTRITIONAL EXCELLENCE

▌ Potassium, for heart and kidney health.

▌ Vitamin C, for immune health.

SEASON

Spring through autumn; available year-round.

VARIETIES

Some fennel bulbs are rather flat and elongated; others are round and plump. I always seek out the round ones because they are fleshier and less stringy.

CHOOSE AND STORE

Choose fat, round bulbs that feel firm and heavy. Flat varieties have a good flavour but are best for using raw as they can be more fibrous when cooked. If the feathery fronds are attached and look lively, it's a sign of freshness. A brown patch on the bottom from where it has been cut is nothing to worry about, but avoid brown patches elsewhere on the bulb. The outer layer may be slightly damaged or dried out, without affecting the inner parts, and this layer can be removed, so don't give up if it's not perfect.

PROCESSED AND PRESERVED

It's unlikely you'll find fennel processed in any way except pickled.

PREP

▌ The dark green tubular row of stems at the top are tough, so should be mostly cut off, but do reserve them to add to vegetable stock as they add a great flavour. Cut off and reserve any perky looking fronds too – these can be scattered over the finished dish for a pretty flash of green. Gently shave off any tuft or brown patch at the bottom without cutting away too much of the outer layer. If the outer layer seems coarse and woody, remove it entirely by pulling it off (it can also be added to stock as long as it's just dry and not rotten). To make beautiful flame-shaped pieces, slice from top to base, cutting crossways through the row of stems. Cut downward into slices 1 cm (½ inch) thick. The core at the bottom should hold the layers together and you should get three to four complete slices out of one medium-sized bulb.

▌ The bulb can also be cut in wedges from top to bottom, or sliced into horseshoe rings by laying the fennel on its side and cutting downwards. Thick-ish single slices make good crudités. Fennel can be shaved on a mandoline or simply cut in half, placed cut-side down and sliced as thinly as possible for eating raw and adding to salads.

Fennel's best mates

Dill, tarragon, parsley, chervil | Thyme, sage, rosemary | Saffron |
Apple | Orange | Black and green olives | Tomatoes | Parmesan, Gruyère |
White wine, sherry, Madeira | Sweetcorn, polenta | Butter, cream |
Nut oils such as walnut

Cook and eat

Sautéed/poached fennel

Sauté in olive oil or butter or cook gently in a small amount of stock, cream or sauce. Fennel tends to go a bit grey when steamed or boiled, and coarse when roasted, plus the charm of its flavour is somewhat diminished, so sautéeing or poaching in a small amount of flavourful liquid is better.

Booze-braised fennel

Fry sliced fennel – both whole flame-shaped slices and long fragments – in olive oil with salt until tinged with gold. Splash in some booze and let it reduce – Pernod will accentuate the liquorice flavour; Madeira wine and sherry are also good.

Fennel and tomatoes

Simmer roughly chopped fennel with some olive oil, fresh chopped tomatoes, garlic and, if you like, a few top-quality black olives, for a lovely nicoise-style sauce for pasta or dipping crusty bread in.

Fennel slaw

Grate, shave or finely slice fennel and mix with a few with spring onions (scallions) and a sweet vinaigrette or a honey–lemon dressing.

A LUSCIOUS, CRUNCHY SALAD buzzing with a riot of sweet and herbal flavours, this dish brings a jolt of freshness to the autumn or winter table, when its components are at their seasonal best and you need a little pick-me-up. It's equally good for the spring or the summer.

Fennel and apple salad with hazelnuts

SERVES 4 | **PREP** 15 MINS | **COOK** 10 MINS + COOLING

30 MINUTES OR LESS | GLUTEN FREE | DAIRY FREE | VEGAN

50 g (1³/4 oz/¹/3 cup) whole hazelnuts

2 crisp and tangy apples, such as Pink Lady, Cox or Russet, quartered, cored and very thinly sliced

1 large or 2 small fennel bulbs, trimmed, quartered and finely sliced (reserve any fronds)

2 spring onions (scallions), finely sliced

1 tablespoon lemon juice

handful of dill

handful of mint sprigs, leaves stripped

2 tablespoons apple cider vinegar

3 tablespoons extra virgin olive oil

sea salt

OPTIONS
Use blanched hazelnuts, or skin-on for extra nutrition. If using skin-on, rub them lightly with a tea towel after roasting and cooling slightly, to remove stray bits of skin.

Serve with fried halloumi slices, hard-boiled eggs or a light omelette to make this dish a main course.

SPECIAL EQUIPMENT
Small baking tray and foil or baking paper.

1 Preheat the oven to 200°C (400°F). Line a small baking tray.

2 Place the hazelnuts on the tray and toast for 5–10 minutes until nicely golden. Remove to a plate and leave to cool. Once cool, chop roughly.

3 In a large bowl, combine the apple, fennel and spring onion. Add the lemon juice, stir and set aside.

4 Chop the dill and mint and stir in, then stir in the vinegar, then the oil and finally season with salt to taste.

5 Transfer the salad to a platter or individual plates. Finish with the hazelnuts and any reserved fennel fronds, chopped. Serve as soon as possible.

SURPRISE! Creamy baked ricotta is a hidden treasure inside baked polenta topped with glistening fennel, glazed in sherry and spiked with chilli. Three strong characters combine to deliver a sublime performance of a dish, with the fennel in the starring role. You'll need three pans to cook this, but each process is dead simple and I promise it's worth the washing up.

I tried cooking polenta in almond milk out of curiosity recently when I had both to hand, and I have never looked back – it makes the best-tasting polenta ever, with no need to add lashings of butter and Parmesan. See also the *Honey-Roast Tomato Polenta* on page 267.

Glazed fennel polenta with secret baked ricotta

SERVES 4–6 | **PREP** 10 MINS | **COOK** 50 MINS

FEAST DISH | GLUTEN FREE

2 fennel bulbs (450–500 g/1 lb–1 lb 2 oz untrimmed weight)

2 tablespoons extra virgin olive oil

sea salt and freshly ground black pepper

100 ml ($3^1/2$ fl oz) sherry, sweet or medium

3–4 thyme sprigs, leaves stripped

$1/2$ teaspoon chilli flakes

1 litre (35 fl oz/4 cups) almond milk (natural unsweetened)

250 g (9 oz) tub ricotta, drained

250 g (9 oz) quick-cook polenta

Parmesan cheese or vegetarian alternative, for grating at the table (optional)

OPTIONS

Substitute soy milk, cow's milk or another nut milk if almond milk is not available, though you may find it tastes bland. Stir in butter and/or grated Parmesan at the end of cooking the polenta to enhance the flavour.

Serve with a simple green salad or juicy sliced tomatoes dressed in balsamic, olive oil and basil.

SPECIAL EQUIPMENT

Large frying pan and a medium oval or rectangular baking dish.

1   Trim off the darker green stems of the fennel bulbs. Slice the bulb from top to base, cutting crossways through the row of stems, into slices 1 cm ($1/2$ inch) thick. You should have at least four to six cohesive slices, and several remaining stray pieces, which will be included too. (Don't worry if all you end up with is stray pieces – not all fennel cuts the same.)

2   Heat a large frying pan over a medium heat and add the oil. Lay the fennel slices in the pan and scatter all the remaining pieces around them. Season well with sea salt and pepper. Cook until the undersides of the slices are golden, then turn everything carefully with tongs and cook the other sides till golden. Pour in the sherry all at once – stand back as it may splutter. Add the thyme sprigs and chilli flakes. Cook, turning once or twice more, until the liquid is completely evaporated and the fennel is glossy. Set aside.

3   Meanwhile, preheat the oven to 200°C (400°F). Place the almond milk in a large saucepan with a little salt and bring to the boil. Brush the baking dish with oil. Plop the ricotta in the centre of the dish, then gently squash it with a spoon to spread it out to the edges.

4   Once the almond milk has come to the boil, reduce to a simmer. Pour in the polenta in a slow and steady stream, stirring constantly. It will soon start erupting like lava; keep stirring a little longer until it is very thick, then remove from the heat. Transfer it immediately into the dish, covering the ricotta completely. Spread it gently to meet the edges of the dish, smoothing the surface, yet keeping the ricotta smothered if possible.

5   Arrange the fennel on the surface of the polenta, pressing in the slices gently and surrounding them with the smaller pieces. Scrape all of the contents out of the pan over any exposed polenta.

6   Bake for 20 minutes until sizzling. Serve at the table, showered with finely grated Parmesan, if desired.

A RATHER ELEGANT AND COLOURFUL PRESENTATION of fennel, this is a tribute to the beauty of this vegetable. It's an easy and impressive dinner party dish if you like to show off a little.

Saffron-infused fennel with a walnut and herb crumb

SERVES 4 | **PREP** 20 MINS | **COOK** 40 MINS

FEAST DISH | GLUTEN FREE | DAIRY FREE | VEGAN

2 large or 4 small fennel bulbs (about 700 g/1 lb 9 oz untrimmed weight)

175 ml (6 fl oz) vegetable stock or hot water mixed with 3/4 teaspoon stock powder

3 large pinches of saffron strands

1 tablespoon extra virgin olive oil

large handful of parsley

5 cm (2 inch) rosemary sprig, leaves stripped

sea salt

100 g (3 1/2 oz) walnuts

1 teaspoon orange zest

OPTIONS
Serve with mashed potatoes, couscous, or *Salt-Baked Celeriac* (page 44).

SPECIAL EQUIPMENT
Baking or casserole dish approx. 20 x 30 cm (8 x 12 inches), foil and a food processor (optional).

1   Preheat the oven to 220°C (425°F).

2   Trim off the darker green stems of the fennel bulbs and reserve any fronds. Slice the bulb from top to base, cutting crossways through the row of stems, into slices 1 cm (1/2 inch) thick. You should have about 8 slices or 10–12 slices total from smaller bulbs. Reserve any extra pieces for another use. Lay the slices in the baking dish.

3   Mix together the (ideally hot) stock, saffron and olive oil. Pour over the fennel. Cover the dish with foil and bake for 20 minutes.

4   To prepare the walnut crumb mixture, whizz the parsley and rosemary with a pinch of salt in a food processor until very finely chopped or chop by hand. Add the walnuts and orange zest and whizz or chop to coarse crumbs.

5   After 20 minutes baking, take the dish from the oven and carefully remove the foil. Use a large spoon to baste the fennel with the cooking liquid. Return the dish to the oven without the foil and reduce the liquid for about 10 minutes more, until the liquid is almost gone but not quite.

6   Remove the dish again and spoon the walnut crumb on top of each slice of fennel. Return to the oven and cook for 5–10 minutes, until the crumb is lightly browned and the liquid is completely reduced, then serve hot or warm, garnished with any reserved fronds, chopped.

Onion and Garlic

... the whole family of alliums, including onions and leeks, equally deserve SuperVeg status.

Onion and Garlic

This section started as one SuperVeg – garlic – renowned for its superlative health-giving properties, versatility, deliciousness, breath-tainting and vampire banishing. But as I started writing, I felt that the whole family of alliums, including onions and leeks, equally deserve SuperVeg status, so please forgive me for cheating a little, but this section is devoted to several blessed members of the same family.

If there were just one SuperVeg that I was forced to choose to take to a desert island or hoard for the apocalypse, it would be onions. With onions, I have flavour. Plus they store better than any other veg, and if I had seed, they are one of the easiest veg to cultivate. It's remarkable how many recipes throughout the world start with the fundamental act of frying an onion in fat. A notable exception is Ethiopia, where they first sweat the onion in a dry pan in its own juices and add a spiced butter later – this gives the dish a unique sweet flavour. But still, a cooked onion is the foundation of deliciousness. It's one of nature's most valuable gifts to humankind.

THE NUTRITIONAL SUPERPOWER

Allicin, in both onion and garlic, reduces cholesterol and is anti-viral, anti-bacterial and anti-fungal, for disease resistance.

OTHER HIGH LEVELS OF NUTRITIONAL EXCELLENCE

▌ Unique phytonutrients for disease prevention, processing toxins and preventing blood clots.

▌ B-complex vitamins, for converting food into fuel and giving us energy.

▌ Garlic contains manganese, for joint health.

▌ Onions also contain high levels of chromium, for stabilising insulin levels.

SEASON

Year-round; wet garlic in spring; wild garlic leaves (ramsons) in early spring.

VARIETIES

BULB ONIONS Come in hundreds of varieties. I usually keep a stock of 'regular' copper-skinned onions, red onions and banana shallots, plus spring onions (in the fridge).

Seek out locally grown garlic, the plumper the better, and often with purple or pink colouring.

WET GARLIC OR 'GREEN' GARLIC Light green stem, graduating to white and purple on the bulb. It has been freshly harvested so the skin will still be soft and damp and the cloves will have a mild, sweet and nutty flavour.

RAMSONS, WILD GARLIC OR RAMPS A pungent green leaf, sometimes with the spring onion (scallion)-like roots attached. The flowers are edible too. Grab in spring if you see them for sale. Better yet, learn how to recognise and forage yourself – even some London parks have patches that I visit in spring.

CHOOSE AND STORE

Onions and garlic should feel heavy and firm without bruises. Avoid garlic that has any visible sprouts and store in a jar with a lid that lets plenty of air in, onions in a breathable bag or box, both in a cupboard away from light. Spring onions, leeks and wild garlic should be stored in a loose bag in the fridge. Wet garlic should be used as soon as possible; if stored like regular garlic, it will harden and keep well.

PROCESSED AND PRESERVED

GARLIC POWDER (OR GRANULES) Awesome in my book! It's perfectly fine for instantly inserting garlic flavour if you are feeling rushed or lazy, or if you find you've run out of fresh. I used to turn my nose up at this stuff, but now I've come round to appreciate it.

PREPARED PURÉED GARLIC Can be found in tubes, jars and frozen cubes. I find it tastes faintly of petrol; powder is a better substitute.

PICKLED GARLIC Delicious as a snack or as a tart addition to a salad. Pickled onions should be treated more like a condiment than a veggie – they are great in a grilled cheese sandwich.

SMOKED GARLIC A fun find. The smoking process cooks it slightly and lessens its pungency. Use quite a lot for a good smoky garlic punch – it's wonderful crushed generously into butter to make garlic bread.

BLACK GARLIC An esoteric gourmet speciality, made using an ancient Korean fermentation process, which caramelises the cloves into squidgy, black stubs. It tastes only faintly of garlic with tones of balsamic and prunes.

PREP

▌ To peel a large amount of garlic, see the two-bowl trick in the intro for *Kerala-Style Garlic Pickle* (page 63).

▌ Have you ever tasted a dish and thought, 'That's TOO garlicky'? It may not be that too much garlic was added, but simply that the raw garlic sprout or germ was allowed to invade. There is one important prep step for garlic that I am very pedantic about, especially if I am using the garlic raw – my garlic mantra: 'Out the sprout'. These sprouts have an unpleasantly pungent flavour and should be removed. Split each clove lengthways with a knife to see if there is a sprout there, and if there is even part of one, use the tip of your knife to pry it out.

▌ Raw garlic tastes best when crushed with coarse salt in a mortar or with the side of a knife on a board – the salt helps release all the flavour and creates a paste.

▌ Wet garlic can be used skins and all – sometimes just one or two drier layers of skin need to be removed. You can top and tail it and slice it across like an onion, and you'll find its mild flavour means you can use a lot more than regular garlic.

When chopping onions, clever cooks will cut the whole onion in half from root to base, then remove the skin, leaving the root intact to hold it together, then place the half bulb cut-side down and slice first from root to tip, then across. The natural layers in the onion will allow it to separate into tiny pieces, though you can make them tinier by also first slicing carefully sideways (knife parallel with the chopping board) towards the root before you cut across.

Red onions tend to require the removal of more layers than other onions. If you find a little mould inside, it can be rinsed off and the onion is still good to use. With all bulb onions, always remove any layers that are a bit papery – cooking will never soften these parts, and someone will end up having to spit them out!

How do you stop the tears? There is no panacea. I do think it helps to hold your nose and breathe through your mouth (the chemical compounds in onions that make you cry travel more quickly to your tear ducts through your nose). It also helps to use a very sharp knife, which avoids crushing the onion's cells and releasing more vapours.

Onion and Garlic's best mates

All good cooking oils | Butter | All good vinegars |
Unrefined sugars, honey | Cream, crème fraîche, yoghurt |
Hard mature cheeses | Lemon, lime | Beans | Tomatoes

Cook and eat

Wet garlic dip

Slice a whole bulb thickly along with the soft skins and fry gently in plenty of olive oil until golden and crisp. Cool and transfer to a bowl, add a few drops of balsamic and some sea salt and use for dipping crusty bread.

Griddled spring onions/calçots

Trim roots and any papery leaves, rinse and dry. Slick the onions with olive oil and cook on a barbecue or scorching chargrill pan, turning occasionally, until charred and soft. Serve with romesco sauce (a quick version can be found in *Bruschlettuce with Two Toppings, page 166)*.

Roasted garlic

Peel just the outer layer off the garlic to keep the bulb intact, slice off the frilly end and wash off any mud. Cut in half equatorially, i.e. through the middle of the cloves rather than top to base. Coat lightly in oil, place in a roasting dish, cut-side up, and roast at 180°C (350°F) for 20–40 minutes until golden. When cool enough to handle, squeeze the roasted flesh out of the skins and spread on bread or blend into butter, sauces and dressings.

VAMPIRES BEWARE: this dish incorporates crisp fried garlic, pickled garlic and a creamy black garlic yoghurt sauce over a backdrop of eggplant (aubergine). Black garlic is slow cooked until caramelised and blackened according to an ancient Korean recipe, and tastes more like liquorice or prunes than garlic – extremely potent. Thanks to chef extraordinaire Yotam Ottolenghi for the inspiration to blend it into a yoghurt emulsion.

Three-garlic and roasted eggplant platter

SERVES 4–6 | **PREP** 20 MINS | **COOK** 20 MINS

30 MINUTES OR LESS | FEAST DISH | GLUTEN FREE

2 eggplants (aubergines)

extra virgin olive oil, for brushing

sea salt and freshly ground black pepper

For the black garlic sauce

100 g (3$\frac{1}{2}$ oz/$\frac{1}{3}$ cup) Greek-style or thick and creamy yoghurt

10–12 black garlic cloves

2 teaspoons lemon juice

1 teaspoon ground cumin

sea salt

For the garlic garnish

3 tablespoons raw sesame seeds

2 tablespoons extra virgin olive oil

3 garlic cloves, sliced

3 pickled garlic cloves, sliced

chilli flakes

chopped parsley

To serve

200 g (7 oz) baby salad leaves such as pea shoots, baby kale, watercress and English spinach

OPTIONS

Add toasted flaked almonds for extra crunch and protein.

If you can't get black garlic, substitute with 2 teaspoons molasses or treacle and 1 crushed garlic clove.

SPECIAL EQUIPMENT

Large baking tray, non-stick foil or baking paper and a blender.

1   Preheat the oven to 220°C (425°F) and line a large baking tray. Cut the stem end off the eggplants and discard. Cut each eggplant into six or eight long wedges. Score the flesh in one diagonal direction, without piercing the skin. Brush generously with olive oil and season with salt and pepper. Roast for 15–20 minutes until completely soft and golden. Keep warm.

2   To make the sauce, place all the ingredients in a blender and whizz until smooth. Taste for seasoning and set aside.

3   For the garlic garnish, heat a small frying pan without oil over a medium heat and add the sesame seeds. Toast, stirring frequently, until golden and popping. Remove from the pan and transfer to a plate to cool. Heat the olive oil in the frying pan over a low–medium heat. Add the garlic slices and cook, stirring gently, until light golden and crisp, then drain on paper towels. Reserve the oil.

4   To assemble, arrange the salad leaves on a platter and top with the warm eggplants. Drizzle the sauce over. Finish with fried garlic, pickled garlic, sesame seeds, chilli flakes and parsley. Add a drizzle of the garlicky oil if desired, and serve.

NOTE

The eggplants can also be served at room temperature, though when slightly warm they carry the flavours beautifully.

THIS RELISH IS A KNOCK-OUT FLAVOUR BOMB. It's perfect scooped up with poppadoms or flatbread, and also makes a sublime accompaniment for curries, lentils or any rice or grain dish. Scatter it on salads, scrambled eggs, baked beans and cheese on toast. I learnt how to make this from a chef I met when visiting Kerala, the southernmost state of India. Get ready for your home to be permeated with a luscious tangy garlic fragrance while it cooks, and for several hours afterwards. The addition of a pinch of fenugreek seeds contributes an outstanding curry aroma, but if not available you can leave it out.

You need a lot of garlic here, and I can imagine you wincing at the thought of peeling it all. But here's a handy trick to make light work of it: separate the garlic cloves from the base of the bulb and from each other. Take two largish equal-sized steel or plastic bowls. Place all the garlic in one bowl and put the other bowl upturned over the top. Hold the edges tightly and shake with all your might for about 1 minute and bam! Most of the garlic skins will be magically loosened or removed.

Kerala-style garlic pickle

SERVES 4–6 | **PREP** 20 MINS | **COOK** 30 MINS

GLUTEN FREE | DAIRY FREE | VEGAN (IF MAPLE SYRUP IS USED)

1 tablespoon coconut oil

100 g (3^1/$_2$ oz) garlic cloves, peeled and medium sliced (about 3 bulbs)

pinch of fenugreek seeds (optional)

^{1}/$_4$ teaspoon cayenne pepper

^{1}/$_4$ teaspoon ground turmeric

sea salt

200 ml (7 fl oz) apple cider vinegar

1 teaspoon maple syrup or honey

OPTIONS
Substitute extra virgin olive oil for coconut oil if desired.

SPECIAL EQUIPMENT
None

1 Heat the coconut oil in a large non-stick frying pan over a low–medium heat. Add the garlic and cook for about 2 minutes, stirring frequently.

2 Stir in the fenugreek, if using, cayenne and turmeric and season with salt, then pour in the vinegar and add the syrup. Bring to the boil, then reduce the heat to a low simmer. Cook, stirring from time to time, until most of the liquid has evaporated.

3 Let the mixture cool, then serve, or transfer to a screw-top jar or sealed container and store in the fridge.

NOTE
Keeps for up to 3 weeks in the fridge.

IF MY **25 SuperVeg** were based strictly on my 25 favourite vegetables, leeks would definitely have their own chapter. They are just brilliant. Here I offer you my 'leek homage potage' – a leek and potato soup that also stars caramelised onions. Leek greens make the most delicious pure soup stock – they just need to be separated layer by layer and washed before simmering in water. Each leek has a 'sweet spot', its most flavourful part, where the white turns light green, and that part is used in a special way here, sliced and poached for the perfect bright, fresh finishing garnish.

Caramelised onion, leek and potato soup

SERVES 4–6 | **PREP** 20 MINS | **COOK** 45 MINS

GLUTEN FREE | DAIRY FREE (IF OPTIONAL GARNISH IS OMITTED AND OLIVE OIL SUBSTITUTED FOR BUTTER) | VEGAN (IF OPTIONAL GARNISH IS OMITTED AND OLIVE OIL SUBSTITUTED FOR BUTTER)

3 large leeks (choose leeks with as much dark green leafage still attached as possible for making stock)

cooking salt

25 g (1 oz/2 tablespoons) butter

1 tablespoon extra virgin olive oil

3 onions (about 300 g/10^1/$_2$ oz), chopped

3 potatoes (about 500 g/1 lb 2 oz), scrubbed but not peeled, cut into medium chunks (floury varieties work best for giving the soup body)

freshly ground black pepper

^{1}/$_4$ teaspoon chilli flakes

To serve

crème fraîche or yoghurt or a handful of grated cheddar cheese (optional)

OPTIONS
Serve with crusty bread.

SPECIAL EQUIPMENT
Potato masher

1   Prepare the leeks. Cut the root end off, then cut out a 5 cm (2 inch) segment where the leek turns from white to light green (the 'sweet spot', which will be reserved for poaching). Reserve all the darker green parts. Set the main white segments aside.

2   Make the leek stock. Separate the dark leaves, cutting them lengthways where necessary, and rinse each layer separately and thoroughly to remove any grit. Place in a large pan with 1.5 litres (52 fl oz/6 cups) water and 1 teaspoon salt. Stir, cover and bring to the boil, then simmer while you prepare the rest of the soup.

3   Melt the butter in a soup pan over a low–medium heat and add the oil. Add the onion and cook for about 10–15 minutes, stirring occasionally, until very soft. Raise the heat and cook for a further 3–5 minutes, stirring frequently, until deep golden and caramelised.

4   Take the main white segments of the leeks and quarter them lengthways, then chop into 1 cm (^{1}/$_2$ inch) pieces. Keeping the heat medium-high, add the chopped leeks and cook for a further 5 minutes, until the leeks are collapsed and starting to colour. Add the potatoes and 1 teaspoon salt, stir well and cover. Cook for 8–10 minutes, stirring frequently and scraping the bottom of the pan to get all the good sticky bits incorporated – this is the stage that really develops the soup's flavour.

5   The mixture should be turning very sticky and dark brown. Lower the heat and ladle in enough stock to fully submerge the veg, stirring between additions. (Take the stock pan off the heat.) Twist some black pepper into the soup and add the chilli flakes. Simmer for 10 minutes until the potatoes are thoroughly cooked.

6   Meanwhile, slice the reserved 'sweet spots' of the leeks into 5 mm (^{1}/$_4$ inch) rounds (inspect to be sure there is no dirt trapped between layers). Place in a small pan with a ladle or two of stock. Cover, bring to the boil, simmer for 5 minutes, then set aside.

7   When the soup is done, remove from the heat and mash with a potato masher to break up the potatoes and thicken the broth.

8   To serve, ladle the soup into warm bowls. Use tongs to place the leeks on the surface and finish with a dollop of crème fraîche, yoghurt or grated cheese, if desired, and a twist of black pepper.

Kohlrabi

… it's a puzzle why this stupendous plant food hero isn't recognised as a superstar throughout the world.

Kohlrabi

Undoubtedly the most obscure of the SuperVeg, kohlrabi is nonetheless right up there with the best of them, delivering top scores across the board, not only for nutrients (being a member of the brassica family, therefore nutritional royalty), but also for its uniquely beautiful flavour and its ability to be eaten raw or cooked in just about every way imaginable. It's a puzzle why this stupendous plant food hero isn't recognised as a superstar throughout the world. It has such character – it's a pale green or bright purple orb with antennae, like a cartoon alien. Just looking at kohlrabi makes me smile. Eating it – now *that* is one of life's great vegetable pleasures.

The main edible body of kohlrabi grows just above ground. Technically it's a stem, with a bulbous shape. Its name comes from the German for 'cabbage-turnip'. Sure, they are shaped like a turnip and kind of resemble a solid cabbage, but in the eating, I would say it could be better described as 'radish-apple'. It has a very faint pepperiness and the sheen of radish, the crispness of an excellent apple, and a delicate but definite sweetness similar to cucumber.

THE NUTRITIONAL SUPERPOWER

Vitamin C, for healthy tissues and disease resistance.

OTHER HIGH LEVELS OF NUTRITIONAL EXCELLENCE

▌ Multiple phytochemicals with antioxidant, anti-cancer and anti-inflammatory properties (like all cruciferous veg).

▌ B-complex vitamins, for converting food into fuel and giving us energy.

SEASON

Late spring through winter.

VARIETIES

'White' kohlrabi is actually light green on the outside and white on the inside and is the most common variety. Purple kohlrabi has a beautiful fuchsia to dark purple skin, but the interior is also white.

CHOOSE AND STORE

If leaves are attached, this is a terrific sign of freshness, plus you get a bonus vegetable – the leaves can be cooked like kale or cabbage (stems are usually too tough to eat). If leaves are attached and wilted, the root should still be good to eat – just snap off where the stems meet the root and discard. Fresh leaves will keep for up to a few days in a plastic bag in the fridge and the root keeps for at least a couple of weeks. If you cut it open and find brown spots it is past its best. Kohlrabi should feel heavy for its size and rock hard.

PROCESSED AND PRESERVED

Kohlrabi makes some of the best pickles, so look out for them, or try your hand at one of the most delicious and easiest home ferments: *Kohlrabi Sauerkraut* (page 71).

PREP

▌ Unless you are lucky enough to have a kohlrabi harvested within just a few days, you will need to remove the skin, as it gets more fibrous as it ages. First snap off or cut off any remaining stems. Cut a thin slice from the top and bottom, stand it on a flat end, and carve away the skin with a sharp knife, cutting downwards across the surface. Depending on how tough the skin is, you may also succeed with a veg peeler.

▌ Once peeled, the white globe can be finely sliced or shaved with a peeler or on a mandoline, grated or julienned for salads, sliced thickly or cut into sticks for crudités, cubed, chunked or cut into wedges for steaming, roasting or boiling.

Kohlrabi's best mates

Rice vinegar, sushi vinegar | Apple cider vinegar | Lemon, lime |
Orange | Honey | Soy sauce | Cream, crème fraîche, yoghurt | Butter |
Parmesan, Gruyère, emmental | Fennel seed | Caraway seed |
Dill, coriander (cilantro), chervil

Cook and eat

Kohlrabi summer rolls

Cut long thin strips or grate kohlrabi, along with strips of red capsicum
(pepper), fresh mango, tofu, spring onions (scallions) and mint or coriander
(cilantro) leaves. Place small clusters of each on soaked rice paper
wrappers, fold, roll up and seal. Serve with soy sauce and sweet chilli sauce
for dipping.

Kohlrabi wrappers

Cut very thin round slices of kohlrabi, sprinkle with salt, leave for
30 minutes or so, rinse and pat dry. The now pliable rounds can be folded
over a filling such as herbed soft cheese, stuffed like a mini taco or wrapped
around or draped over other ingredients.

Buttered kohlrabi

Cut into small chunks and pan-fry very gently in a generous amount
of butter until soft.

Kohlrabi fries

Cut into 1 cm (½ inch) diameter sticks or wedges. Toss with olive oil
and sea salt. Place on a lined baking tray and bake at 200°C (400°F) until
golden, turning once.

I WAS KEEN TO INCLUDE ONE RECIPE in this volume as an introduction to the wonderful world of fermentation. Home fermenting is a wild and complex subject, but this lacto-fermented kohlrabi might just be the simplest, most satisfying and foolproof recipe you are likely to try. A great starting point, this is a delicious use for kohlrabi – even tastier than cabbage sauerkraut, I would argue.

It takes about 30 active minutes of preparation, then the wild microbes do the rest of the work. After 3–6 days (depending on conditions), you will be rewarded with a delicious relish that keeps for months in the fridge (if you need it to). Eating it boosts your gut health with natural probiotics. Use it just as you would cabbage sauerkraut – toss in salads, fill a baked potato or eat with cottage cheese and alfalfa sprouts. It tastes amazing in a toasted rye or sourdough bread sandwich, laid on in a thick layer, with melting cheese and a slick of mustard.

Kohlrabi sauerkraut

SERVES 6 | **PREP** 30 MINS | 3–6 DAYS FERMENTATION

LOW CALORIE | GLUTEN FREE | DAIRY FREE | VEGAN

3 large kohlrabi (about 700–800 g/
1 lb 9 oz–1 lb 12 oz total), as fresh as possible, with leaves – if no leaves are attached, you will need 1 large cabbage leaf (any type but red), for covering the kraut

1 tablespoon sea salt

1 litre (35 fl oz/4 cups) still natural mineral water

OPTIONS
Add whole spices such as caraway seeds, cumin seeds or dried chillies.

SPECIAL EQUIPMENT
Large preserving jar (500 ml/17 fl oz +), washed and dried and something to weigh down the ferment at the top of the jar (I use a zip-seal plastic bag filled with mineral water). If you have a food processor with a grating attachment, use it to grate the kohlrabi (your arm will thank you for it) or use a box grater.

1   Remove any leaves from the kohlrabi and reserve two. Peel the kohlrabi, then grate coarsely, using a food processor or box grater. Place the grated kohlrabi in a large non-metallic bowl. You should have 500–600 g (1 lb 2 oz–1 lb 5 oz).

2   Wash and dry your hands and add the 1 tablespoon salt to the bowl. Mix with your hands. Cover the bowl with plastic wrap and set aside at room temperature for 1–2 hours to release the juices.

3   Meanwhile wash the 2 reserved kohlrabi leaves or 1 large cabbage leaf and dry well. Also be sure your preserving jar is clean and dry.

4   Once the grated kohlrabi looks collapsed and juicy, wash your hands and grab a handful at a time, squeezing as much liquid as possible back into the bowl, and pack each squeezed-out handful into the jar. Once all the kohlrabi is transferred, pour the liquid into the jar.

5   Cover the surface with the clean leaves to reach the edges and tuck in. Gently pour in enough mineral water to come 5 cm (2 inches) above the surface. Weigh down (see left). Close the jar, though not air-tight – leave just ajar for a little breathing room.

6   Now it's time to leave it alone for a few days. Place the jar in a shallow bowl (in case any eruptions occur) and leave it in a draught-free place for 3–6 days. It will start to turn an unappetising brownish colour. This is good!

7   After 3 or so days, test for doneness. Using a wooden tool such as a chopstick or wooden spoon handle, lift the covering leaf and grab out a little kraut. It should smell pleasantly tart. If it tastes satisfyingly sour, it is done. If it is not sour enough, leave for a few more days. If it is too sour or tastes bad, well, sorry, but you will have to bin it and start again. This is highly unlikely, but there are lots of variables at work here and sometimes it fails.

8   Once ready, discard the leaves and store the sauerkraut in the fridge. It will continue to develop flavour slowly in storage. Serve the sauerkraut drained. Use within 6 months.

IF YOU ARE A LOVER OF THE THAI GREEN PAPAYA SALAD called *som tam*, you will adore this. Kohlrabi is an ideal substitute for the elusive unripe papaya, plus it delivers all the nutritional super powers of the cabbage family.

If you're not familiar with tempeh, it's a protein-packed, fermented soya bean slab with a nutty flavour, originating in Indonesia. It's available in health food shops and some Asian groceries, often in the frozen section. You could use tofu instead, cooked as for the *Pumpkin and Tofu Malay Curry* on page 245. The tempeh or tofu is optional, but it does make this a complete light main course. Add noodles or rice for more substance.

Hot and sour kohlrabi salad with roasted tempeh

SERVES 4 | **PREP** 30 MINS | **COOK** 25 MINS

LOW CALORIE | GOOD SOURCE OF PROTEIN | GLUTEN FREE (IF TAMARI IS USED) | DAIRY FREE | VEGAN (IF MAPLE SYRUP IS USED)

For the tempeh (if using)

200 g (7 oz) tempeh, defrosted if frozen

4 teaspoons light soy sauce or tamari

1 tablespoon sesame oil

For the salad

2 large kohlrabi (about 500–600 g/ 1 lb 2 oz–1 lb 5 oz total)

1 red capsicum (pepper), deseeded and cut into thin strips

100 g (3½ oz) green beans, thinly sliced crossways

4 spring onions (scallions), thinly sliced diagonally

2 handfuls of mint leaves

50 g (2 oz/ ⅓ cup) toasted peanuts or cashews, lightly crushed

coriander (cilantro), to garnish (optional)

For the dressing

80 ml (2½ fl oz/⅓ cup) lime juice

80 ml (2½ fl oz/⅓ cup) light soy sauce or tamari

2 tablespoons maple syrup or runny honey

1 garlic clove, crushed

1 teaspoon chilli flakes

SPECIAL EQUIPMENT
Baking tray, non-stick foil or baking paper and a box grater or julienne tool.

1 For the tempeh, preheat the oven to 200°C (400°F) and line a baking tray. Cut the tempeh into two rectangles, then slice thinly, about 5 mm (¼ inch) thick. Place on the tray in a single layer and drizzle over the soy sauce. Turn the pieces to coat. Brush each piece with sesame oil on both sides and cook for 20–25 minutes until crisp and golden. Keep warm.

2 For the salad, pull any leaves off the kohlrabi and peel with a veg peeler or paring knife. Use a grater or julienne cutting tool to cut into shreds. Place in a large bowl and add the capsicum, beans and spring onion.

3 For the dressing, combine all the ingredients thoroughly in a small bowl.

4 Just before serving, stir half of the dressing through the salad. Transfer to a serving platter or individual plates. Top with the tempeh. Tear the mint leaves and scatter over, then add the crushed peanuts. Pour over the remaining dressing, finish with coriander sprigs, if using, and serve right away.

NOTE
The dressing is a great all-round Southeast Asian sauce with a good balance of sweet, sour, salty and hot. It can also be used as a dipping sauce or a marinade for tofu etc.

THINLY SLICED KOHLRABI HAS A JUICY, SUPER-CRISP BITE, similar to an extra-firm apple without the acidity, but with plenty of delicate sweetness. The poppy seeds add an extra component of nutrition here, being packed with vitamins and minerals. This simple salad looks gorgeous with its demure pale green colour flecked with tiny grey-black seeds and verdant mint leaves, and its flavour is fresh, clean and textural. There should be a bold statement of mint here – don't hold back on the quantity; think of the mint as a salad leaf rather than a herbal garnish.

Kohlrabi and mint salad with sweet poppy seed dressing

SERVES 4–6 | **PREP** 20 MINS | **COOK** 0 MINS

30 MINUTES OR LESS | LOW CALORIE | GOOD SOURCE OF PROTEIN | GLUTEN FREE

2 large kohlrabi (about 500–600 g/ 1 lb 2 oz–1 lb 5 oz total)

1 bunch of mint, leaves stripped from about 8–10 sprigs

For the sweet poppy seed dressing
120 g (4¼ oz) Greek-style or thick and creamy yoghurt

4 teaspoons apple cider vinegar

6 teaspoons maple syrup or runny honey

2 tablespoons poppy seeds

1 tablespoon extra virgin olive oil

sea salt and freshly ground black pepper

OPTIONS
Substitute dairy-free yoghurt to make it vegan.

Serve as a side salad or great with *Tomato and Feta Grain Roast* (page 269).

SPECIAL EQUIPMENT
None

1   Pull any leaves off the kohlrabi and peel with a veg peeler or paring knife. Using a large knife, cut each in half top to bottom, then place cut-side down on the chopping board. Make a long cut downwards through the middle equatorially, then cut across and downwards as thinly as possible into slices. Place in a bowl.

2   To make the dressing, mix all the ingredients together until smooth, whisking in the oil at the end. Taste for seasoning.

3   Just before serving, stir the dressing through the kohlrabi or leave to serve on the side. Pluck the mint leaves and roughly tear most of them into the bowl, leaving a few for garnish. Transfer the salad to a serving dish, and finish with a few whole mint leaves. Eat right away.

NOTES
The dressing may become thinner upon standing. It's best to mix the dressing and assemble the salad shortly before serving. Any saved portion will still taste good, but if it seems too watery, simply add a bit more yoghurt to thicken.

This dressing is excellent with all kinds of salad leaves and raw vegetables so use it anywhere you fancy a creamy, sweet-and-sour flavour.

Sweet Potato

... their sexy colour, velvety texture
and sweetness is irresistible.

Sweet Potato

I feel I should give ordinary potatoes an honourable mention here. They didn't make the cut to star as one of my 25 SuperVeg, not because they aren't wonderful in every way, and healthy too, but sweet potatoes (incidentally, no botanical relation to potatoes) possess a spud-trumping talent – their orange pigment, which actively protects your health, supplying beta-carotene (and other nutrients) in abundant quantity and quality. In addition, sweet potatoes' starch causes the body's blood sugars to release more slowly than potatoes' starch, giving you sustained energy rather than a sugar crash. Good old potatoes are super in every other way for their deliciousness, versatility and basic carb-based energy, but they just don't hold a candle to sweet potatoes for what they can deliver in the health department. Sorry spuds!

Sweet potatoes are enjoying a bit of a renaissance in modern healthy cookery, and rightly so. They are cheap, they store well, they have a sexy colour, and their velvety texture and sweetness is irresistible. At some point, I reckon around the inception of the internet, they became 'cool' and since then the demand for sweet potatoes has just exploded.

THE NUTRITIONAL SUPERPOWER

Vitamin A/beta-carotene, an antioxidant and anti-inflammatory – mostly in orange and purple varieties; the highest of any root veg.

OTHER HIGH LEVELS OF NUTRITIONAL EXCELLENCE

- Amylose, a slow-releasing starch for maintaining energy levels.
- B-complex vitamins, for converting food into fuel and giving us energy.
- Minerals, especially iron, for blood health.
- Vitamin C, for healthy tissues and immunity.

SEASON

Year-round; best in autumn through winter where they are locally grown.

VARIETIES

ORANGE-FLESHED VARIETIES Always the ones to go for, not just because their colour is fabulous, but because orange = beta-carotene/vitamin A, which is this vegetable's strongest (but not only) nutritional strength, plus the orange ones are dependably sweet, nutty and creamy-fleshed.

WHITE-FLESHED VARIETIES Can turn a bit greyish when cooked. There are also some purple-fleshed varieties. It's sometimes hard to tell what colour the flesh is by the skin, which can be any shade of dark beige to purplish red – if you're not sure, either ask the greengrocer or surreptitiously use your thumbnail to scratch off a tiny bit of skin to check the flesh colour underneath – just don't get caught vandalising the produce!

CHOOSE AND STORE

Blemishes on sweet potatoes are nothing to fret about – they can easily be cut off, but avoid roots with wrinkles, mould, soft patches or sprouts. The most important thing is that they are rock hard and heavy. For baking like a jacket potato, long and spindly roots resembling thick carrots aren't as desirable – find more round and plump ones for this if you can. Otherwise any shape fits most purposes. Store without washing in a breathable box or bag (not plastic) in a dark, cool place, as you would ordinary potatoes.

PROCESSED AND PRESERVED

Frozen sweet potato chunks are suitable to cook from frozen for steaming, boiling or roasting. Frozen jacket sweet potatoes have added vegetable oil and are a handy fast food – though fresh roots are quick and easy to cook as 'baked' in a microwave (see page 80). Tinned sweet potatoes are a relic from the mid twentieth century and are best avoided.

PREP

It's not essential to peel sweet potatoes, plus the skin contains bonus nutrients. But they usually have a few knobbles, hairs or blemishes that need to be cut off, especially from the ends. Do peel them to capitalise on their velvety texture in soups, purées and mash, using a veg peeler.

Sweet Potato's best mates

Nutmeg, cinnamon, cardamom, anise | Paprika, smoked paprika |
Ground cumin | Fennel seeds | Ginger | Chilli | Garlic | Sage, rosemary, thyme |
Cream, crème fraîche, yoghurt | Butter | Soy sauce | Honey, maple syrup |
Almonds, amaretto | Cashews | Coconut | Sweetcorn

Cook and eat

Oven-baked sweet potato jackets

Preheat the oven to 200°C (400°F). Stab each potato several times with a fork. Rub all over with a little olive oil and salt. Place directly on the oven rack, also placing a lined tray on a lower rack to catch any seeping syrup. Bake for 40–50 minutes or until soft throughout, turning halfway with tongs.

Speedy microwave-baked jackets

For two sweet potatoes, weighing about 250–300 g (9–10$\frac{1}{2}$ oz) each, stab several times with a fork. Wrap each one in a paper towel and place both on a suitable plate in the microwave. Cook at high power for about 5 minutes, then use tongs to turn over. Cook for 3 more minutes, then leave to stand for 2 minutes. Test with a skewer or sharp knife that they are soft throughout. (Microwaves vary.)

Smoky sweet potato wedges

Cut chunky wedges, leaving the skin on. Toss in olive oil and sea salt, then arrange on a lined baking tray and bake at 200°C (400°F) for about 30–40 minutes until tender, turning once. Sprinkle with a little smoked paprika and serve.

Super crisp sweet potato fries

Peel and cut into thin wedges and strips about 5 mm ($\frac{1}{4}$ inch) thick. Place in a sealable plastic bag or bowl and toss with a couple of spoonfuls of cornflour (cornstarch) or potato starch mixed with fine salt to taste. Next toss them in a light coating of olive oil and spread in one layer on a lined baking tray. Bake at 200°C (400°F) for about 20–25 minutes until crisp and golden, turning just once.

ESSENTIALLY THIS IS SOUP BY ANOTHER NAME. Cool, creamy, velvety and sweet, it makes a bone-clinging breakfast that's also packed with nutrients. Boil up some sweet potatoes in the evening and chill, then they're ready for the blender first thing in the morning. As with most root veg, you can leave the skin on for maximum nutrition – sweet potato skins contain iron, potassium, fibre and vitamin E. Just scrub the root well and cut off the ends and any blemishes before cutting into chunks and boiling for 15 minutes or until tender, then drain, cool, pop into a bag and chill. Alternatively use leftover baked sweet potatoes.

The addition of turmeric here brightens the colour, and it's also functional for health – turmeric has powerful anti-inflammatory and antioxidant properties.

Sweet potato and almond power smoothie

SERVES 2 | **PREP** 5 MINS | **COOK** 0 MINS (+ SWEET POTATO COOKING TIME – SEE ABOVE)

30 MINUTES OR LESS | GOOD SOURCE OF PROTEIN | GLUTEN FREE | DAIRY FREE | VEGAN (IF MAPLE SYRUP IS USED)

250 g (9 oz) cooked sweet potato chunks, chilled

500 ml (17 fl oz/2 cups) almond milk, chilled

1–2 tablespoons maple syrup or honey, or to taste

1 teaspoon ground turmeric

1 teaspoon ground cinnamon

large pinch of sea salt

1 teaspoon pure vanilla extract

$1/2$ teaspoon pure almond extract

OPTIONS
Add other warm spices such as ground cardamom or nutmeg.

Substitute soy milk or another nut milk for almond milk.

SPECIAL EQUIPMENT
Blender

Whizz all the ingredients together in a blender at high speed until completely smooth. Bear in mind this may take a bit of extra blitzing if you've left the skins on the sweet potato.

NOTE
The smoothie keeps well in the fridge for up to 24 hours.

SCRUMPTIOUS, MULTICOLOURED AND COOKED in one large oven tray, this does lend itself well to a lazy weekend brunch or breakfast, but it can be devoured at any time of day. Enjoy the seductive aroma of garlic, capsicums (peppers), sage and thyme as they permeate the kitchen. If you aren't familiar with using fennel seeds, you'll see how much of a lovely surprise element they add here – I'm a big fan of roasting them with any veggies, and they work particularly well with sweet potato.

Sweet potato breakfast tray

SERVES 3–4 | **PREP** 20 MINS | **COOK** 35 MINS
GOOD SOURCE OF PROTEIN | GLUTEN FREE | DAIRY FREE

700 g (1 lb 9 oz) sweet potatoes (about 3 medium), scrubbed but not peeled, cut into bite-sized chunks

2 large banana shallots, quartered, or 4–6 small French shallots, left whole

4 garlic cloves, left whole

1 red capsicum (pepper), cut into chunks

2 green chillies, halved from stem to base

150 g (5^1/2 oz/1 cup) frozen sweetcorn (or use fresh or tinned)

8 sage leaves

4 thyme sprigs

1 teaspoon fennel seeds

50 ml (1^3/4 fl oz) extra virgin olive oil

sea salt and freshly ground black pepper

4 eggs

OPTIONS
Substitute eggs with tofu, in large chunks – toss together with the veg before roasting.

Serve with toast and fruit or steamed green veg or a salad.

SPECIAL EQUIPMENT
Large baking tray (covering most of an average oven shelf) and non-stick foil or baking paper.

1 Preheat the oven to 200°C (400°F) and line a baking tray. Place all the ingredients except the eggs on the tray and toss together with your hands to coat evenly with the oil and seasoning. Spread out in a single layer.

2 Bake for 30 minutes, stirring halfway through.

3 Remove from the oven and make four gaps in the veg to cook the eggs in. Carefully crack the eggs into the gaps and season the eggs with salt and pepper. Return to the oven for 3–4 minutes, until the egg whites are cooked and the yolks are still runny; longer if you prefer them well done. Serve right away.

THE LEMONY GARLIC MUSHROOMS here are a little tapas trick I learnt from a Spanish chef – it's a super simple way to make ordinary mushrooms extraordinary. Along with all their juices, they make a delicious foil for the sugary creaminess of sweet potatoes. A crown of melting mozzarella fuses it all together for your eating pleasure in about 30 minutes if you use a microwave to speed-bake the spuds.

Smothered sweet potatoes with tangy mushrooms and mozzarella

SERVES 2–4 | **PREP** 15 MINS | **COOK** 15 MINS

30 MINUTES OR LESS | GOOD SOURCE OF PROTEIN | GLUTEN FREE

2 sweet potatoes (about 500–600 g/ 1 lb 2 oz–1 lb 5 oz total weight)

2 tablespoons extra virgin olive oil + more for brushing

3 garlic cloves, sliced

250 g (9 oz) chestnut or portobello mushrooms, medium sliced

sea salt and freshly ground black pepper

1 tablespoon lemon juice

handful of parsley, chopped

100 g (3^{1}/$_{2}$ oz) pizza mozzarella, grated (or other hard cheese)

OPTIONS

Serve with a green salad, wilted greens or steamed broccoli.

SPECIAL EQUIPMENT

Microwave for cooking sweet potatoes (alternatively, oven-bake for 40–50 minutes at 200°C/400°F), baking tray and non-stick foil or baking paper.

1   Preheat the oven to 200°C (400°F) and line a baking tray.

2   Scrub the sweet potatoes and cut off any major blemishes. Stab them several times with a fork. Wrap each one in a paper towel and place both on a suitable plate in the microwave. Cook at high power for 5 minutes, then use tongs to turn them over. Cook for 3 more minutes, then leave to stand for 2 minutes. (Microwave cooking times vary.)

3   Carefully unwrap the sweet potatoes and test first with a knife or skewer, which should penetrate without resistance. Slice open in half lengthways and check again that they are cooked throughout. (If not, rewrap and cook for 1–2 minutes more plus standing.)

4   Place the four halves on the baking tray, at first cut-side down, then brush with oil. Flip over so that they face cut-side up and use a fork to fluff the flesh slightly, keeping it contained in the skins.

5   Meanwhile, cook the mushrooms. Heat a frying pan over a medium heat and add the oil and garlic. Cook until the garlic starts to turn golden, then add the mushrooms and salt. Cook, stirring occasionally, until the mushrooms are soft and have released the maximum amount of juice – the juicier the better. Take the pan off the heat and stir in the lemon juice and parsley, then add several twists of black pepper.

6   Strain the mushrooms over a jug. Pour the reserved juice on to the sweet potatoes to season the fluffed flesh. Pile the mushrooms evenly over the top of the sweet potatoes. Top each with cheese.

7   Place in the oven and cook for 10 minutes, until the cheese is melted and tinged with gold.

NOTE

Ordinary mushrooms work best here – wild mushrooms would be dominated by the lemon and cheese.

Shoots and Leaves

Asparagus
Broccoli
Cabbage and Brussels Sprouts
Cauliflower
Witlof
Globe Artichoke
Cavolo Nero and Kale
Lettuce
Mushrooms
Chard and Spinach
Watercress

Asparagus

... is a really special vegetable – a high priestess, demanding
the utmost respect and reverence.

Asparagus

Asparagus is a really special vegetable – a high priestess, demanding the utmost respect and reverence. I gorge on it during its short season and then I rarely taste it for the rest of the year. It wasn't until I grew asparagus myself that I understood its true amazingness and the importance of its seasonality. It occupies a permanent small patch in my allotment and starts emerging all of a sudden and incredibly quickly in April when there is little else to eat in the garden – a total bonanza! Suddenly it's asparagus for dinner every other day and sometimes that's all you need – heaps of it, steamed and buttered – because it's so damn delicious. It comes thick and fast and then, just when it's really going full tilt in June, on Midsummer's Day, you must stop harvesting it so it can grow into tall feathery ferns and take in strength from the sun and replenish, helping it to come back and do the same the next year. Frustrating, but by then there are many other things to harvest, so you just move on.

I'll never forget biting into my first spear of homegrown asparagus, cut from the soil, straight into my mouth. It was a flavour I had never experienced, and suddenly I fully understood the value of homegrown veg – when it's just harvested, the flavour is simply incomparable to anything you can buy, no matter how fresh.

Year-round imported asparagus is just OK. It is really not worth the expense or the carbon footprint in my opinion. But I am lucky enough to live in the UK, which I do believe produces the best asparagus on earth for 2 months a year.

THE NUTRITIONAL SUPERPOWER

Asparagusic acid, which not surprisingly is unique to asparagus, is a powerful antioxidant, plus saponins, which are super-powerful anti-inflammatories.

OTHER HIGH LEVELS OF NUTRITIONAL EXCELLENCE

▌ Zinc, for healthy immunity and metabolism, male reproductive health, plus sensory organ and skin health.

▌ Vitamin K, for brain health.

▌ B-complex vitamins, for converting food into fuel and giving us energy.

▌ Folate, for cell vitality.

▌ A unique combination of phytonutrients, for disease resistance.

▌ Copper, for bone and tissue health.

▌ Iron, for blood health.

SEASON

Spring to early summer.

VARIETIES

There are two basic and very polarising varieties: green and white. I'm talking about green asparagus here in my worshipful eulogy. (Purple varieties fall into the green category and are delicious.) Many Europeans only like white asparagus.

WHITE ASPARAGUS This is almost a different vegetable and requires different treatment. It is a forced albino, grown against nature's wishes; it is not allowed to photosynthesise and is laboriously kept under mounds of soil to stay white. It is pointless to argue which type is better because white asparagus lovers are patriots too. It just comes down to personal taste, familiarity and maybe a cultural divide. (I have tried the best possible white asparagus – freshly picked from a field in the southwest of France in May, and cooked it on the same day and I still don't see the appeal. It was bland, stringy and bitter. I have also tasted it exquisitely prepared by a French master chef who no doubt got it from the same local farm and subjected it to complex and skilled preparation to enhance its delicateness. I'm still not convinced.)

'WILD ASPARAGUS' This is available in some specialist food shops and is a cultivated relative, which is prettier than it is tasty – mostly just an ornament for the plate.

CHOOSE AND STORE

As soon as asparagus is harvested, it starts to lose flavour. So if you know how far it has come, that will indicate whether it's worth buying – the more local, the better. But it's easy to use your senses to evaluate it. Simply examine the tips. They should have no damage or fraying and should be fully intact. Next – and always do this even if they look perfect – sniff the tips. One inhalation will reveal the truth of their freshness. Even a slight whiff of rot and it's a no go. Use asparagus as soon as you get it home if you can, and store in the fridge in a plastic bag until then.

Asparagus is usually sorted in bunches by thickness – various shapes and sizes emerge from the same plant. Some people prefer the thin grassy 'sprue' and others prefer thick and juicy spears. The medium thickness is the most popular.

PROCESSED AND PRESERVED

Asparagus in jars is widely available, but it's a mushy ghost of its former self. In some places it is adored – in Spain if you order asparagus on a restaurant menu, even when it is in season, you will most likely be served a plate of white stems out of a jar. At least that has been my experience several times.

PREP

Asparagus has a woody end where it's cut from the ground. Modern kitchen wisdom says that if you snap asparagus towards the bottom it will break where the woodiness stops. That is open to debate, but it is still an easy way to get the spears ready for cooking and is reliable enough. Snap and rinse and you're ready to cook. Or just slice an inch or two off the bottom of the whole bunch.

Asparagus's best mates

Lemon | Balsamic vinegar | Sushi vinegar | White wine vinegar | Olive oil | Flaxseed oil | Soy sauce | Miso | Toasted sesame seeds | Eggs cooked any style | Peas, pea shoots | Ginger | Hollandaise sauce | Butter | Parmesan | Ricotta

Cook and eat

Raw

Cut the stems in thin diagonal slices or shave long strands from the stems with a peeler and leave in ice water to curl up. Reserve the whole tips and add both to salads.

Cooked and chilled for salads and crudités

Blanch in plenty of boiling salted water for 1 minute, run under cold water until cool, then drain and chill.

Steamed

This is the best way to cook asparagus to maintain its delicate flavour (and the colour of purple asparagus, which is lost by boiling). Sprinkle with salt and steam for just 3 or 4 minutes (depending on how thick it is) until it's bright green, and when the lower stem just allows a knife tip to penetrate, it is perfect.

Roasting, chargrilling and barbecuing

Intensifies sweetness and brings out a nutty flavour. Toss in olive oil and salt and cook for just a few minutes until bright green and slightly blackened if on the grill. It can also be grill-cooked inside a foil parcel with a little butter if desired.

HERE'S A LOVELY WAY OF MAKING ASPARAGUS YOUR MAIN COURSE with the help of some miso-infused, high-protein tofu for breakfast, lunch or dinner. It can also be served as part of a feast of sharing platters. Scrambling tofu is one of the easiest ways to give it an appealing texture, and it's a good partner for the firm and juicy asparagus.

Asparagus and miso tofu scramble

SERVES 2–4 | **PREP** 5 MINS | **COOK** 20 MINS

30 MINUTES OR LESS | LOW CALORIE | GOOD SOURCE OF PROTEIN | GLUTEN FREE | DAIRY FREE | VEGAN

2 tablespoons coconut oil or extra virgin olive oil

250 g (9 oz) green asparagus (about 14 spears, trimmed weight), tips cut about 2 cm (^{3}/4 inch) long, stems cut on the diagonal into 1 cm (^{1}/2 inch) long segments

sea salt

300 g (10^1/2 oz) block firm fresh tofu, drained, left whole and wrapped in paper towel

1 spring onion (scallion), thinly sliced on the diagonal

freshly ground black pepper

For the miso sauce

2 tablespoons white miso

1 tablespoon lemon juice

1 tablespoon mirin

OPTIONS
Serve this with grains or noodles for a heartier meal.

SPECIAL EQUIPMENT
Large non-stick frying pan

1   Heat a large non-stick frying pan over a high heat. Add 1 tablespoon of the oil and the asparagus with a pinch of salt. Stir-fry for about 3 minutes, until bright green and charred in places. Remove the asparagus to a plate and set aside.

2   Return the pan to the heat, lowering it to medium–high. Add the remaining 1 tablespoon oil. Take the tofu and break it into rough, crumbly pieces with your hands into the pan, leaving it quite chunky. Add a pinch of salt. The idea now is to cook the water out of the tofu and crisp it up a bit. Stir it occasionally and turn it gently without breaking it down too finely – it should resemble the curds of scrambled eggs. Adjust the heat so that the tofu is gently browning, but not in danger of burning. Cook for about 10 minutes. The tofu should have released most of its water and start looking golden and crisp in places.

3   While the tofu is cooking, mix together all the miso sauce ingredients until smooth.

4   When the tofu is cooked, add half of the miso sauce to the pan. Stir for about 2 minutes until it is absorbed. Now add the asparagus and cook until completely heated through.

5   Transfer to a serving platter or individual plates or bowls. Drizzle over the remaining sauce and finish with a few spring onion slices and black pepper.

THE UMAMI-RICH SESAME BALSAMIC DRESSING here is perfect for glorifying asparagus without interfering with its delicate flavour, and also marries beautifully with eggs that have been boiled until butter-yolked. It's a filling and fuss-free salad for spring. As an abundant sharing platter, it looks verdant and dashing on the table.

Roasted asparagus and egg with sesame balsamic

SERVES 4 | **PREP** 15 MINS | **COOK** 15 MINS

30 MINUTES OR LESS | FEAST DISH | LOW CALORIE | GOOD SOURCE OF PROTEIN | GLUTEN FREE (IF TAMARI IS USED) | DAIRY FREE

4 large eggs

400 g (14 oz) green asparagus spears, lower part of stems snapped

2 teaspoons extra virgin olive oil or melted coconut oil

sea salt

100 g (3^{1}/$_{2}$ oz) baby salad leaves (rocket/arugula, baby kale, watercress, pea shoots)

For the sesame balsamic dressing

2 tablespoons raw sesame seeds

1^{1}/$_{2}$ tablespoons best balsamic vinegar

1^{1}/$_{2}$ tablespoons dark soy sauce or tamari

2^{1}/$_{2}$ tablespoons extra virgin olive oil

OPTIONS
Substitute baked tofu for eggs (see prep as for *Pumpkin and Tofu Malay Curry*, page 245).

SPECIAL EQUIPMENT
Large baking tray and non-stick foil or baking paper.

1   Preheat the oven to 220°C (425°F). Line a baking tray.

2   Place the eggs in a small saucepan and cover with cold water. Cover and bring to the boil, then simmer for 6 minutes. Drain and rinse the eggs under cold water until completely cool, then peel and cut into halves or quarters. (This cooking technique should result in yolks that are slightly undercooked and buttery – not powdery like hard-boiled eggs. Cook them 5 minutes longer if you prefer them well done.)

3   Meanwhile, place the asparagus on the baking tray and add the oil. Toss with your hands to coat evenly. Sprinkle with a touch of salt. Roast for 5 minutes until bright green and just tender.

4   For the dressing, heat a small frying pan without oil over a medium heat and add the sesame seeds. Toast, stirring frequently, until golden and popping. Remove from the pan and transfer to a small bowl to cool. When cool, combine all the ingredients thoroughly in the bowl.

5   Arrange the salad leaves on a platter or individual plates and top with asparagus (warm or cold) and the eggs. Pour the dressing over and serve right away.

ASPARAGUS SEGMENTS ARE BRIEFLY ROASTED here with a crunchy crumble of polenta, ground almonds and Parmesan (or see vegan suggestion, below). Nibble as a snack or side dish, use as an adornment on top of an omelette or scrambled eggs, or serve as the crowning glory for a bowl of egg-fried rice.

Asparagus with polenta crumb

SERVES 2–4 | **PREP** 10 MINS | **COOK** 20 MINS

30 MINUTES OR LESS | GLUTEN FREE | VEGAN (IF USING OPTION BELOW)

250 g (9 oz) green asparagus spears, lower part of stems snapped off, cut into 2 cm (³/4 inch) pieces

1 tablespoon extra virgin olive oil

1 tablespoon polenta

1 tablespoon ground almonds

20 g (³/4 oz) Parmesan cheese or vegetarian alternative, finely grated

sea salt

OPTIONS
Substitute 10 g (¹/4 oz) nutritional yeast flakes for Parmesan to make this vegan.

Serve with lemon wedges (see also suggestions above).

SPECIAL EQUIPMENT
Small baking tray and non-stick foil or baking paper.

1 Preheat the oven to 200°C (400°F) and line a baking tray. Place the asparagus in a bowl and stir through the olive oil to coat evenly.

2 In a small bowl, mix together the polenta, ground almonds and grated Parmesan and season with salt. Add to the asparagus and stir through. Spread the asparagus with every last crumb of coating in one layer on the baking tray.

3 Bake for 15–20 minutes until golden and sizzling. Cool for about 2 minutes, then transfer to individual plates or bowls and eat right away.

Broccoli

... no amount of bad PR can ever take this
stupendous vegetable down.

Broccoli

Poor old broccoli. It's burdened with an unfair cultural stereotype: for many kids who refuse to eat their greens, it represents the enemy. People who hate broccoli are quite outspoken about it, I find. Former US President George Bush Snr. famously declared in 1990, 'I do not like broccoli! I haven't liked it since I was a little kid and my mother made me eat it. And I'm president of the United States, and I'm not going to eat any more broccoli!' This comment not only endeared him to millions, it also prompted broccoli farmers to send 10 tons of the controversial vegetable to the White House as a gift, along with recipes for preparing it in exciting ways, in the hopes they might change the president's mind. So, even broccoli has had a short infamy as a political issue in the free world. But no amount of bad PR can ever take this stupendous vegetable down.

     Everyone knows broccoli is good for you, so that fact alone makes some people recoil from it right off the bat. Like all of its extended family members in the cabbage clan, overcooking it causes chemical changes that release sulphurous compounds and make it taste bad. I can see how a child who has tasted badly cooked broccoli would never go near it again. It should be cooked in intense heat for a short time to deliver its best qualities.

     For those who love it, I share your passion deeply. Broccoli is the one vegetable I always have to have in the fridge. As a voracious herbivore, I feel I need to eat it every day if possible, and it's super quick and mindless to prepare. It's my rescue remedy and also my best pal. Broccoli is my SuperVeg BFF, without question.

THE NUTRITIONAL SUPERPOWER

Extremely high concentration of multiple phytonutrients with anti-inflammatory and anti-cancer properties, for disease protection and eye health.

OTHER HIGH LEVELS OF NUTRITIONAL EXCELLENCE

- Quercetin, which is anti-viral, anti-microbial, anti-inflammatory and anti-allergic.
- Folate, for cell vitality.
- Vitamin C, for healthy tissues and immunity.
- Vitamin K, for brain health.
- B-complex vitamins, for converting food into fuel and giving us energy.

SEASON

Year-round; sprouting broccoli in late winter/early spring.

VARIETIES

Ordinary broccoli is a perfect staple and, once all its florets are used up, you still have its thick stem, one of its best attributes (see Prep opposite). There are many types of sprouting broccoli, which can be cooked whole with their slender stems – purple and white, broccolini/tender stem and broccoli raab/cima di rapa/rapini (the latter is actually the greens of a type of turnip, but it is used as a broccoli).

CHOOSE AND STORE

With ordinary broccoli, scan the surface and avoid heads with bruised or yellow patches, or saggy limbs. Pick up the head and shake it – it should be totally rigid and not floppy – same for sprouting broccoli, although flimsy leaves are fine. Pre-cut florets are OK but will spoil faster. Keep broccoli in a loose or sealed plastic bag in the fridge crisper drawer.

PROCESSED AND PRESERVED

Frozen broccoli is a good standby as an emergency green veg, especially when you are having a fast feed such as a bowl of ramen with broth or miso soup; it can be a little stringy once cooked.

PREP

Rinse the head thoroughly, letting water flow underneath and through the florets. For a large broccoli head, use a small knife to cut away individual florets with about 2 cm (3/4 inch) stems attached. Any leaves attached are good to eat too. Don't forget the stem, which will deliver several more delicious edible pieces from its tender core, it is one of the sweetest parts of the vegetable. Think of the broccoli as a tree, and treat the stem as the trunk. Carefully pare away the outer 'bark' of the trunk to reveal the pale, sweet flesh underneath.

Broccoli's best mates

Lemon | Orange | Soy sauce | Toasted sesame, sesame oil | Balsamic vinegar |
Apple cider vinegar | Cream, crème fraîche, yoghurt | Butter | Breadcrumbs |
Most cheeses | Chilli | Garlic | Ginger | Almonds, cashews, walnuts

Cook and eat

Whizzed raw

I call it microbroccoli – a lovely and easy way to eat broccoli raw. See
Microbroccoli Super-Tabbouleh (page 105).

Microwave steamed

The most convenient and quickest cooking method. You'll need to
work out the right timings for your microwave – if it overcooks or too
much water is used, it gets stringy. For my 800w oven, I use around 300 g
($10^1/_2$ oz) florets for two people, with just the water left on it from washing
it, or about a teaspoon more if it's dried off, plus a little sea salt, in a
microwave container with a breathable lid. Two minutes on high power and
standing for 1 minute and it's done to perfection.

Roasted

Broccoli's tiny buds taste wonderful when roasted until crisp. Place
florets in a sealable plastic bag and add a little oil. Seal the bag and massage
the oil thoroughly into the broccoli. (You can also add a little flavouring to
the bag such as crushed garlic or chilli flakes.) Spread the broccoli in one
layer on a lined baking tray, sprinkle with salt and roast at 220°C (425°F) for
about 15–20 minutes until the tops are deep golden and crisp.

Broccoli on the barbie

Cut large pieces so they are easier to turn and won't fall through the
grill bars. Prepare as for roasted broccoli (above). Turn over the coals until
nicely charred.

BROCCOLI JUST LOVES TO BE ROASTED – its sweetness intensifies and the tiny buds of its florets can take on a delicate crispness if the right amount of oil is applied (not too oily, not too dry). Chickpeas take on a surprising crunchy charm in the oven too, and the two are a happy match, especially with this versatile cumin yoghurt sauce bonding them as one.

Roasted broccoli and chickpea crunch

SERVES 2 AS A MAIN, 4 AS A SIDE | **PREP** 15 MINS | **COOK** 30 MINS

GOOD SOURCE OF PROTEIN | GLUTEN FREE

400 g (14 oz) tin chickpeas, drained

4 tablespoons extra virgin olive oil

sea salt

400 g (14 oz) broccoli florets, cut into bite-sized pieces

1/2 teaspoon chilli flakes

For the cumin yoghurt sauce

150 g (5 1/2 oz) plain yoghurt

1 teaspoon grated lemon zest

1 tablespoon lemon juice

1 teaspoon ground cumin

1 garlic clove, crushed

sea salt

OPTIONS
Serve with baked or mashed sweet potatoes or cooked grains, and a crunchy side salad.

SPECIAL EQUIPMENT
2 large baking trays, non-stick foil or baking paper and a large zip-seal plastic bag.

1   Preheat the oven to 200°C (400°F). Line two baking trays.

2   Pat dry the drained chickpeas between pieces of paper towel. Place them in a bowl, stir through 2 tablespoons of oil and season with sea salt. Pour the entire contents of the bowl onto one of the baking trays. Place on the middle shelf of the oven and bake for 10 minutes.

3   Place the broccoli in a large zip-seal plastic bag and add the remaining 2 tablespoons oil, the chilli flakes and salt. Seal the bag and toss and massage the broccoli so that it is well coated. Spread out the broccoli on the other baking tray. When the chickpeas' 10 minutes are up, stir them, then move them to the bottom oven shelf. Place the broccoli on the middle oven shelf.

4   Bake for another 10 minutes, then stir both the chickpeas and broccoli. Crank the oven up to 220°C (425°F) and cook for 10 minutes more – both the chickpeas and broccoli tips should be crisp but not burnt.

5   Meanwhile, make the sauce. Mix all the ingredients together and season with salt.

6   Serve the broccoli topped with chickpeas on a platter or individual plates and drizzle with the sauce.

NOTE
This sauce is also designed for the *Smoky Greens and Beans* (page 153), another great (but very different) marriage of brassicas and beans (cavolo nero and butter beans). It also pairs well with roasted roots or Mediterranean veg such as eggplants (aubergines), zucchini (courgettes) and capsicums (peppers), as well as baked potatoes and sweet potatoes.

MICROBROCCOLI IS MY NAME FOR RAW BROCCOLI WHIZZED TO CRUMBS in a food processor, reducing it to its most easily consumable form (no jaw work). Like its cousin cauliflower couscous (page 122), it can stand in for grains in grain-based salads as it does here, standing in for burghul (bulgur) wheat. It also works beautifully in a 1:1 ratio with quinoa as a basic side dish. It's alluringly green and you won't even notice you are consuming a large quantity of raw broccoli, which resides near the top of the list of nutrient powerhouse vegetables and does have extra benefits when eaten raw.

The addition of feta makes this already dense and filling salad a complete light meal, but if you prefer a purely plant-based side salad, it can be left out.

Microbroccoli super-tabbouleh

SERVES 4–6 | **PREP** 20 MINS | **COOK** 0 MINS

30 MINUTES OR LESS | LOW CALORIE | GOOD SOURCE OF PROTEIN | GLUTEN FREE | DAIRY FREE (IF FETA IS OMITTED) | VEGAN (IF FETA IS OMITTED)

200 g (7 oz) broccoli florets (from about 1 average head)

3 spring onions (scallions), sliced

100 g (3^1/$_2$ oz) cherry tomatoes, halved

1 baby cucumber or ^{1}/$_3$ English cucumber, diced

large handful of parsley, leaves stripped and chopped

2^1/$_4$ tablespoons lemon juice

60 ml (2 fl oz/^{1}/$_4$ cup) extra virgin olive oil + more to serve

sea salt

100 g (3^1/$_2$ oz) feta cheese

large handful of mint leaves

OPTIONS
Add boiled eggs, walnuts or toasted almonds for extra protein and substance.

SPECIAL EQUIPMENT
Food processor for whizzing broccoli (alternatively hand chop as finely as possible).

1 Place the broccoli in a food processor and whizz until reduced to crumbs the size of couscous. Scoop the crumbs into a mixing bowl.

2 Stir through the remaining ingredients except the feta and mint. Taste for seasoning and transfer to a serving platter or individual plates or bowls.

3 Crumble the feta over the top, then tear the mint leaves over to finish. Add an extra drizzle of olive oil, if desired. Best served right away.

PURPLE SPROUTING BROCCOLI, broccolini or ordinary broccoli all work well here. Pile all this saucy deliciousness on top of a steaming bowl of wholegrains for an uber-healthy main course or side dish.

Hot and spicy wok-charred broccoli bowl

SERVES 2 AS A MAIN, 4 AS A SIDE | **PREP** 10 MINS | **COOK** 10 MINS

30 MINUTES OR LESS | GOOD SOURCE OF PROTEIN | GLUTEN FREE (IF TAMARI IS USED) | DAIRY FREE | VEGAN

2 tablespoons coconut oil or extra virgin olive oil

75 g (2½ oz/½ cup) raw cashew nuts

5 cm (2 inch) thumb very fresh ginger, cut into thin matchsticks (see NOTE)

4 plump garlic cloves, sliced

1 red chilli, thinly sliced

250 g (9 oz) broccoli, cut into 5 cm (2 inch) pieces (include stems, peeled if thick, sliced diagonally)

sea salt

2 tablespoons dark soy sauce or tamari

3 tablespoons mild sushi vinegar

cooked brown rice or quinoa, to serve (optional)

OPTIONS
If sushi vinegar isn't available, use 2 tablespoons rice vinegar and 1 tablespoon mirin or sherry.

Add tofu for extra protein: stir-fry it in the wok first, then set aside and add it to the broccoli at the end, or bake it as for the *Pumpkin and Tofu Malay Curry* (page 245).

SPECIAL EQUIPMENT
Wok or large frying pan.

1   If serving this with cooked grains, get that sorted and standing by; the broccoli will be ready in less than 10 minutes once cooking starts.

2   Heat a wok or large frying pan over a medium–high heat and add the oil. Add the cashews with the ginger, garlic and chilli. Cook, stirring frequently, until everything turns a deep golden brown. (Keep an eye on the garlic and stop cooking if it starts to get dark before the rest.) Pour the contents of the pan, including most of the oil, into a medium bowl and set aside.

3   Return the pan to the heat and raise to high. Add the broccoli and a couple of pinches of salt and stir-fry for 3–4 minutes, until starting to soften and appear charred in places. Finish the cooking by splashing a little water (2–3 tablespoons) in the pan and stir until evaporated. The broccoli should be bright green and just tender. Remove from the heat.

4   Add the soy sauce and vinegar to the bowl of cashews and whisk with a fork. Divide the rice or quinoa, if using, amongst warm serving bowls. Top each with the broccoli and spoon the sauce over. Serve right away.

NOTE
To peel the ginger, use the tip of a teaspoon. Slice thinly, then stack the slices and cut into thin matchsticks.

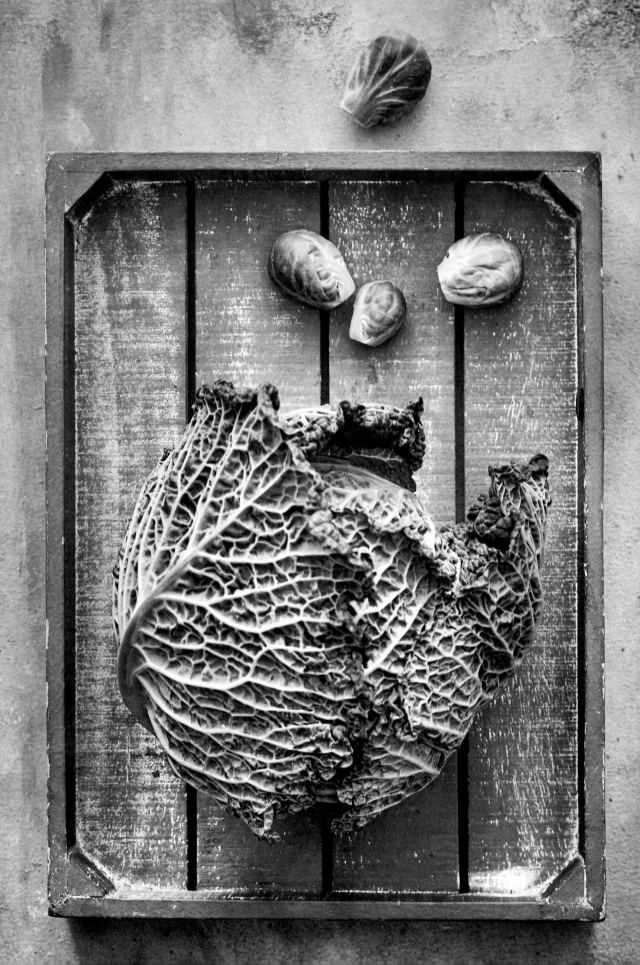

Cabbage and Brussels Sprouts

... all types of cabbages are SuperVeg.

Cabbage and Brussels Sprouts

All types of cabbages are SuperVeg, and there are so many of them. I have given cavolo nero (black cabbage/Tuscan kale) its own separate section along with kale and other leafy dark cruciferous greens because they have unique uses and status and are mostly interchangeable. So here I pay homage to the rest of the cabbages, highlighting my favourite types, including red cabbage and Savoy cabbage, which evolved in Europe, and Chinese leaf (Napa cabbage) and the bok choy (pak choy) sisters, which originated in Asia – all quite different vegetables. This book would not be complete without acknowledging the mighty brussels sprout, so I have included it here under the cabbage umbrella – after all, each sprout is an adorable miniature cabbage, designed as if for a doll's house kitchen.

THE NUTRITIONAL SUPERPOWER

A rich concentration of multiple phytochemicals, which lower cholesterol, stimulate the immune system, support cardio and stomach health, and fight infection, inflammation and cancer – especially brussels sprouts and red cabbage.

OTHER HIGH LEVELS OF NUTRITIONAL EXCELLENCE

- Indole-3-carbinol, which neutralises carcinogens, supports the immune system, and is important for oestrogen metabolism.
- Vitamin C, for healthy tissues and immunity.
- Vitamin K, for brain health.
- B-complex vitamins, for converting food into fuel and giving us energy.

SEASON

Year-round – best in winter.

VARIETIES

Each cabbage variety is a character all its own, lending itself to specific uses. Here are some common and favourite types:

RED, WHITE AND GREEN CABBAGES Round with sturdy, compact leaves, these are easy to shred and are ideal for salads and stir-fries or for cooking slow with vinegar, wine and sugar.

SAVOY CABBAGE The exquisite veiny leaves are wonderful for stuffing.

SWEETHEART (HISPI/POINTED CABBAGE) This has a tulip shape and looser leaves, which are thin and great for using as wraps, or for slicing and steaming or stir-frying.

CHINESE LEAF (NAPA CABBAGE) Shaped like a zeppelin, this is also perfect for wraps, and has a dual texture in the leaves of both lettuce-like parts and juicy, crunchy ribs.

BRUSSELS SPROUTS Green is standard; purple varieties taste much the same. A frilly variety called flower sprouts or 'Kalette' is available in winter and is a tasty crossbreed with kale.

BOK CHOY (PAK CHOY) Along with its sisters choy sum and tatsoi, they share the textures of Chinese leaf and its delicate flavour. Baby specimens are perfect for cutting lengthways in half or quarters and stir-frying.

CHOOSE AND STORE

In general, heaviness indicates a good moisture content and hence freshness. Avoid heads with dry, yellow or black patches. Store in a loose plastic bag in the fridge. Most cabbages (except the choys) are excellent keepers and may stay fresh for up to 3 weeks. Outer leaves that wilt in storage can be removed and discarded. If you only use part of a cabbage, cut surfaces may turn grey after a few days in the fridge, but they can be cut off when you are ready to use the remainder. Brussels sprouts are handy to have in stock for frequent use, as you can use a few at a time, instead of hacking into a large cabbage head periodically.

PROCESSED AND PRESERVED

Pickled or brined cabbage leaves can be found in eastern European, Turkish and Asian grocery stores. They are sturdy and good for stuffing. Sauerkraut (fermented shredded white cabbage) is an acquired taste, but incredibly healthy due to its natural probiotics – Korean kimchi is also made mostly of cabbage. Tinned brussels sprouts exist but are not to be trusted.

PREP

COMPACT CABBAGES (RED, WHITE AND GREEN) Remove any damaged leaves and rinse on the outside. Cut through from top to bottom into quarters. Chop out the hard core near the base and cut as necessary.

LOOSE CABBAGES (CHINESE LEAF, BOK CHOY ETC) Either cut away individual leaves and rinse, or cut the whole thing in quarters through the stem, rinse and drain well. Leave the hard core in to hold the leaves together, or cut it out before slicing or chopping the leaves.

Cabbage and Brussels Sprouts' best mates

Wine, sherry, Madeira | All good vinegars | Lemon | Orange, marmalade | Honey, maple syrup | Chilli | Garlic | Caraway | Cumin | Fennel seed | Coriander seed | Cloves, nutmeg | Dill, chervil, parsley | Rosemary, sage | Caramelised onions | Red lentils | Kidney beans, white beans | Chestnuts

Cook and eat

Raw

All the cabbages mentioned here are a welcome addition to a salad, for texture, flavour and nutrition – and are best finely shredded and raw. Red cabbage is especially fab, shredded and salted, then dressed in citrus juice to make it brighter and softer, to feature as a major salad ingredient (see *Bombay Slaw*, opposite). Whole Chinese cabbage leaves are ideally shaped for presentation and can also be wrapped round fillings. The light green parts can be torn and used as a pale, interesting salad leaf, and the sliced ribs are a sensation all their own, bursting with sweet juice between the teeth. Brussels are excellent raw and shredded as a salad ingredient.

Stir-fry

Cabbage and a wok get on like a house on fire. Intense heat and a little oil amplify cabbage's sweetness and maintain its crunch. In general, cut medium slices and stir-fry with a good pinch of salt over the highest possible heat with a small amount of oil until you get golden caramelised edges, before adding any sauce to the wok. Chinese leaf, bok choy (pak choy) and shredded brussels sprouts cook in about 1–2 minutes in a hot wok.

Roast

Cabbage wedges are fabulous roasted, especially looser leaved ones like sweetheart, Chinese and the central parts of Savoy. Coat with olive oil and season with sea salt and black pepper, place on a lined baking tray and cook at 200°C (400°F) for about 30 minutes or more until deep golden, turning once. For roasted brussels, cut the sprouts in half (include any stray leaves in the roasting – they will go crisp). Coat well with oil and season, then roast in a single layer on a lined baking tray at 220°C (425°F) for just 15–20 minutes, until darkened in places but still slightly firm. See more methods for cooking brussels sprouts on page 116.

RED CABBAGE TURNS A SEXY MAGENTA WITH THIS TREATMENT, creating a vibrant and beautiful raw salad base, which joins forces here with the surprising texture and spice bomb of Bombay mix. It's a colourful scene-stealer, perfect for entertaining as part of a summer buffet or BBQ, but it makes a great winter salad as well, when cabbage is at its best. It's a simple recipe, easily multiplied if you need to feed the masses.

Not familiar with Bombay mix? It's a whole family of protein-rich snack mixtures, from chickpea-based gram flour noodles, crisp fried lentils, chickpeas and nuts, laced with chilli and curry spices. Choose any variety you can find for the 'wow' factor in this slaw. See substitution suggestion below.

Bombay slaw

SERVES 4 | **PREP** 20 MINS + 1 HOUR SALTING | **COOK** 0 MINS

GLUTEN FREE (IF GLUTEN-FREE BOMBAY MIX IS USED) | DAIRY FREE | VEGAN (IF MAPLE SYRUP IS USED)

250 g (9 oz) red cabbage (about $1/2$ small or $1/4$ large), cored

1 teaspoon fine salt

1 tablespoon lime juice

1 tablespoon maple syrup or runny honey

2 spring onions (scallions), sliced diagonally

2 mild red chillies, deseeded and thinly sliced

100 g ($3^1/2$ oz) Bombay mix

handful of fresh coriander (cilantro) leaves (optional)

OPTIONS
Add a drained and rinsed tin of kidney beans, boiled eggs or chunks of feta or tofu as a garnish to make this a main-course salad.

Substitute 60 g ($2^1/4$ oz) dry-roasted peanuts, crushed and tossed with 1 teaspoon curry powder in place of the Bombay mix – not quite the same, but still tasty!

Serve with baked potatoes or sweet potatoes.

SPECIAL EQUIPMENT
None

1 Slice the cabbage as thinly as possible and place in a large bowl. Sprinkle with the salt and toss it through with your hands. Transfer to a large colander and set it over the bowl or the sink to drain and soften for about 30 minutes–1 hour.

2 Place the drained cabbage in the rinsed and dried bowl and stir through the lime juice and maple syrup until evenly mixed. Toss through the spring onion and chilli.

3 Arrange the salad on a platter. Just before serving, scatter over the Bombay mix and coriander leaves, if using. Serve right away.

NOTE
The cabbage base can be made well ahead and refrigerated, leaving the Bombay mix and the coriander to scatter over just before serving.

THE GORGEOUS VEINED LEAVES OF THE SAVOY CABBAGE are ideal for stuffing, and I have used them a lot over the years rolled up around various fillings as Mediterranean-style 'dolmas'. I'm quite skilled at the rolling process after so much practice, but some people might consider it too fiddly, so I wanted to come up with a simpler format. Here's what I dreamt up – half-moons or *mezzelune* (shown here cut in half) – dead easy and even tastier than dolmas, as it turns out, because they hold a lot of filling and take on a special flavour around the crisped-up edges. Long live the Savoy mezzelune!

I've included two ricotta-based fillings here to choose from – one is rich and elegant, with porcini mushrooms and finished with rich sage-garlic butter; one is light and zingy, with dill, mint and lemon. Have fun dreaming up your own mezzelune fillings – the possibilities are endless!

Savoy mezzelune with two fillings

SERVES 4 | **PREP** 30 MINS | **COOK** 25 MINS

FEAST DISH | GOOD SOURCE OF PROTEIN | GLUTEN FREE

For the porcini filling

40 g (1½ oz) dried porcini mushrooms

500 g (1 lb 2 oz) ricotta, drained

40 g (1½ oz) Parmesan or vegetarian substitute, finely grated

sea salt and freshly ground black pepper

50 g (1¾ oz/3 tablespoons) butter or 3 tablespoons olive oil

12–16 fresh sage leaves, roughly chopped

1 garlic clove, crushed

For the lemon, dill and mint filling

500 g (1 lb 2 oz) ricotta, drained

2 heaped tablespoons chopped dill

1 teaspoon dried mint (ideally from a peppermint teabag)

1 teaspoon lemon zest

2 teaspoons lemon juice

1 garlic clove, crushed

sea salt and freshly ground black pepper

For the cabbage wrapping

1 Savoy cabbage

cooking salt

3 tablespoons extra virgin olive oil

SPECIAL EQUIPMENT
Large pan, large baking tray and non-stick foil or baking paper.

1   To make the porcini filling, place the mushrooms in a small saucepan and add just enough water to cover. Bring to the boil, then stir and simmer for 10 minutes. Drain (reserving the liquid for another use such as a soup or sauce) and allow the mushrooms to cool, then squeeze out any excess moisture and chop finely. In a bowl, beat the ricotta until smooth, then stir in the mushrooms and Parmesan and season with salt and pepper.

2   To make the lemon filling, beat all the ingredients together.

3   Preheat the oven to 200°C (400°F). Bring a large pan of salted water to the boil. Prepare a tray or countertop with a clean tea (dish) towel or layers of paper towel for drying the cabbage. Line a large baking tray and brush generously with olive oil.

4   Remove any dark, tough outer leaves from the cabbage by cutting individually at the base. Cut away eight whole leaves, removing them carefully from the core so that they don't rip. (The unused leaves and core can be added to soups or stir-fries.)

5   Blanch the leaves, four at a time, for 2 minutes. Remove to a colander and run cold water over until cool. Lay the leaves on the towel-lined tray and allow them to dry thoroughly. Place each leaf on a chopping board and cut a 3–4 cm (1¼–1½ inch) long slit through the bottom of the thick rib. Flatten each leaf completely.

6   With the core-side of each leaf facing up, spoon a generous heap of your chosen filling on to one side of the central stem of the leaf, then fold over the other side and press the edges together, forming a half-moon shape. (The leaf edges will not really stick together, but the filling should hold them in place.) Place each stuffed leaf on the baking tray. Brush with the oil. Bake for 20 minutes, then turn off the oven and leave the mezzelune in for another 5 minutes to crisp up the edges.

7   To make sauce for the porcini filling, melt the butter in a frying pan. Once it starts foaming, stir in the sage and garlic and remove from the heat. Leave for 2 minutes while the sage crisps up.

8   Serve two mezzelune per person and spoon the sage-garlic butter over for the porcini ones.

THESE ADORABLE MINIATURE CABBAGES have endured a maligned existence due to being obliviously overcooked. Light cooking is essential with sprouts; they quickly reach a stage where they release unappetising sulphur compounds. Brussels sprouts are a winter vegetable, but they are brilliant on the barbie – below are two delicious and easy options with very different results.

Brilliant brussels sprouts

Zesty maple sprouts

For traditional roast dinners and festive feasts such as Thanksgiving and Christmas, this is my go-to sprout treatment – no fuss, just maximising the best of the brussels. Trim (and halve if large) 500 g (1 lb 2 oz) sprouts and place in a small to medium saucepan with a lid that will fit the sprouts snugly. Add 2 tablespoons water, 50 g (1¾ oz/3 tablespoons) butter, 2 tablespoons maple syrup, 2 teaspoons finely grated lemon zest and sea salt, to taste. Cover and bring to the boil over a high heat, then stir and reduce to a simmer. Keep covered and cook, stirring gently two or three times, until the sprouts are bright green and tender throughout, about 5–7 minutes. Lift the sprouts out of the pan with a slotted spoon into a warm serving dish and cover. Place the pan with the juices back over a medium-high heat and reduce for a couple of minutes until thickened, then pour over the sprouts and serve immediately.

Skewered sprouts

Trim the sprouts and stab each one all over a few times with the end of a skewer. Place in a bowl and drizzle over some soy sauce and toss. Leave for a few minutes. Thread the sprouts onto skewers through the base. Brush all over with olive oil. Cook over hot coals or gas flames, turning occasionally, until slightly charred and just tender.

Balsamic parcel sprouts

Trim the sprouts and halve if large, leave whole if small. Make a parcel by folding up the edges of a double or triple-layered square of foil. Place the sprouts in it, drizzle with balsamic vinegar and olive oil and season with sea salt and black pepper. Toss to coat. Scrunch the parcel to seal, allowing a little space for them to steam within. Place the parcel on the grill over hot coals or gas flames for about 5–10 minutes, until the sprouts are steaming, bright green and tender. The parcel can also be baked in the oven at 220°C (425°F) for 15 minutes or until the sprouts are tender.

SKEWERED
SPROUTS

ZESTY MAPLE
SPROUTS

BALSAMIC
PARCEL
SPROUTS

Cauliflower

... one of the most versatile of all veg, speaking every language of flavouring, and adaptable to just about any method of preparation.

Cauliflower

Cauliflower is indeed a flower. Actually, it's an enormous cluster of flowers in the bud stage that grows from a tall and sturdy stem as thick as your wrist. It can take up to 1 cubic metre of space to grow one cauliflower, and some varieties take nearly a year to grow from seed to harvest. It's hard to imagine how that's economically viable for a cauliflower farmer, when they only cost loose change to buy. Cauliflower's value is immeasurable – it is one of the most versatile of all veg, speaking every language of flavouring, and adaptable to just about any method of preparation, from barbecuing to whizzing into raw couscous-like crumbs. To top it off, it's abundantly nutritious, yet low in calories.

Whether larger than your head or smaller than your fist, cauliflowers usually come with some pale green, elegantly curvaceous leaves attached to the base. Everyone is accustomed or instructed to strip these off and discard them – but why? These are like a bonus vegetable that comes with the package! The leaves have a delicate cabbage flavour and can be treated any way you might use cabbage – steamed, stir-fried, added to soup or shredded raw in a salad. If the leaves have thick stems, as long as they don't seem too woody, chop and cook them up, along with the dense white core and stem of the cauliflower. It's all good stuff.

THE NUTRITIONAL SUPERPOWER

One of the best sources of indole-3-carbinol, which neutralises carcinogens, supports the immune system, and is important for oestrogen metabolism.

OTHER HIGH LEVELS OF NUTRITIONAL EXCELLENCE

- Multiple phytonutrients, which are anti-cancer, anti-bacterial and anti-viral (present in all cruciferous vegetables).

- B-complex vitamins, for converting food into fuel and giving us energy.

- Vitamin C, for healthy tissues and immunity.

- Vitamin K, for brain health.

SEASON

Year-round.

VARIETIES

Cauliflower heads come extra large, large to medium, and in baby size. Babies are best cooked by steaming whole, leaves and all. If you are lucky enough to find purple or orange cauliflower, or the gorgeous green Romanesco with its psychedelic fractal-patterned florets, these are best broken into individual florets and steamed (never boiled) or served raw, to make the most of their natural beauty.

CHOOSE AND STORE

The surface of the florets should always be perfectly even in colour and unblemished. Small blemishes can be cut off. Any type of cauliflower has excellent longevity when stored in a sealed plastic bag in the fridge – up to 2 weeks if bought very fresh. Pre-cut florets have a shorter lifespan – greying on the cut surfaces can be cut away and they should still be good to use. A sniff and a squeeze should confirm this – bin them if there's a pong or if they lack firmness.

PROCESSED AND PRESERVED

Frozen cauliflower florets are an OK standby, but can be a little bit stringy once cooked. Cauliflower 'rice' or 'couscous' – whizzed into grain-like pieces – is now available chilled and in long-life packets – it's convenient but the high price is hard to justify for what it is. Pickled cauliflower is a rare treat to find, and it's quite delicious as a snack or salad addition, in small quantities.

PREP

Cutting florets: cut away any leaves and the stem and reserve for another use (see opposite). Slice the cauliflower in half through the base. Cut the florets away from the V-shaped core, or pull them off and tear or cut to your preferred size.

Cauliflower's best mates

Cardamom, nutmeg, cumin | Fennel seeds | Saffron | Chilli |
Coconut milk | Toasted sesame seeds | Tahini | Cream, crème fraîche,
yoghurt | Mustard | Honey | Capers | Truffle | Parmesan,
mature cheese | Blue cheese

Cook and eat

Cauliflower couscous

This is a great low-cal and low-carb substitute for grains. Break the cauliflower into florets, wash and drain. Place in a food processor and whizz until reduced to crumbs the size of couscous. It can be eaten raw or cooked. To cook 250 g (9 oz), scrape into a microwave-safe container and sprinkle with salt, distributing it evenly with your fingertips (no need to add water). Cover and cook for 3 minutes, then stand for 2 minutes. (Microwaves vary: the cauliflower should be cooked through.)

Cauliflower steaks

A sexy cross section of cooked cauliflower makes a fab alternative side veg, or a stand in for carbs. Cut a 1 cm ($^1/_2$ inch) or 2 cm ($^3/_4$ inch) thick slab right from the middle of the cauliflower, cutting through the stem. Save the remainder for another use. You can cut more steaks, but they will be smaller and uneven sizes. Brush the steak with oil and season with salt, then cook in a chargrill pan or roast in a 200°C (400°F) oven until tender. Alternatively cook on a barbecue, turning regularly, until blackened in places and tender when prodded with a knife or skewer.

Cauliflower sauce

Simmer small florets in just enough milk or nut milk to cover along with garlic and seasoning until very soft, then purée until completely smooth.

Roast florets

Cauliflower gets super sweet when roasted, and tastes heavenly when slightly charred. Toss raw florets with oil and salt, and whole spices such as cumin seeds if desired, then roast in a 200°C (400°F) oven until golden. Cook for a few minutes more at 220°C (425°F) for charred edges.

CAULIFLOWER BECOMES DELICATE AND CREAMY when cooked to within an inch of its life with nutty brown rice, fragrant whole spices and sultanas. Just wait for the incredible aromas given off by this vibrant yellow dish, festooned with twinkling pomegranate seeds and golden almonds. Spice alert! You might want to warn your diners that they may be biting into whole cardamom pods and cloves, which burst with flavour between the teeth, but are best chewed a bit and then discarded as any pilau-lover is accustomed to. If this is a concern, just leave those two spices out.

Jewelled cauliflower pilau rice

SERVES 4–6 | **PREP** 15 MINS + 30 MINS SOAKING | **COOK** 50 MINS

FEAST DISH | GLUTEN FREE | DAIRY FREE | VEGAN

250 g (9 oz/1^1/$_4$ cups) brown basmati rice

1 tablespoon coconut oil or extra virgin olive oil

1 onion, finely sliced

1 teaspoon ground turmeric

^{1}/$_2$ teaspoon cumin seeds

12 cardamom pods

6 cloves

2 bay leaves

5 cm (2 inch) cinnamon stick or a few shards of cassia bark

500 g (1 lb 2 oz) cauliflower, including the stem and leaves – break off medium-size florets and roughly chop the stem and leaves

2 teaspoons sea salt

4 tablespoons sultanas (golden raisins) or currants

To serve

2 handfuls of fresh pomegranate seeds (optional)

4 tablespoons flaked or slivered almonds, toasted (optional)

OPTIONS

If serving as a main course for four, a dollop of creamy yoghurt is a nice addition, as is a boiled or poached egg for extra protein.

Substitute freekeh (green whole-wheat grain) for rice for an exotic smoky flavour.

Serve with *Smoked Eggplant Dal* (page 205).

SPECIAL EQUIPMENT

Deep, wide pan with a lid, as you would use for cooking rice.

1   Soak the basmati rice in cold water for 30 minutes, then drain thoroughly.

2   Heat a deep, wide pan over a medium heat and add the oil. Add the onion and cook until translucent, then add the spices. Cook until fragrant, about 1 minute, then add the cauliflower and salt and stir. Cover and let the cauliflower release some of its juice for about 5 minutes, stirring once or twice.

3   Add the drained rice and sultanas and stir for 1 minute. Add 650 ml (22^1/$_2$ fl oz) water, stir, cover and bring to the boil. The mixture should be just barely submerged in water. If it is not, add a little more. Later in cooking, as the water gets absorbed, the top layer becomes steamed, while the bottom layer simmers in liquid. Simmer, covered, without stirring, for 20–30 minutes, or until all the water is absorbed and every grain of rice is tender – check by sticking a wooden spoon down to the bottom of the pan and pushing the contents aside. If the rice is cooked and there is still liquid in the pan, remove the lid and cook until the water has disappeared. Check from time to time that it has not dried out completely underneath.

4   Spoon onto a warm platter or individual plates and garnish with pomegranate and toasted almonds, if using.

ONE OF AMERICA'S FAVOURITE JUNK FOOD SNACK INDULGENCES – Buffalo wings – can be morphed into a scrumptious, healthier alternative starring the mighty cauliflower. I can't take credit for thinking of cauliflower in place of chicken wings – they are popping up on bar snack menus all over the place – but I've taken the idea and made it my own with a rather addictive cornflake crumb coating, which bakes to crisp perfection in the oven. These taste wicked, but are actually angelic, and are perfect party fodder or great for slovenly munching in front of the TV. Please read about the cornflake coating in the intro for *Pea Fritters* (page 237).

Cauliflower wings and hot sauce

SERVES 2–4 | **PREP** 20 MINS | **COOK** 20 MINS

LOW CALORIE | GLUTEN FREE (IF GLUTEN-FREE CORNFLAKES ARE USED) | DAIRY FREE

cooking salt

250 g (9 oz) cauliflower florets, about walnut size – 2–3 cm (1 inch) wide

100 g ($3^1/2$ oz) cornflakes (opt for a natural, additive-free brand)

sea salt

2 eggs

coconut oil spray or other oil spray

For the hot sauce

1 tablespoon coconut oil or extra virgin olive oil

4 tablespoons tomato ketchup

$1/2$ tablespoon Sriracha or other hot chilli sauce, or to taste

2 teaspoons apple cider vinegar or rice vinegar

1 teaspoon light soy sauce

1 small garlic clove, crushed or $1/2$ teaspoon garlic powder

OPTIONS
Add 1–2 tablespoons toasted sesame seeds to the cornflake crumbs for extra flavour.

SPECIAL EQUIPMENT
Baking tray, non-stick foil or baking paper and a food processor for whizzing cornflakes (alternatively crush them in a sealed plastic bag).

1   Bring a pan of well-salted water to the boil. Add the cauliflower and blanch for 1 minute, then remove and rinse under cold water until cool. Drain thoroughly.

2   Preheat the oven to 200°C (400°F) and line a baking tray. Whizz the cornflakes in a food processor until they resemble very fine breadcrumbs. Place in a shallow bowl and stir through a good pinch of sea salt.

3   Beat the eggs in a small bowl. Dip each floret first in cornflakes, then in the egg, then in the cornflakes again until well coated and place on the baking tray.

4   Spray each piece of cauliflower a few times with oil. Bake for 20 minutes, or until crisp and firm.

5   Meanwhile, make the hot sauce. Combine all the ingredients in a small saucepan and gently bring to the boil, stirring frequently. Take off the heat, taste for seasoning and set aside.

6   Once the wings are cooked, transfer the hot sauce to a dipping bowl and the wings to a sharing plate. Eat right away.

ROASTED WHOLE CAULIFLOWER HAS BECOME A MODERN CLASSIC and presents infinite options for creativity. Cauliflower takes centre stage in all its glory here. This is so much fun to make; you simply must try it! The whole thing – I've included leaves and all – bakes in a golden, deliciously spiced yoghurt coating. Cut it into wedges at the table, displaying the cauliflower's enchanting anatomy in each cross section. The cooked greens at the bottom of the dish are (almost) the best bit.

Spiced whole roast cauliflower

SERVES 4–6 | **PREP** 20 MINS | **COOK** 1 HOUR 5 MINS

FEAST DISH | GLUTEN FREE

1 large whole cauliflower, with some leaves attached

cooking salt

1 teaspoon ground turmeric

For the spiced coating

300 g (10^1/$_2$ oz/1^1/$_3$ cups) Greek-style or another thick and creamy yoghurt

1 teaspoon grated fresh ginger

1 garlic clove, crushed, or ^{1}/$_2$ teaspoon garlic powder or granules

1 teaspoon lemon or lime juice

^{1}/$_2$ teaspoon ground cumin

^{1}/$_2$ teaspoon ground coriander

^{1}/$_2$ teaspoon ground cardamom (optional)

^{1}/$_2$ teaspoon ground turmeric

^{1}/$_2$ teaspoon nutmeg, ideally freshly grated

^{1}/$_4$ teaspoon cayenne pepper, or to taste

1 teaspoon paprika

sea salt

1 tablespoon melted coconut oil or extra virgin olive oil

OPTIONS

If you don't have every one of the spices listed here, don't let that stop you making it! Just use what you have – it will still be delicious.

Serve with a green salad spiked with some nuts such as walnuts or toasted almonds.

SPECIAL EQUIPMENT

Large pan to fit a whole cauliflower and a baking dish, ideally round, about 25–28 cm (10–11^1/$_4$ inch) diameter, to fit the cauliflower plus a little space around it.

1 Bring a large pan of well-salted water to the boil. Prepare a plate or tray lined with paper towels for draining the cauliflower.

2 To prepare the cauliflower, trim off all the leaves, keeping all those that are fresh and lively. Rinse the leaves, then shred them quite finely, including their stems. Cut a flat base off the bottom of the cauliflower stem so it will sit upright steadily.

3 Once the water has boiled, add the turmeric and stir. Now gently lower the whole cauliflower into the water – it might help to use a large flat slotted spoon if you have one. It will partially float. Boil for 5 minutes, then rotate the cauliflower to submerge the other half and cook for another 5 minutes. Carefully lift it out, letting as much water as possible drain back into the pan, then place it on the towel-lined plate to dry.

4 Now add the shredded leaves to the water and cook for 1 minute, then lift them out with a slotted spoon or strain over the sink. Leave to drain thoroughly.

5 Arrange the oven racks so that the cauliflower will be in the middle of the oven, the dish sitting on a lower rack. Preheat the oven to 180°C (350°F).

6 Place the yoghurt in a large pouring jug. Using a fork, beat in all the remaining ingredients, including a generous dose of sea salt, and beating in the oil last. Taste for seasoning.

7 Now oil your baking dish. Spread the blanched greens in a layer over the bottom, leaving a clearing in the middle. Place the cauliflower in the centre. Start pouring the yoghurt mixture slowly and gently over the top of the cauliflower, letting it ooze all over the sides, coating most of the surface and pooling at the bottom over some of the greens.

8 Place in the oven and bake for 45–55 minutes, until the cauliflower is deep golden.

9 Remove from the oven and cool for 5 minutes, then transport to the table and use a sharp knife to cut into wedges. Add the greens on the side of each portion. Enjoy!

NOTE

Leftovers can be cooled, covered and refrigerated and will reheat well in a microwave or can be heated as pre-cut wedges in a 200°C (400°F) oven. Ideally use within 24 hours.

Witlof

... the gorgeous members of the witlof family assert
their bitterness with pride, for our eating pleasure.

Witlof

Bitterness is the predominant flavour characteristic of this family of leaf bundles. Bitterness is not generally a flavour one seeks out. In fact, it is usually best avoided; sometimes a hint of unintentional bitterness can ruin a whole dish. However in the right context, and with conviction, bitterness can be addictively delicious – think dark chocolate, gin and tonic or sweet and tangy grapefruit. Like these, the gorgeous members of the witlof (chicory) family assert their bitterness with pride, for our eating pleasure.

The witlof are also an arrestingly good-looking family. From achingly pale yellow endives to ravishing reddish purple radicchios with fancy flecks and stripes, they add glamour to the plate like no other leaf can. They are abundant in winter, so along with cabbages, they are the go-to salad leaf for cold days.

THE NUTRITIONAL SUPERPOWER
Its bitter compound, called lactucopicrin, is a powerful pain killer and anti-malarial agent.

OTHER HIGH LEVELS OF NUTRITIONAL EXCELLENCE

▌ Inulin, a prebiotic that helps support a healthy gut bacteria balance.

▌ Multiple phytochemicals with antioxidant properties; radicchio is particularly rich in compounds that support eye health.

▌ B-complex vitamins, for converting food into fuel and giving us energy.

▌ Folate, for cell vitality.

SEASON
Autumn through spring.

VARIETIES
BASIC WITLOF Called Belgian endive in the US, chicory in the UK, witloof or white leaf in Belgium and Holland, and chicons in France. Light yellow or red and white, these tightly packed leaf clusters are the most common variety available in the UK. The individual raw canoe-shaped leaves make ideal mini receptacles for fillings, as party finger food (see *Beetroot and Blue Cheese in Witlof Leaves*, page 21).

RADICCHIO CHIOGGIA The most common radicchio, round and somewhere between the size of an orange and a grapefruit, and a deep purply-red with white veins.

RADICCHIO TREVISO Either elegantly oblong, like a small purple romaine (cos) lettuce, or they have striped leaves with an inward curl on the tips and look like a purple squid swimming at full speed – handsome and delicious, raw or cooked.

RADICCHIO CASTELFRANCO The glam darling of the witlof family, and a sight to behold – a gushing blossom of delicate pale yellow leaves flecked with pink. Use raw to preserve their beauty.

ESCAROLE AND FRISEE A loose mass of frilly to scraggly light green leaves, like a lettuce on a bad hair day, and are mostly used for salads.

PUNTARELLE Pretty rare to find. This huge, swirling mass of spiky green leaves holds a tender secret at its heart: pull apart the jungle of greenery and at its base you will find a core mass of tangled tendrils that look like asparagus from Mars. The dandelion-like leaves can be sautéed or eaten in salads, but it's the 'cespo', the central tuft of hollow crunchy tendrils, which is the real delicacy.

CHOOSE AND STORE
Witlof should feel heavy, be free of brownish patches, and look lively and crisp. Store in a loose plastic bag in the fridge. Loose-leaved witlof have less staying power than those with tight heads, but all should keep for at least a week or more if bought very fresh.

PROCESSED AND PRESERVED
Like lettuce, I have never come across anything other than fresh witlof.

PREP

▌ Witlof and radicchio heads can be halved lengthways or quartered before cooking, or the leaves can be separated for using raw.

▌ Puntarelle's tendrils at its core should be separated from the base, thoroughly washed and the tough white end removed, then sliced lengthways. Typically they are then blanched to lessen the bitterness before cooking, or sliced very finely and soaked in ice water for about an hour so they curl up.

Witlof's best mates

Balsamic vinegar | Wine vinegar | Sherry, Madeira, port | Lemon | Orange | Grapefruit | Chestnuts | Walnuts, almonds | Rosemary, thyme, sage | Blue cheese | Parmesan | Cream, crème fraîche | Garlic | Chilli | White beans | Tomatoes | Pears | Apples

Cook and eat

Raw

All witlof can form the dominant base of a salad (see *Witlof and Pear Salad with Blue Cheese Dressing*, page 136), or can be used in small quantities amongst other salad leaves to add colour and the occasional bitter bite. Try witlof leaves – especially Castelfranco – as the base of a simple salad with orange or grapefruit slices, olive oil, white wine vinegar and salt, topped with Parmesan shavings.

Pan-fry and simmer

Cut witlof or radicchio into long wedges or slice into long shreds. Fry in olive oil or butter with sea salt and black pepper until tinged with gold. You can add crushed garlic and chilli at the end and serve. Or you can add sherry, port or Madeira wine to the pan and reduce until sticky, turning the witlof occasionally.

Roasted/grilled radicchio

Cut into wedges, brush with olive oil, season with sea salt and black pepper, and roast on a lined baking tray in a 220°C (425°F) oven. Alternatively, turn over barbecue coals or on a chargrill and finish just before serving with a top-notch balsamic vinegar. The bitterness can be reduced by blanching the wedges first in salted water. See *Roasted Radicchio and Pasta with Sage and Walnut Pesto* (page 135).

I LIKE THE BITTERNESS OF WITLOF (chicory), but especially when it's matched in battle with other ingredients that have an alpha flavour profile. Here I choose sweet orange as the opponent, with a little backup from its citrus sourness and bitter zest. It tames the bitterness of the witlof, but also makes it welcome to offset all that sweetness from the juice and syrup. The chestnuts are an affable companion, absorbing the flavours and delivering them as a rich embellishment at the end.

Witlof vary in size – use enough to fit cut-side down on the bottom of a large non-stick frying pan, but don't force any extra in. Use ready-peeled chestnuts from a tin or vacuum pack – they are one of life's great convenience foods. Freeze any leftover chestnuts from the pack if you won't use them soon.

Sticky orange-glazed witlof with chestnuts

SERVES 2 AS A MAIN, 4 AS A SIDE | **PREP** 10 MINS | **COOK** 15 MINS

30 MINUTES OR LESS | FEAST DISH | GLUTEN FREE | DAIRY FREE | VEGAN (IF MAPLE SYRUP IS USED)

1 tablespoon extra virgin olive oil

3–4 heads of witlof (chicory) (about 400 g/14 oz total), cut in half lengthways

2 large oranges

2 teaspoons maple syrup or runny honey

sea salt and freshly ground black pepper

120 g (4^1/$_4$ oz) peeled chestnuts

2 thyme sprigs, leaves stripped

OPTIONS
Serve as a main course with a wedge of mature cheese for extra protein or with a bean or lentil dish.

As a side, serve as part of a classic roast dinner.

SPECIAL EQUIPMENT
Large non-stick frying pan

1 Heat a large non-stick frying pan over a medium–high heat. Add the oil, then the witlof halves cut-side down. Cook for 5 minutes, until golden underneath.

2 Meanwhile, finely grate the zest from one of the oranges and squeeze the juice of both. You should have ^{1}/$_2$ teaspoon zest. Measure 100 ml (3^1/$_2$ fl oz) of the juice and mix in the zest and maple syrup or honey.

3 When the witlof are golden underneath, flip over with tongs. Season with salt. Allow to cook for a couple of minutes, then add the chestnuts and thyme in the gaps between the witlof. Pour the juice mixture over the witlof, then flip them over again. Allow to bubble and reduce for another 5–7 minutes, until all the liquid has evaporated. Turn the chestnuts from time to time and break them up a bit if you wish, but don't disturb the witlof.

4 When all the liquid has evaporated, the chestnuts and witlof will start to caramelise quickly. Turn each witlof over to expose the flat side: if they are deep golden and glossy, that's perfect. If not, turn the ones that need it back over and leave a little longer. Stir the chestnuts. Once in caramelising mode, it will get very sticky, so be careful not to burn the chestnuts. Lift the witlof onto a serving platter and scrape all the sticky chestnuts from the pan to join it. Serve right away.

RUSTIC AND RAVISHING PURPLE WEDGES OF RADICCHIO crown this generous and deeply flavourful pasta platter. Blanching the radicchio lessens its bitterness and gives it a well-seasoned and juicy texture, but you can leave out this step if you (and all your diners) really love that bitter edge, and roast it from raw. The blanching turns the water a strange colour, and even though it strips the bitterness, it doesn't transfer it to the pasta, so you can reuse the same water for cooking the pasta.

Roasted radicchio and pasta with sage and walnut pesto

SERVES 4–6 | **PREP** 15 MINS | **COOK** 20 MINS

30 MINUTES OR LESS | FEAST DISH | GLUTEN FREE (IF GLUTEN-FREE PASTA IS USED)

500 g (1 lb 2 oz) radicchio (about 2–3 large)

2 tablespoons extra virgin olive oil

cooking salt, sea salt and freshly ground black pepper

250 g (9 oz) wholemeal (whole-wheat) pasta, such as penne

For the pesto

75 g (2^1/$_2$ oz/^{1}/$_2$ cup) walnut pieces

2 handfuls of fresh sage leaves

50 g (1^3/$_4$ oz) Parmesan or vegetarian alternative, grated + more for the table

2 garlic cloves, roughly chopped

sea salt

1 teaspoon grated lemon zest

1 tablespoon lemon juice

125 ml (4 fl oz/^{1}/$_2$ cup) extra virgin olive oil

OPTIONS

Serve with a cluster of watercress or baby leaf salad with a light lemon dressing.

SPECIAL EQUIPMENT

Food processor or hand blender, large baking tray and non-stick foil or baking paper.

1   Put a large pan of well-salted water on to boil. Preheat the oven to 220°C (425°F) and line a baking tray.

2   Cut the radicchio in half from stem to base, then each half into three or four wedges through the core. (Save any stray leaves for a future salad.) Once the water has boiled, drop the radicchio wedges in a few at a time and blanch for 1 minute, then remove with a slotted spoon and drain very well. Gently place them on the baking tray and brush all over with olive oil. Roast for 10–15 minutes, until steaming and showing some golden edges. Remove from the oven and keep warm.

3   Cook the pasta until done to your liking. Drain and toss with a few drops of oil, then keep warm.

4   Meanwhile, make the pesto. Whizz all the ingredients together to a thick but spoonable paste – add more oil if it is too solid.

5   Stir half the pesto through the pasta and scoop into a warm serving dish. Arrange the radicchio on top and dollop the remaining pesto over it. Serve right away, with extra grated Parmesan, if desired.

IF THERE'S ONLY ONE WAY YOU EAT WITLOF (chicory), this should probably be it. Witlof and pears are perfect partners and they love blue cheese, so here I've appeased them both with mashed blue cheese thinned with vinegar and water to create the simplest sharp and creamy dressing imaginable, and jazzed up the party with crunchy toasted hazelnuts. It all adds up to quite a bombshell of a winter salad – great as part of a dinner party spread or as a light lunch with bread. ·

Witlof and pear salad with blue cheese dressing

SERVES 4 | **PREP** 20 MINS | **COOK** 0 MINS

30 MINUTES OR LESS | FEAST DISH | GOOD SOURCE OF PROTEIN | GLUTEN FREE

For the dressing

150 g (5$\frac{1}{2}$ oz) blue cheese such as Stilton or Gorgonzola

1 tablespoon white wine vinegar

For the salad

3 large heads of witlof (chicory), cut into 2 cm ($\frac{3}{4}$ inch) pieces (save 6–8 whole leaves for decorating, if desired)

2 pears, cored and sliced, dressed with a squeeze of lemon juice

50 g (1$\frac{3}{4}$ oz/$\frac{1}{3}$ cup) hazelnuts, toasted, coarsely chopped

freshly ground black pepper

handful of parsley, coarsely chopped

OPTIONS

Expand the salad base with watercress, rocket (arugula) or baby kale.

Serve with crusty bread, if desired.

SPECIAL EQUIPMENT

None

1   To make the dressing, roughly crumble the blue cheese into a bowl and add the white wine vinegar and about 2 tablespoons of tepid water. Mash it with a fork until amalgamated but still a little chunky. Add a little more water if necessary to make a thick, spoonable dressing.

2   Arrange the witlof on a platter or individual plates and top with the dressed pears. Spoon over the dressing, then scatter over the hazelnuts. Finish with a few twists of black pepper and chopped parsley. Eat right away.

Globe Artichoke

... to the uninitiated, one glance at an artichoke begs the question, 'How on earth are you supposed to eat this thing?'

Globe Artichoke

Artichokes do not immediately present themselves as a delicious edible vegetable. To the uninitiated, one glance at an artichoke begs the question, 'How on earth are you supposed to eat this thing?' And possibly, 'Why would anybody want to eat this thing?' Artichokes are the bud of a giant thistle. Our ancient ancestors who discovered that these were a delectable snack must have been very hungry indeed! Much of the artichoke, especially when mature, is completely inedible: the outer spiky-tipped leaves are tough as old boots, and the internal hairy bristles, called the 'choke', could actually choke you (or at least make you cough a lot) if you swallowed it the wrong way, which is why that bit should always be removed.

But once you know how to get to the tenderest bit of a fresh artichoke, the core just above the stem, referred to as the heart, it is one of life's most ambrosial eating pleasures. The tough leaves also carry a pocket of tender flesh, mostly near the base of each leaf, which can be scraped off with the teeth, and each leaf gets softer as you approach the centre. The flavour is slightly sweet and unlike any other vegetable, except Jerusalem artichokes, which are unrelated but so named because of the similarity in taste.

If I am ever forced to choose a last supper, it will be a whole boiled artichoke with a dipping sauce of good-quality mayonnaise mixed with lemon juice, sea salt and black pepper.

THE NUTRITIONAL SUPERPOWER

Cynarin, unique to artichokes, is a powerful liver cleanser and lowers cholesterol. It is also thought to increase bile production, which helps with fat digestion and to prevent gallstones.

OTHER HIGH LEVELS OF NUTRITIONAL EXCELLENCE

- Antioxidants, which protect against disease and lower cholesterol.

- B-complex vitamins, for converting food into fuel and giving us energy.

- Folate, for cell vitality.

- Vitamin C, for healthy tissues and immunity.

- Vitamin K, for brain health.

SEASON

Spring through autumn.

CHOOSE AND STORE

Avoid artichokes that appear dry, shrunken or shrivelled. They should feel heavy.

Ideally they should also have leaves that are tightly closed and there will be less choke to remove. As mentioned before, the artichoke is a giant thistle bud, and once the thistle blooms, it reveals a dazzling flush of purple, pollen-loaded stamen – these are the hairs of the choke before they emerge.

Artichokes vary greatly in size – some are the size of a melon. These are wonderfully fleshy, so long as they are still round and unopened. Smaller specimens are often sold in bunches and are also best when they are tightly closed.

Artichokes keep well in the fridge, in an airtight container or plastic bag in the vegetable drawer. Depending on how fresh they were when purchased, they can be kept refrigerated for up to 3 weeks.

PROCESSED AND PRESERVED

Artichokes can be found tinned in brine, in jars in brine or a marinade, or in oil, and also frozen. All of these are convenient, easy to find and perfectly respectable as an ingredient, but quite a different animal from the freshly prepared ones. Artichoke hearts in tins or jars are usually the whole or quartered core of baby artichokes that are so young that the choke is edible. Larger, meatier processed artichokes are usually sold as 'bottoms' in large jars in brine or frozen. These saucer-shaped artichokes are particularly tasty and convenient for baking with a stuffing (see *Pesto Artichokes*, page 143).

PREP

WASH Before any real prepping can be done, the artichokes need to be washed well under a strong stream of water. They often harbour small insects deep between the leaves, so if you have time, soak them in warm water doused with vinegar and the bugs will make a swift exit.

LARGE FRESH ARTICHOKES If the leaves have dangerously thorny tips, snip off the tips with kitchen scissors. Slice off the stem flush with the base. Snap off the smaller leaves near the base, as they are usually bitter. Slice the inedible top third clean off the artichoke. Rub the cut parts with a cut lemon to prevent them discolouring, if desired.

MEDIUM AND SMALL FRESH ARTICHOKES Follow the directions in the recipe method for *Crackling Artichokes* (page 145), steps 1 and 2 only.

Globe Artichoke's best mates

Salt | Eggs any style | Coconut oil, coconut milk | Truffle oil, truffle salt |
White wine vinegar, red wine vinegar | Sweet balsamic glaze |
Creamy yoghurt, crème fraîche | Lemon, lime | Parmesan, cream cheese |
Black olive purée, green olive purée, sweet red pepper purée | Tomato |
Garlic | Roasted mild green chillies, mild pickled chillies | Saffron |
White wine | Tarragon, basil, oregano | Toasted breadcrumbs |
Toasted almonds, cashews | Toasted sesame seeds, sesame oil

Cook and eat

Steam

Arrange in a steamer over at least 4 cm (1^1/$_2$ inches) simmering water. Cover and steam for up to 45 minutes, depending on the size. (This is not my preferred method of cooking, as you don't get the penetrating seasoning from the salt and vinegar as you do with boiling.)

Boil

Use a large lidded pan and add plenty of cold water. It is essential to thoroughly salt the water – it should be as salty as you would make water for pasta – as salty as the sea. Another very important addition to the water is vinegar or lemon juice. This should be an extremely generous glug – about 100 ml (3^1/$_2$ fl oz) per 2 litres (70 fl oz/8 cups) of water. The salt and the vinegar really season the artichokes properly and bring out the best flavour. Add the prepared artichokes and bring to the boil. Reduce the heat to a simmer and cook large artichokes for about 45 minutes to an hour, smaller artichokes for 25–35 minutes. They are done when a leaf pulled from near the centre comes away easily. Use tongs to grab out the artichokes and drain bottom-side up in a colander until cool enough to handle. They are best eaten warm or at room temperature.

Microwave

This is a good method if you are in a hurry. Place the prepared artichokes in a microwave-safe container with a couple of tablespoons of water and sprinkle with salt. One large (300 g/10^1/$_2$ oz +) artichoke or a few smaller ones will take 8–9 minutes to cook on high power. Leave to stand, covered, for 5 minutes, then test for doneness.

'ARTICHOKE BOTTOMS' ARE A BRILLIANT PREPARED ARTICHOKE PRODUCT worth seeking out. They are quite different from the commonly found tinned hearts – they are the round, stripped-down, shallow, cup-shaped prize of large globe artichokes, grown more mature than the babies that are used for hearts. They can be found preserved in large jars in brine and also frozen – check Mediterranean and Middle Eastern grocery shops. Their saucer shape just begs to be stuffed.

This stuffing has all the components of pesto, but loose instead of crushed to a paste – all ingredients that marry beautifully with artichokes and form a neat and cohesive nugget of deliciousness when baked. This is a cracking party dish or appetiser. If you can't find artichoke bottoms, substitute whole hearts from a tin: cut each in half and pile the filling on the cut side – not quite as neat in design, but still scoring top marks for yum.

Pesto artichokes

SERVES 4–6 | **PREP** 20 MINS | **COOK** 15 MINS

FEAST DISH | GOOD SOURCE OF PROTEIN | GLUTEN FREE

12 artichoke bottoms, drained or defrosted

2 tablespoons extra virgin olive oil + extra for brushing

2 garlic cloves

sea salt and freshly ground black pepper

large handful of basil, chopped

100 g ($3^1/_2$ oz/$^2/_3$ cup) pine nuts

40 g ($1^1/_2$ oz) Parmesan cheese or vegetarian alternative, finely grated

few drops of lemon juice

OPTIONS
Substitute halved artichoke hearts (tinned) for artichoke bottoms.

Serve as a canapé, starter or side dish.

SPECIAL EQUIPMENT
Mortar and pestle (alternatively use a garlic press), a large baking tray and non-stick foil or baking paper.

1 Preheat the oven to 200°C (400°F) and line a large baking tray. Place the artichoke bottoms on the tray and brush all over with olive oil.

2 Pound the garlic with a pinch of sea salt or crush it, then combine with the basil, several twists of pepper, pine nuts, Parmesan, 2 tablespoons oil and a squeeze of lemon juice. Mix well and taste for seasoning.

3 Using a teaspoon, fill the concave side of each artichoke bottom, pressing gently to make a compact little mound of filling on each one.

4 Bake for 15 minutes, until golden and sizzling. Serve hot, warm or at room temperature.

IF YOU ARE NOT FAMILIAR WITH FRESH ARTICHOKES, this recipe will teach you everything you need to know as you get intimately engaged with this unique vegetable's armour and anatomy. You will also be duly rewarded with the delicious results of your labour, and experience glorious abandon as you make one heck of a mess when eating them.

With the exception of simple boiled artichokes (with salt and vinegar, page 142), I feel this is the best way I have found of cooking them yet. Trust me: I grow several abundant artichoke plants on my veg plot, and I have cooked them many, many ways, and this is tops. So named because of the sexy crackling noise they make when they emerge from the oven.

Crackling artichokes

SERVES 4 | **PREP** 40 MINS | **COOK** 35 MINS

GLUTEN FREE | DAIRY FREE | VEGAN

1/2 lemon, for acidulating the water

4 small–medium globe artichokes

sea salt

up to 80 ml (2^1/$_2$ fl oz/^{1}/$_3$ cup) extra virgin olive oil

lemon wedges, to serve

OPTIONS
Serve as a light meal or single course, with crusty bread, if desired.

SPECIAL EQUIPMENT
Scissors, large baking tray and non-stick foil or baking paper.

1   Fill a large bowl with cold water and squeeze half the lemon in it (this is for stopping the blackening of the chokes through oxidation as you prep them).

2   Cut the stem of the artichokes to about 5 cm (2 inches) in length. Snip off any thorny leaf tips, then snap off three rows of leaves from the stem up. Cut each artichoke in half through the stem, top to bottom. Using a teaspoon, carefully scrape out just the actual hairy choke, leaving as much of the flesh around it intact as possible. Drop the artichokes into the acidulated water as you finish each one.

3   Now they must be par-cooked. This is easiest in a microwave, but you could also steam them. Taking half of them from the bath at a time, place in a microwave-safe bowl, splash in a little water and season with salt. Cook on high power for 3 minutes, then stand for 2 minutes (microwaves vary). Test with a skewer or fork – they should just allow piercing near the base. (If steaming, use the same test.) Drain in a colander cut-side down. Repeat with the other half of the batch, then leave them until cool enough to handle.

4   Preheat the oven to 250°C (500°F) or its highest setting and line a large baking tray. Place the artichokes in a bowl and pour the oil over them – the recommended amount should be about right, but it depends on their size – be generous. Get your hands in and massage each one gently between the leaves and over every surface to coat as evenly as possible, then place in the baking tray cut-side up.

5   Season them again with a little salt. Place the tray on the bottom shelf of the oven (this should help them to crisp without burning). Cook for about 15–20 minutes, until golden and sizzling. Remove from the oven and hear the crackle!

6   Once they are cool enough to handle, transfer them to a platter or individual plates, adding lemon wedges. Bring a large bowl to the table for the scraps. Don't forget the napkins (or possibly bibs). Devour them by hand and enjoy the savagery.

NOTE
These will keep well. If they have been refrigerated, return to room temperature before eating.

GREAT NEWS: artichokes from a tin lose none of their nutrients and all the fiddly preparation has been eliminated. Tinned artichoke hearts are whole-cooked babies, yummy to munch straight from the tin. Here's a simple treatment that elevates them to delectable, concentrating their unique natural sweetness without added sugar, imparting a meaty texture and making them sing with garlic and chilli.

Caramelised artichokes

SERVES 2–4 | **PREP** 5 MINS | **COOK** 25 MINS

30 MINUTES OR LESS | LOW CALORIE | GLUTEN FREE | DAIRY FREE | VEGAN

400 g (14 oz) tin whole artichoke hearts (240 g/8$^{1}/_{2}$ oz drained weight), drained and patted dry

1 tablespoon extra virgin olive oil

2 garlic cloves, crushed, or 1 teaspoon garlic powder/granules

$^{1}/_{2}$ teaspoon chilli flakes or $^{1}/_{4}$ teaspoon chilli powder, or to taste

pinch of sea salt

OPTIONS
Add to an omelette or frittata.

For a main course salad, serve with boiled eggs, salad leaves, sprouts and toasted sesame seeds.

Serve on their own as a snack or canapé, with cocktail sticks.

Serve on toasted pita bread spread with cream cheese or Greek-style yoghurt.

SPECIAL EQUIPMENT
Small baking tray and non-stick foil or baking paper.

1 Preheat the oven to 200°C (400°F) and line a baking tray.

2 Cut the artichoke hearts into quarters. Place in a bowl with the remaining ingredients and toss gently but thoroughly to coat the artichokes well.

3 Transfer to the tray and spread out in a single layer, scraping every last drop of dressing over the artichokes.

4 Bake for 25 minutes, until slightly crisp and patched with gold. Eat hot, warm or at room temperature.

Cavolo Nero and Kale

... seemingly overnight, kale launched into a meteoric rise
from shabby peasant food to 'superfood' poster girl
for the twenty-first century healthy eating movement.

Cavolo Nero and Kale

Kale is the Cinderella of vegetables. Her glass slipper is a metaphor for a sea change in popular food culture that was a perfect fit for kale's innate gifts of nutrient density and versatility. Seemingly overnight, kale launched into a meteoric rise from shabby peasant food to 'superfood' poster girl for the twenty-first century healthy eating movement.

Farmers who grow kale must feel truly blessed – one day it was hardly worthy of animal feed, and the next they can't grow enough of the stuff. One farmer in Lancashire, England, has been growing kale since the 1980s. Originally his crop was a minor sideline to other more profitable veg. The bulk of the demand for kale was from fishmongers, who used it to decorate their fish counters – hardly any was sold for eating. By 2013, demand for kale went ballistic and he decided to devote his entire farm to growing several varieties of kale and cavolo nero. By 2017 he was shifting up to 600 tons of green kale alone per year for the UK market, and rising.

So while kale is the rock star, it's here I am also singing the praises of her dark leafy cruciferous sisters, in particular cavolo nero (black cabbage/Tuscan kale), which is interchangeable with kale but looks very different, and some other varieties (see opposite).

English spinach and chard are not part of this botanical family, yet they are often mistakenly grouped together with this clan. They have their own devoted section in this book.

THE NUTRITIONAL SUPERPOWER

Extremely high in lutein, an antioxidant benefitting eye health.

OTHER HIGH LEVELS OF NUTRITIONAL EXCELLENCE

- Multiple phytochemicals with antioxidant, anti-cancer and anti-inflammatory properties (like all cruciferous veg).

- Glucosinates, which are anti-inflammatory, cancer-protective and anti-microbial.

- Vitamin K, for brain health.

- Folate, for cell vitality.

- B-complex vitamins, for converting food into fuel and giving us energy.

- Copper and calcium, for bone and tissue health.

- Iron, for blood health.

SEASON

Year-round; best in winter through spring.

VARIETIES

CAVOLO NERO Sometimes referred to as a variety of kale, but its Italian name, black cabbage, describes it better. Its long, slender leaves are slightly thicker than kale and yes, it's so dark green it's almost black.

KALE The most common variety is green curly, but seek out other varieties such as purple, red Russian, white/purple queen and frizzy kale. A baby-leaf variety of green curly kale is available as a salad leaf. Each leaf is no bigger than my thumb and it is amazingly delicate and delicious.

SPRING GREENS AND COLLARD GREENS Large, dark green leaves with a soft texture and sweet flavour. They have less in the way of strings and hard stalks than kale.

MUSTARD GREENS Bright to dark green or reddish black, these have a delicate lettuce-like texture, but they pack a pungent hot mustard punch, which is tempered by cooking. Mustard greens' stems and stalks are tender enough to cook too. They come in a variety of shapes, but their assertive taste makes them less versatile.

ROCKET (ARUGULA) Should also be mentioned in this section as it is in the same family and should be eaten in abundance for its wonderful peppery taste and comparative nutrient value, raw or lightly cooked.

CHOOSE AND STORE

Buy whole leaves (as opposed to pre-shredded) in bunches, bags or loose, and turn away from anything wilted, yellowing or less than perky. Store in the fridge in a sealed plastic bag – a damp paper towel in the bag will prolong life.

PROCESSED AND PRESERVED

Frozen kale and other dark leafy greens are a perfectly good stand-by for adding to soups or cooking as a side veg (but fresh is best).

PREP

Cavolo nero and kale leaves have a tough central stalk, which is usually too tough to eat raw or cooked. Simply hold the end of each stalk and pull the leafage off, or cut it out of cavolo nero. Pre-shredded kale usually has this tough inner stem still attached, so by the time you've got rid of those you might have well just shredded whole leaves from the start! You can still cook it with those stems, but they are likely to be annoyingly woody to eat.

Cavolo Nero and Kale's best mates

Dried fruits | Pistachios, almonds, cashews, walnuts, hazelnuts | Coconut | Balsamic vinegar, wine vinegar, cider vinegar | Lemon | Orange | Roasted capsicums (peppers) | Chillies | Parmesan | Beans, lentils | Eggs any style

Cook and eat

Raw

It needs taming, but raw is the best way to eat it for max nutrition. Small pieces benefit from being massaged with oil, which you can do by popping them inside a sealed plastic bag with a little oil and working them until softened. Otherwise whizz the de-stalked leaves in a food processor, pulsing until they're finely chopped and look like chopped curly parsley, but stopping the machine before they turn into sludge. See *Kale and Smacked Cucumber Salad* (page 156).

Stir-fry

It can take a little longer than other stir-fry veggies, so for best results steam-fry it first as outlined below, then stir it in to any other wok-fried ingredients at the end. Heat the wok over the highest possible flame, add a little coconut oil or olive oil and the kale with a pinch of salt. Stir for 1 minute, then splash in a little water to help it steam. Continue stir-frying until it is cooked to your liking – around 5 minutes or up to 8 depending on how much you have in the wok.

Pesto

A good way to sneak raw kale into someone who would otherwise turn their nose up at it! Stir through just-drained pasta or spread on toast. For 3–4 servings: remove stalks to produce 100 g (3$\frac{1}{2}$ oz) of kale or cavolo nero leaf, wash and drain. Proceed as for *Watercress Pesto* (page 193), replacing the watercress. Use the pesto as soon as possible as the flavour lessens as it stands – if serving with pasta, make it while the pasta cooks.

HERE'S AN EASY WAY to incorporate more dark greens into your diet. A one-pan meal that's ready in about 20 minutes, this is near instant gratification for the busy, health-minded and hungry cook – real fast food. Eat this as it is as comforting bowl food for two or extend it for four with a bed of grains as the balancing accompaniment for satisfaction and nutrition. This needn't add time or effort if you stock convenient packets of cooked wholegrains or quinoa; or you can make couscous in a flash.

The smoky element comes from Spanish smoked paprika, or pimentón, a brilliant spice for adding instant depth and – dare I say – a 'meaty' quality to all sorts of dishes, especially beans. Use regular paprika if it's not available. Look out for beans sold in a jar rather than a tin – they may be a bit more pricey, but in my experience, they are always superior.

Smoky greens and beans

SERVES 2, OR 4 WITH GRAINS | **PREP** 10 MINS | **COOK** 10 MINS
30 MINUTES OR LESS | LOW CALORIE | GOOD SOURCE OF PROTEIN | GLUTEN FREE

4 tablespoons extra virgin olive oil

200 g (7 oz) cavolo nero or kale, stripped from stems (trimmed weight), washed and roughly chopped

large pinch of sea salt

freshly ground black pepper

3 garlic cloves, finely sliced

400 g (14 oz) tin or jar butter beans, drained (240 g/8^1/$_2$ oz drained weight)

1 teaspoon smoked paprika, hot or mild, to taste

1 tablespoon lemon juice

To serve

cooked grains or couscous (optional)

1 x cumin yoghurt sauce from *Roasted Broccoli and Chickpea Crunch* (page 103)

OPTIONS
Substitute any leafy green veg such as chard or English spinach for the cavolo nero or kale (cooking time may vary).

Any white beans or chickpeas can be used in place of butter beans.

SPECIAL EQUIPMENT
Wide, lidded saucepan or wok with a lid.

1 If serving this with cooked grains, get that sorted and standing by; the smoky beans will be ready in less than 10 minutes once cooking starts.

2 Prepare the cumin yoghurt sauce. Mix all the ingredients together and set aside.

3 Heat a wide, lidded pan or wok over a medium heat and add 2 tablespoons of oil. Add the greens (take care as they may splutter if wet), salt and pepper and cook with the lid on, stirring frequently, for about 5–6 minutes until the greens are steamed and wilted.

4 Add the garlic and stir until fragrant, then add the butter beans and cook, stirring, until heated through. Add the remaining 2 tablespoons of oil and then the smoked paprika. Stir until evenly combined and the paprika turns dark and fragrant. To finish, take the pan off the heat, quickly splash in the lemon juice and stir. Taste for seasoning and cover the pan until you plate up.

5 Plate up the grains, if using, and top with the greens mixture, then drizzle with the sauce and eat immediately.

CONTEMPORARY KALE AFICIONADOS will be familiar with oven-baked kale crisps, from either making them at home or buying them in snack bags (at an alarming price). I offer you my own perfected technique here, using a zip-seal plastic bag, which ensures foolproof results. If you can't get whole kale leaves, a pack of ready-cut kale can be used, but you'll need to pick through and pull the kale leaves off the stub of thick stem.

This recipe is as much about the cashew fairy dust as the kale. CFD started out as an idea to develop a Parmesan stand-in. At first I combined it with various ingredients, but eventually I stripped it back to cashews and salt alone, and it took on its own identity. So, it has accidentally become my go-to magic flavour enhancer and protein booster for pretty much anything. Fling it over salads and soups, curries and casseroles, porridge and ice cream for instant umami – the fifth taste – aka savoury deliciousness – aka glutamates, abundant in cashews.

This quantity of CFD is more than you need for the kale – store it in a screw-top jar and experiment with enchanting your food. You can cheat by making it with ready roasted and salted cashews, however the mix might not turn out quite as dust-like, due to oil added to the cashews.

Kale crisps with cashew fairy dust

SERVES 4 | **PREP** 30 MINS | **COOK** 25 MINS

LOW CALORIE | GLUTEN FREE | DAIRY FREE | VEGAN

For the cashew fairy dust

100 g (3^1/$_2$ oz/^{2}/$_3$ cup) raw cashew nuts

^{1}/$_2$ teaspoon sea salt

For the kale crisps

200–250 g (7–9 oz) kale, washed and dried

1 tablespoon extra virgin olive oil

sea salt

OPTIONS
Serve as a nibble with cocktails or bubbly.

SPECIAL EQUIPMENT
Medium baking tray, blender or food processor, 2 large baking trays, non-stick foil or baking paper and a large zip-seal plastic bag.

1   To make the cashew fairy dust, preheat the oven to 200°C (400°F). Place the cashews on a baking tray and roast for 5 minutes or until golden. Toss onto a cold plate and cool completely, then whizz in a blender or food processor with the salt to a powder, stopping before it becomes pasty. Transfer to a screw-top jar to store.

2   To make the kale crisps, preheat the oven to 150°C (300°F). Line two large baking trays.

3   Tear the kale leaves away from the inner stems into pieces. If you have just washed the kale, it must be thoroughly dried. Run it through a salad spinner, lay out on paper towels and pat dry. (You should have about 100 g/3^1/$_2$ oz of prepared leaves for one tray.)

4   Put the kale pieces in a large zip-seal plastic bag and add the oil. Seal the bag and toss the kale around in it, then massage the kale to ensure that each piece has a light slick of oil all over.

5   Arrange the kale on the baking trays in a single layer. Do not crowd the leaves – give each piece a little space or else they won't get crisp. Sprinkle lightly with salt. Use a bit less salt than you think you need because the kale shrinks and the salt intensifies.

6   Bake for about 15–20 minutes, until the kale is crisp and golden in places.

7   Using a teaspoon, scatter a couple of spoonfuls of cashew fairy dust lightly over the kale while still warm. Transfer to a wide bowl. Eat with fingers right away.

NOTE
Sadly the crisps do not keep well – as soon as they start to absorb moisture in the atmosphere they lose their crisp appeal.

FANCY VENTING SOME AGGRESSION ON A CUCUMBER? It's fun! Smacked cucumber is a classic and ingenious Sichuan dish that is made by whacking the living daylights out of a cucumber to make it pulpy so it instantly absorbs a pungent dressing. I've combined it here with very finely chopped raw kale and hulled (skinned) hemp seeds to deliver a quite substantial and uber-healthy salad with max flavour and texture impact.

The hulled hemp seeds could elevate this dish from a mere side salad to a light main course, especially if you added some grains or noodles. Hemp seeds are brilliant for sprinkling on salads and much more, and I wouldn't be without them at home. Hemp seeds with the shell still on have a popcorn-like crunch and are great for adding to bread and baking, but the hulled version is much more versatile and easy to eat. They are widely available in health food shops, and are powerfully nutritious, being high in omega-3 fats, protein, iron and magnesium. I try to get at least a handful in me every day with cereal, yoghurt or just munching them by the spoonful as a snack – they are totally scrumptious.

Kale and smacked cucumber salad

SERVES 4 | **PREP** 20 MINS | **COOK** 0 MINS

30 MINUTES OR LESS | LOW CALORIE | GLUTEN FREE | DAIRY FREE | VEGAN

75 g (2^{1}/$_{2}$ oz) kale or cavolo nero, stripped from stems, washed and drained

1 cucumber (about 300–350 g/10^{1}/$_{2}$–12 oz)

^{1}/$_{2}$ teaspoon fine salt

For the dressing

4 teaspoons light soy sauce

2 teaspoons rice vinegar

1 teaspoon maple syrup or runny honey

^{1}/$_{4}$ teaspoon chilli flakes

1 garlic clove, crushed

To serve

4 tablespoons hulled (skinned) hemp seeds

2 teaspoons chilli oil (optional)

OPTIONS

Hulled hemp seeds can be replaced with finely chopped raw cashew nuts, toasted sesame seeds or *Cashew Fairy Dust* (page 155).

Serve with cold cooked quinoa or noodles to make it a main course.

SPECIAL EQUIPMENT

Food processor (optional) and a rolling pin.

1   Pulse the kale in a food processor until it is finely chopped and has the appearance of chopped curly parsley. (Alternatively, chop very finely by hand.) Choose a medium mixing bowl that will fit in the fridge and scoop the kale into it.

2   Smack the cucumber. Place it on a chopping board and whack it several times all over with a rolling pin (or another unbreakable heavy object) until it is slightly flattened and cracked, though not completely pulverised. The cucumber should be broken and the core slightly pulpy. Now cut it lengthways into quarters, then cut on the diagonal into 1 cm (^{1}/$_{2}$ inch) pieces. Add to the bowl of kale. Add the salt and stir. Place in the fridge for 10 minutes.

3   Mix together the dressing ingredients in a small bowl.

4   Take the kale and cucumber from the fridge and empty into a sieve to drain off the liquid. Return to the bowl and mix through the dressing.

5   Place the mixture in a serving bowl or individual bowls and top with the hulled hemp seeds. Add a few drops of chilli oil, if desired. Eat right away.

NOTE

Although this is best eaten immediately, leftovers will keep refrigerated for 24 hours.

Lettuce

... by all means consume lettuce at every opportunity – it does you more good than you might realise.

Good old lettuce is not to be forgotten in this realm of greenery fighting to be top dog in the health race and gourmet stakes. Lettuce ranks high in nutrient density, and it's easy to consume it in large quantities too, since it's mostly water. So by all means consume it at every opportunity – it does you more good than you might realise.

There are about as many lettuce varieties as stars in the sky, but to me, the best lettuce has varied textures of leaf and crunch, and expels a fresh sweetness in its watery contents. For this I usually reach for romaine (cos) lettuce and its baby sisters, little gems. The Average Joe of lettuces, iceberg, delivers in the crunch department, but has virtually no flavour at all – it's like eating tap water. Despite being bland, even iceberg offers an abundance of nutrients but, in general, lettuces with darker, more open leaves (unlike the tightly packed, pale head of the iceberg) have more pigmented surfaces exposed to sunlight, which they photosynthesise into available nutrients and flavour to boot.

It's easy to grasp the hidden potency of lettuce's inner workings when you consider that it can be used as a psychoactive drug. If lettuce is left to over-grow, its watery juices turn milky and bitter, becoming 'lettuce opium', which has been used since the time of the ancient Greeks as a sleep-inducing medicine.

THE NUTRITIONAL SUPERPOWER

Zeaxanthin plus beta-carotene make a powerful combination for boosting eye health.

OTHER HIGH LEVELS OF NUTRITIONAL EXCELLENCE

▌ Vitamin K, for brain health.

▌ Folate, for cell vitality.

▌ Vitamin C, for healthy tissues and immunity.

SEASON

Year-round.

VARIETIES

ROMAINE (COS) This takes its name from the early Greeks (from the island of Kos) and later the Romans who cultivated them. They dominate to this day as our go-to lettuce. Little gems are miniature versions of these. Both are used as the foundation of the ubiquitous Caesar salad. Individual leaves are sturdy enough for wrapping and holding fillings. See *Thai Mushroom and Cashew Larb* (page 176) and *Bruschlettuce* (page 166).

ROUND LETTUCE AND BUTTERHEAD These have floppy bright green leaves with a mineral flavour note, and are also good for wrapping and filling.

DARK AND DELICATE LETTUCES Varieties such as oakleaf and lollo rosso have a good earthy flavour and striking colour.

FRISEE LETTUCE This is as frilly as it sounds and is technically a witlof, not a lettuce. It has a bitter edge, so it's best used in tandem with other leaves in a salad.

BABY LEAVES AND MACHE (CORN SALAD) These are intensely nutritious lettuces with a delicate flavour.

CHOOSE AND STORE

Visual clues are pretty obvious indicators – avoid anything wilted, browning or with cracked ribs. Most lettuces, especially romaine and little gem, are always best bought as whole heads – pre-packed cut pieces will have diminished flavour and will go bad quickly. Pre-packed baby leaves are wonderful, but inspect the bag carefully for any dead leaves, which will soon poison the whole lot. It's best to obey the use-by dates on bagged lettuce. If you've found a bag in your fridge that's a bit past it, a good sniff should tell you if it's salvageable or not.

PROCESSED AND PRESERVED

Fresh is all there is!

PREP

The outermost leaves of romaine and little gems may need to be removed if they are damaged – check the ribs near the base and if they are cracked or rusty looking, these leaves should be discarded. Once sliced or torn it's best to rinse and spin-dry, even though they look perfectly clean, as they can harbour insecticide and fine grit.

Only wash lettuce right before you are about to use it. If you have a large quantity, first separate the whole leaves from the stem or core and rinse them under cold running water, then fill a clean sink with cold water, swish the leaves around in it and leave them to float to the top while any remaining grit settles on the bottom of the sink. After a few minutes, lift out the leaves, drain in a colander, dry in a salad spinner, then tear or chop.

Lettuce's best mates

Salt | All good oils, nut oils | All good vinegars | Pomegranate molasses | Lemon | Orange | Mint, dill, parsley | Parmesan | Cottage cheese

Cook and eat

Chilled lettuce soup

Refreshing on a hot day. In a food processor or blender, whizz together 250 g (9 oz) lettuce, 250 g (9 oz) plain yoghurt, a crushed garlic clove, 1 teaspoon finely grated fresh ginger, sea salt, a handful of mint leaves, the juice of $\frac{1}{2}$ lemon and about 150– 200 ml (5–7 fl oz) water to get the desired consistency. Chill before serving and garnish with chopped walnuts, torn mint leaves and freshly ground black pepper.

Lettuce on the barbie

Brief, fierce cooking brings all the lettuce juices to the fore. Cut hearts of romaine in half lengthways, brush with olive oil and flash on a hot barbecue or cook on a scorching chargrill pan for 1–2 minutes each side. Serve with a mustardy vinaigrette poured over and Parmesan shavings.

Peas cooked in lettuce

The juices of the lettuce act to steam peas or fresh broad beans and impart an incredibly clean, sweet flavour. Line a small, lidded saucepan with lettuce leaves. Add a knob of salted butter. Wet your hand and sprinkle a few drops of water in. Add a few handfuls of fresh peas or broad beans, cover the pan and place over a medium heat for about 3 minutes until the lettuce is wilted and the peas or beans are just tender. Eat the buttery cooked lettuce and all.

Crunchtastic noodle salad

For a toothsome salad sensation, break up 2–4 packets of dry ramen noodles into bite-sized pieces and spread on a lined baking tray. Cook at 200°C (400°F) for about 6–8 minutes until golden, then cool. Toss with plenty of roughly chopped romaine or little gems, some chopped spring onions (scallions), toasted flaked almonds and toasted sesame seeds. Dress with the *Sweet Soy and Ginger Dressing* (opposite).

SAY THE WORD 'SALAD' and a mental image of lettuce is probably the first thing that springs to mind. The word derives from the Latin word *salata*, or 'salted'. The Romans were fond of lettuce dressed simply in olive oil, vinegar and, most importantly, salt.

Fab salad dressings and accessories

Dressings

All of the following dressings are best made in a 250 ml (9 fl oz) screw-top jar and can be stored in the fridge for up to 5 days. For each recipe, add everything but the oil and shake vigorously, then add the oil and shake until emulsified. Shake again just before using.

Best balsamic vinaigrette

2 tablespoons best balsamic vinegar, 1/2 teaspoon garlic granules or 1 small crushed garlic clove, 1 teaspoon Dijon mustard, 1 teaspoon runny honey, sea salt and freshly ground black pepper and 5 tablespoons extra virgin olive oil.

Tangy lemon dressing

1 teaspoon finely grated lemon zest, 3 tablespoons lemon juice, 1 teaspoon maple syrup or runny honey, 2 large pinches of sea salt and 5 tablespoons extra virgin olive oil.

Sweet soy and ginger dressing

1 teaspoon finely grated fresh ginger, 2 tablespoons maple syrup, 1 tablespoon dark soy sauce, 2 tablespoons rice vinegar, lots of freshly ground black pepper and 4 tablespoons extra virgin olive oil.

Pomegranate molasses, oil and salt

My favourite way to dress a large bowl of mixed lettuce leaves is with these ingredients, direct in the salad bowl. Drizzle the prepared leaves very sparingly with pomegranate molasses and sprinkle with sea salt, then toss. Taste a leaf in case you want more of either. Lightly drizzle with the best extra virgin olive oil and toss again. Done. It's important to eat immediately.

Accessories

Good lettuce and a good dressing can be good enough. But some little nuggets of texture can complete the outfit. Maybe just a few toasted nuts or croutons. Or these:

Sweet seed clusters

Heat a non-stick frying pan over a medium heat. Toss in 25 g (1 oz) hulled (skinned) sunflower seeds, drizzle 1 teaspoon maple syrup or honey over them and add a pinch of salt. Cook, stirring frequently, for about 3–4 minutes until the syrup coats the seeds and they turn golden. (The seeds tend to stick to your stirring implement, so you may need to use a small spoon to scrape them off back into the pan from time to time.) Remove the sugared seeds to a plate to cool, then crumble into pieces.

Sesame tofu croutons

Pat dry 250 g (9 oz) fresh firm tofu and cut into 5 mm (1/4 inch) matchstick pieces. Preheat the oven to 200°C (400°F) and line a large baking tray with non-stick foil or baking paper. Brush with a little oil, then lay the tofu pieces on it. Brush more oil gently on the tofu. Sprinkle each piece lightly with salt, then 1 tablespoon hulled (skinned) hemp seeds (see *Kale and Smacked Cucumber Salad*, page 156) or raw sesame seeds. Bake for about 20–25 minutes, until golden and crunchy.

Pink baby corn blossoms

Slice 3–4 baby corn cobs crossways into 5 mm (1/4 inch) rounds. Place the sliced corn in a small bowl or jar with 4 tablespoons beet vinegar from a jar of pickled beetroots (beets) and stir well. Cover and refrigerate for several hours or overnight. Drain well before using.

THE 'WEDGE SALAD' IS AN AMERICAN CLASSIC consisting of iceberg lettuce quarters, usually smothered in blue cheese dressing, bacon and tomatoes. It's one way to make an iceberg appetising, though romaine (cos) or gem lettuce is a richer foundation for a salad where the lettuce is the star ingredient. Here I've smothered it in a spicy peanut-coconut sauce and added a few classic Indonesian gado gado accompaniments, including egg, cucumber and tomato. Here's how to turn a lettuce into a main course with ease, plus it looks rather spectacular. Ground toasted rice is optional, but it is a dead easy trick appropriated from Thai cooking that adds a punchy crunch and a delicious toasty accent. See the recipe in *Thai Mushroom and Cashew Larb* (page 176).

Gado gado wedge salad

SERVES 4 | **PREP** 20 MINS | **COOK** 0 MINS

30 MINUTES OR LESS | FEAST DISH | GOOD SOURCE OF PROTEIN | GLUTEN FREE (IF TAMARI IS USED) | DAIRY FREE

For the gado gado dressing

125 g (4$\frac{1}{2}$ oz) salted roasted peanuts

1 small garlic clove, halved

1 tablespoon runny honey

2 teaspoons apple cider vinegar

2 tablespoons dark soy sauce or tamari

2 teaspoons chilli sauce, such as Sriracha

$\frac{1}{4}$ teaspoon cayenne pepper, or to taste

200 ml (7 fl oz) coconut milk

For the salad

2 romaine (cos) lettuce hearts, quartered lengthways (alternatively use 4 litle gem lettuces, quartered lengthways)

4 eggs, hard-boiled, peeled and quartered

3 tomatoes, chopped in small dice

$\frac{1}{2}$ cucumber, deseeded and chopped in small dice

2 spring onions (scallions), sliced diagonally

handful of coriander (cilantro) leaves

1 tablespoon ground toasted rice (page 176) or toasted sesame seeds (optional)

few slices of red chilli (optional)

OPTIONS
Substitute the egg with small cubes of fried tofu or tempeh.

SPECIAL EQUIPMENT
Blender or food processor.

1 Place all the dressing ingredients in a blender and whizz until completely smooth. Taste for seasoning, adding a little more soy sauce, vinegar, honey or cayenne to get a good balance of flavour if necessary. If it is very thick, thin with a little water.

2 Arrange the lettuce cut-side up on a platter or individual plates. Pour the dressing over and around the lettuce, then scatter the rest of the ingredients on top and serve right away.

YEP, MY NAME FOR BRUSCHETTA USING LETTUCE INSTEAD OF GRILLED BREAD. But wait, I promise I am not suggesting that lettuce should ever be a replacement for bread, this is just a great way to get more lettuce in you. It's basically a salad you eat with your hands. Compact little gem hearts sliced lengthways make a crisp vehicle for toppings, especially a topping with the approximate consistency of hummus, so it holds its own but also seeps gently into the layers of gem leaves. So try it with hummus, baba ghanoush and similar purées.

Here are two quick and moreish toppings, which complement each other, or can stand alone, too. If you make both recipes, you'll have 16, enough for 8 people at 2 each; the recipes can be easily halved. The toppings will keep for 3 days in the fridge and they also taste great on toasted bread!

Bruschlettuce with two toppings

SERVES 8 | **PREP** 15 MINS + CHILLING | **COOK** 5 MINS

30 MINUTES OR LESS | GOOD SOURCE OF PROTEIN | GLUTEN FREE | FEAST DISH

Tomato and almond Romesco

This combo is inspired by the Catalan classic. It's so easy to make and delivers big time flavour.

90 g (3¼ oz/1 cup) flaked almonds

230 g (8 oz) tinned tomatoes with juice (½ a tin)

4 teaspoons red wine vinegar

3 tablespoons extra virgin olive oil

2 garlic cloves, crushed

pinch of cayenne pepper, to taste

sea salt and freshly ground black pepper

4 little gem lettuce hearts, to serve

SPECIAL EQUIPMENT
Baking tray, food processor or hand blender.

1   Preheat the oven to 200°C (400°F). Scatter the almonds on a baking tray and toast for 3 minutes until golden. Toss onto a plate and leave to cool.

2   Reserve a handful of almonds for serving. Whizz the remaining almonds with the other ingredients, except the lettuce, until smooth. Taste for seasoning.

3   Remove a couple of layers of leaves from the gem hearts and save for another time. You should have a fairly compact core, about 7.5 cm (3 inches) long. Cut in half lengthways and set aside any leaves that fall off. Arrange cut-side up on a platter or individual plates, spoon the Romesco mixture onto them and scatter almonds over the top to finish.

Chia cheese with chives

Uber-healthy chia seeds soak up the whey in the cottage cheese and make it firm in a flash.

250 g (9 oz) cottage cheese

3 teaspoons chia seeds

sea salt and freshly ground black pepper

handful of chives

4 little gem lettuce hearts, to serve

SPECIAL EQUIPMENT
None

1   Combine the cottage cheese and chia seeds, season with salt and pepper and mix very thoroughly.

2   Cover and refrigerate for at least 20 minutes (longer is fine), to allow the chia seeds to expand.

3   Remove a couple of layers of leaves from the gem hearts and save for another time. You should have a fairly compact core, about 7.5 cm (3 inches) long. Cut in half lengthways and set aside any leaves that fall off. Arrange cut-side up on a platter or individual plates, spoon the chia cheese mixture onto them and snip chives over the top to finish. Add extra black pepper if desired.

Mushrooms

... eating a lot of mushrooms is likely to prolong your life, so get in.

Mushrooms

Mushrooms are not technically a vegetable or a fruit or even a plant! They are a unique and mysterious life form classed in solitary splendour as fungi. It's a bit of a macabre thought, but imagine how many of our ancestors died an agonising death eating poisonous fungi before the wisdom to identify the delicious edible ones was established. We're not talking a little tummy ache here, but a seriously gruesome end, and yet their peers and offspring persisted in eating them. Springing up from nowhere overnight in fields before any other wild fruit was ripe, or emerging from the forest floor and blooming out of rotting logs as autumn set in and food was getting scarce, mushrooms must have been a welcome and essential source of nourishment for our hunter-gatherer forebears between feasting on animals. But they learned to be wary.

It's a shame that so few people still possess wild mushroom wisdom. Informed foraging is a dying art, one that hasn't really ever existed in the UK, unlike most of Europe. In France, pharmacists are trained to identify edible mushrooms, so you can take your foraged mushrooms to any pharmacy to confirm whether or not they're edible. Wild mushrooms are usually expensive to buy, but the skill of the forager and peace of mind justifies the price. Store-bought common mushrooms and exotic cultivated mushrooms (like shiitake and oyster) are a weekly staple for me, and you might be surprised to learn how incredibly and uniquely nutritious they are. Basically, eating a lot of mushrooms is likely to prolong your life, so get in.

THE NUTRITIONAL SUPERPOWER

Powerful phytochemicals, which stimulate the immune system, fight cancer and inhibit blood clots.

OTHER HIGH LEVELS OF NUTRITIONAL EXCELLENCE

- Zinc, for healthy immunity and metabolism, male reproductive health, plus sensory organ and skin health.

- B-complex vitamins, especially pantothenic acid, for a high functioning metabolism.

- Copper, for bone and tissue health.

- Selenium, for detoxification and thyroid support.

- Iron, for blood health, especially shiitakes.

SEASON

Year-round for cultivated mushrooms; some species of wild appear in spring (St George, morels), others through summer and autumn.

VARIETIES

COMMON CULTIVATED MUSHROOMS These include button, chestnut, cremini, flat and portobello (these are grown-up creminis). Dark brown or black gills on the underside of the caps are a basic indication that the mushroom will have good flavour. I prefer chestnut (tan coloured with a closed cap so no visible gills, firm texture) to white closed-cap (including button) mushrooms for flavour. Flat and portobello are wonderfully juicy and a good size for roasting and stuffing.

EXOTIC CULTIVATED MUSHROOMS These include oyster (delicate flavour and texture), king oyster (eryngii) (meaty and firm – great for grilling in slices, especially the trunk-like stem), shiitake and shimeji (both bursting with umami flavour but not so juicy), and enoki (pretty elfin white mushrooms with long stems, but very little flavour).

FAVOURITE WILD MUSHROOMS These include ceps (porcini), St George, chanterelles, girolles and morels. Chicken-of-the-woods is an extraordinary, huge, apricot-coloured fungus that grows on trees in spring through early autumn. It has a dense texture and really does mimic chicken when sliced and fried.

CHOOSE AND STORE

Choose firm, unblemished mushrooms; avoid anything shrivelled or wet looking. If they aren't pre-packaged, give them a sniff and choose only those that smell earthy – your nose knows to reject them if they smell of anything stronger. It's good to store mushrooms in an airtight container or bag in the fridge, but it's important to wrap them first in a dry paper towel to help keep them from rotting. If they come in a shrink-wrapped packet, just leave them as is and store in the fridge. Try to use them as soon as possible, and once you open the packet, have a sniff to confirm they are still good to eat.

PROCESSED AND PRESERVED

Dried mushrooms are an absolute godsend – a kitchen cupboard essential with an indefinite shelf life. Dried ceps (porcini) and shiitake are the best. Their flavour is concentrated, and they can be restored almost to their fresh former selves in minutes. Simply rinse lightly first, then proceed with either of these methods; place them in a small bowl and pour boiling water over them to cover and leave for about 20–30 minutes; or place them in a small saucepan and pour boiling water over them to cover, then bring to the boil and simmer for 10 minutes.

In both cases, save the water strained off them and use as a flavourful stock.

Look out for powdered dried shiitake or ceps, which can be used as a seasoning, or make your own powder by whizzing them in a spice grinder. Add to tomato sauce or any mushroom dish such as a risotto or soup to add depth of flavour.

PREP

Any tough stems should be snapped or pulled off, especially from shiitake mushrooms. Unless you are using wild mushrooms that are obviously caked in dirt, do not wash mushrooms because they act like sponges and absorb the water, making them soggy. Use a damp paper towel to gently wipe the caps if necessary. If you want chunky pieces rather than sliced or finely chopped, it is sometimes easier to just tear them into pieces rather than trying to manage them wobbling around on a chopping board.

Mushroom's best mates

Salt | Olive oil | Butter | Garlic, chives, wild garlic (ramsons) | Red wine, white wine, Madeira, sherry | Balsamic vinegar | Lemon | Black pepper | White pepper | Truffle | Thyme, rosemary, sage | Dill, parsley | Paprika | Cumin, coriander, nutmeg | Chilli | Soy sauce | Miso | Most cheeses | Eggs any style

Cook and eat

Raw

Personally I'm not a fan of raw mushrooms on their own or added to a salad. But they can be really delicious marinated, as for *Mushroom Ceviche* (see opposite).

Crispy mushrooms

Some people object to the texture of mushrooms, but this might set them straight – they take on a texture a bit like bacon. Slice chestnut or white mushrooms as thinly as possible and cook in olive oil with salt and lots of black pepper until all the liquid has evaporated and they start to sizzle in the oil. Cook until they are extremely shrunken, golden and crisp. This can also be done with shiitakes and will take less time as they release less moisture. The resulting pieces will be very small and blackened, but a total taste sensation.

Stuffed BBQ mushrooms

Flat cap sandwiches enclosing oozing garlicky cheese – divine. Take 8 large mushroom caps and cut the stem out. Score with a knife over the gills, not cutting through to the other side. Choose pairs of equal size. Lay one of each pair gill-side up on the worktop. First season with salt and pepper, then add 1 tablespoon vermouth or white wine, followed by a little chopped garlic and thyme, and finishing with a mound of grated Gruyère or cheddar cheese. Place its paired mushroom on top. Drive a cocktail stick through from the top to secure together. Brush all over with olive oil. Cook over hot coals, turning frequently and carefully, until very soft, juicy and melting inside. These can also be cooked in a 220°C (425°F) oven until soft and juicy, turning once.

PERU'S WONDERFUL TECHNIQUE for quick-curing raw fish can also be applied to raw mushrooms, resulting in high-impact flavour and a succulent texture. This refreshing dish is a perfect light meal for a sweltering hot day, or a stimulating first course as a prelude to something rich and indulgent.

Ordinary white mushrooms or chestnut mushrooms work best in this recipe because they are nice and firm, although oyster mushrooms (especially king oysters (eryngii), which are very firm) or shiitake also work well. The ice-cube bath for the onions makes them mild, sweet and crunchy.

Mushroom ceviche

SERVES 4 AS A STARTER OR SIDE | **PREP** 25 MINS | **COOK** 0 MINS

30 MINUTES OR LESS | LOW CALORIE | GLUTEN FREE | DAIRY FREE | VEGAN (IF MAPLE SYRUP IS USED)

$1/2$ red onion, finely sliced

2–3 ice cubes

100 g ($3^1/2$ oz/$^2/3$ cup) frozen sweetcorn, thawed in boiling water (alternatively use tinned or fresh)

70 ml ($2^1/4$ fl oz) fresh lime juice

$1/2$ teaspoon maple syrup or runny honey

sea salt

2 tablespoons freshly squeezed orange juice

1–2 red chillies, finely chopped

250 g (9 oz) mushrooms, finely sliced

handful of coriander (cilantro) leaves, chopped + small sprigs to decorate

OPTIONS
Serve with chunks or slices of avocado dressed in lime juice.

1   Place the sliced onion in a small bowl and add a few ice cubes, then cover with cold water. Set aside.

2   Place the thawed, well-drained sweetcorn in a bowl and stir in 2 teaspoons lime juice, syrup or honey and a good pinch of sea salt. Cover and chill.

3   Whisk together the remaining lime juice, orange juice, chilli and a generous seasoning of salt. Place the mushrooms in a bowl and stir through the juice mixture, ensuring every piece is coated. Stir through some chopped coriander. Drain the onions and stir them through the mixture. Set aside for at least 10 minutes, or longer if possible (see NOTE).

4   Serve the mushroom ceviche with a side of the sweetcorn and sprigs of coriander.

NOTE
The ceviche can be left to marinate for longer (ideally chilled) and in fact develops even more flavour if you do so.

MY DAD IS THE WORLD'S GREATEST mushroom soup fan, so I perfected this especially for him. When I'm visiting home in Colorado, I love to make him a huge batch and freeze it in single portions – it makes him very happy while it lasts. Which isn't very long, as he tends to devour it like wildfire!

If you can get fresh wild mushrooms, they make a luxurious embellishment, simply sautéed and scattered on top of the soup. Alternatively you could use dried ceps (porcini) or other dried mushrooms – see NOTE on how to use them in this recipe. You could even go extra luxe and add a spoonful of crème fraîche and even a few drops of truffle oil on top of each bowl.

Ultimate mushroom soup

SERVES 4 | **PREP** 10 MINS | **COOK** 35 MINS

LOW CALORIE | GOOD SOURCE OF PROTEIN | GLUTEN FREE | DAIRY FREE | VEGAN (IF VEGAN WINE IS USED)

2 tablespoons extra virgin olive oil

1 onion, coarsely chopped

3 garlic cloves, sliced

500 g (1 lb 2 oz) chestnut, white or portobello mushrooms or a mixture, coarsely chopped

sea salt and freshly ground black pepper

leaves stripped from a few thyme sprigs or 1 teaspoon dried thyme

150 ml (5 fl oz) Madeira, medium sherry or Marsala wine

600 ml (21 fl oz) vegetable stock

For the optional garnish

100 g (3¹/2 oz) mixed fresh wild mushrooms, or exotic varieties such as shiitake, brushed or wiped clean; or 20 g (³/4 oz) dried wild mushrooms (see NOTE)

1 tablespoon extra virgin olive oil

truffle oil, to finish (optional)

OPTIONS
Serve with crusty bread or croutons.

SPECIAL EQUIPMENT
Hand blender

1   Heat the oil in a lidded pan over a low–medium heat and add the onion. Cook until soft and translucent, then add the garlic. Fry for a minute or 2 to release the fragrance, then add the chopped mushrooms. Add a generous dose of salt and plenty of pepper and stir. Cover and cook for about 10 minutes, stirring occasionally, until the mushrooms are collapsed and stewing in their juices.

2   Add the thyme and wine. Bring to the boil, then lower the heat to a simmer. Cook, uncovered, for 5 minutes, until the liquid is slightly reduced and the alcohol has evaporated. Add the stock, return to the boil and simmer for 10 minutes.

3   Remove from the heat and cool briefly. Purée the soup with a hand blender until smooth or, if you prefer a chunky texture, purée partially. Check the seasoning. The thickness of the soup may vary depending on how juicy your mushrooms are. If you feel it is too thick, dilute with a little boiling water, then taste for seasoning again.

4   Meanwhile, if making the wild mushroom garnish, tear or slice them into bite-sized pieces. Heat the 1 tablespoon of oil in a frying pan over a medium heat. Add the wild mushrooms, a little salt and several twists of pepper. Cook until softened and tinged with gold. Remove from the heat and set aside.

5   To serve, ladle the soup into warm bowls. Scatter the sautéed wild mushrooms, if using, over the surface. Finish with a few drops of truffle oil, if using, and eat right away.

NOTE
If using the 20 g (³/4 oz) dried mushrooms for the topping, reconstitute them first in the 600 ml (21 fl oz) vegetable stock (they will add extra flavour to the stock). Bring the stock to the boil in a saucepan, add the dried mushrooms and simmer for 10 minutes. Lift them out with a slotted spoon, cool and pat dry, then sauté them as instructed in step 4.

'LARB' IS A PHONETIC SPELLING FOR THE THAI NAME of a light but filling main course salad of spiced minced chicken or pork with herbs, often served in lettuce leaves. Here, ordinary chopped mushrooms and cashew nuts are cooked together to create a nutritious mock-meat mince infused with the knockout flavours of lemongrass, ginger and chilli. The result is to die for! Cucumber goes really well alongside this too, and the toasted rice (see NOTE) is a traditional but optional accompaniment – a few pinches adds an extra dimension of crunch.

Thai mushroom and cashew larb

SERVES 4 AS A LIGHT MAIN, 8 AS A SIDE | **PREP** 20 MINS | **COOK** 35 MINS

FEAST DISH | LOW CALORIE | GOOD SOURCE OF PROTEIN | GLUTEN FREE | DAIRY FREE | VEGAN

500 g (1 lb 2 oz) mushrooms

1 tablespoon coconut oil or extra virgin olive oil

sea salt

100 g (3^1/2 oz/^{2}/3 cup) raw cashew nuts

2 lemongrass stems, white part only, sliced

4 garlic cloves, halved

1 French shallot, roughly chopped

2 cm (^{3}/4 inch) piece fresh ginger, peeled and roughly chopped

2 small red chillies, snipped

1 tablespoon toasted sesame oil

3 tablespoons light soy sauce

2 tablespoons lime juice

little gem lettuce leaves or Chinese leaf (Napa cabbage) leaves, to serve

cucumber slices, to garnish

handful of mint leaves

1 tablespoon ground toasted rice (see NOTE) (optional)

OPTIONS

Chestnut mushrooms work well in this dish, but ordinary white mushrooms or any firm mushrooms will work well here. Wild mushrooms would be lost in this dish, so the more common the mushroom, the better!

Serve with cooked rice or noodles for larger portions if desired.

SPECIAL EQUIPMENT

Wide frying pan or wok and a food processor.

1   Place the mushrooms in a food processor and pulse until they are chopped finely, but not ground to a purée (think pinky- nail-sized pieces).

2   Heat a wide frying pan or wok over a medium–high heat and add the coconut or olive oil. Add the mushrooms and a sprinkling of salt and stir well.

3   While the mushrooms start to cook, add the cashews to the food processor and process until finely chopped, but not ground to a powder. Add to the mushrooms.

4   Cook for about 20–30 minutes, stirring frequently, until the liquid has evaporated and you have a loose, slightly dry mixture that is turning golden.

5   Meanwhile, wipe out the food processor and add the lemon grass, garlic, shallot, ginger and chilli. Whizz until ground as finely as possible.

6   Clear a space in the middle of the pan and add the sesame oil, then scrape the lemongrass mixture into the oil and stir it through. Stir everything together in the pan, fry for 2 minutes and enjoy the fragrance. Add the soy sauce and cook for 3 minutes more, stirring frequently.

7   Take the pan off the heat and add the lime juice. Mix thoroughly and set aside. Taste for seasoning.

8   Arrange the lettuce or Chinese leaves on four plates. Spoon the mushroom mixture onto each leaf and add a few cucumber slices, if desired. Chop the mint and scatter over the plates, along with a few pinches of toasted rice, if using, and serve right away.

NOTE

Toasted rice is a simple and tasty sprinkle for salads and keeps well in a jar for weeks. Take 3 tablespoons uncooked Thai glutinous rice (available in Asian food shops) and place in a dry frying pan. Cook over a medium heat, stirring constantly, until deep golden. Cool completely and grind with a pinch of sea salt using a mortar and pestle until fine. Store in an airtight container for up to 3 weeks.

Chard and Spinach

... they are both incredibly versatile, delicious and,
for the most part, interchangeable.

Chard and Spinach

Spinach is the ever-popular queen of the greens, and chard is the slightly less robustly verdant sister in her shadow. They are both incredibly versatile, delicious and, for the most part, interchangeable (along with beetroot/beet greens, their cousin). Both are also immensely nutrient dense, but iron is not their biggest strength, as many are led to believe. Yes they both contain a great deal of iron, and calcium too, but they also contain oxalic acid, which makes the iron and calcium less easily absorbed by the body, so you're better off with kale and co. for these nutrients. Oxalic acid is the chemical in their behemoth cousin rhubarb's leaves that renders them poisonous if eaten in quantity (don't ever eat rhubarb leaves). It's also what makes your teeth feel abrasive and metallic sometimes when you eat cooked spinach or chard – this can be reduced by cooking them with a dairy element such as butter or cream.

Despite having their iron and calcium cancelled out, they deliver plenty more health enhancers (see opposite). Both have the uncanny ability to shrink down to nothing when cooked; this means you can put away a large quantity for a serious health boost once collapsed. But it can make it difficult to judge quantities – 100 g (3½ oz) raw English spinach or young chard will shrink to barely enough for one portion. Wilting or light sautéeing, steaming or eating raw is best for max nutrition benefits.

THE NUTRITIONAL SUPERPOWER

Multiple phytochemicals including beta-carotene, which are anti-inflammatory, reduce cancer risk and lower cholesterol, plus chlorophyll, which increases satiety.

OTHER HIGH LEVELS OF NUTRITIONAL EXCELLENCE

- Flavonoids, which are anti-inflammatory and cancer-protective.

- Vitamin K, for brain health.

- Nitrates, for gut health and increasing blood flow to the brain.

- Zinc, for healthy immunity and metabolism, male reproductive health, plus sensory organ and skin health.

- Vitamin C, for healthy tissues and immunity.

- Folate, for cell vitality.

- Magnesium, for bone health.

- Betaine, in chard, is a powerful antioxidant, excellent for heart health and detoxifying the body.

SEASON

Year-round.

VARIETIES

CHARD This can also come in baby size and mature. The large leaves can get pretty huge and their thick, celery-like stems make them a vegetable of two very different textural components. The two main types are Swiss chard, with a white stem, and Rainbow chard, with brightly pigmented stems and veins of fuchsia, orange and yellow. Perpetual spinach is a chard with a light green stem. Chard is one of the easiest greens to grow in a garden or window box.

ENGLISH SPINACH Has many botanical varieties, but the basic types are baby leaf or mature, the latter sometimes having a large flat leaf, others with curled leaves. Baby is best for eating raw; mature is best for cooking. Perpetual spinach is actually a type of chard.

CHOOSE AND STORE

Always look for bright green leaves that are lively enough to stand up if they were in a flower vase, without any dark, cracked or slimy patches. Super-fresh mature spinach bunches should make a delicious squeaking sound when you handle them. If they have a pink blush at the base of the stems, this is a sure sign of freshness. Baby spinach in bags should be inspected first to make sure there are no dead leaves inside, which will soon spoil the whole bag. Chard's stems should be rigid, not floppy. Store both (if not pre-packaged) wrapped in paper towels in a loose bag in the fridge and use as soon as possible.

PROCESSED AND PRESERVED

Frozen chard is not something I have come across, which is a puzzle because it does freeze well – I freeze heaps of it from my allotment after a quick blanching.

Frozen spinach comes in leaf form and chopped. Both are quite convenient, eliminating the laborious washing, plus it's already shrunk down, but neither can compete with fresh for vitality and flavour. Frozen leaf spinach can be chucked straight into a pan with butter or oil and only really has to defrost and heat up before serving, or it can be stirred into soup. Frozen chopped spinach usually comes in little pellets that are more like nuggets of frozen purée than chopped.

PREP

- Discard any darkened, soggy or wilted leaves, or tear these parts off leaves that are otherwise OK. Spinach stems can be left on if you want to cook a bunch whole to serve as a side dish by blanching it for just a few seconds in salted boiling water (well washed first, of course). Otherwise, either chop or remove spinach stems. Chard stems can either be cut away from the leaf and cooked separately, or chopped and cooked with the chard.

- Both chard and spinach need to be thoroughly washed. Spinach harbours a lot of dirt, and if it's not organic you'll want to remove all traces of insecticide.

Chard and Spinach's best mates

Cream, crème fraîche, yoghurt | Most cheeses | White wine vinegar |
Garlic | Ginger | Chilli | Nutmeg | Lemon | Orange | Dill, parsley, mint |
Pine nuts, walnuts, cashews, almonds | Toasted sesame seeds | Tahini |
Dried fruits | Tomatoes | Soy sauce | Miso

Cook and eat

Wilted English spinach

There is no need to add water when wilting spinach – there should be enough still clinging to it from washing it, plus it releases its own water as soon as it meets the heat. Dry ready-washed spinach may only require a splash flung from wet fingertips. Just cram it all in a lidded deep pan and place over a medium heat, adding a pinch of salt if desired. Cover and cook, stirring occasionally to bring the wilted leaves from bottom to top, until completely collapsed. This will take only a couple to a few minutes, depending on how much spinach is used. Drain, or grip with tongs and lift from the pan juices to serve.

Raw spinach tahini salad

Toss young raw English spinach with the dressing used for *Raw Carrot and Orange Salad with Tahini Dressing* (page 34). Add some toasted pine nuts and chopped sun-dried tomatoes if desired.

Creamed greens

Chop chard, mature spinach or beetroot greens along with their juicy stems. Fry some chopped onion and garlic in a little olive oil or butter and when soft, add a spoonful of plain (all-purpose) flour. Cook for a couple of minutes, then splash in a little milk and stir to make a roux. Once smooth and thickened, add the greens and a little salt. Cover the pan and stir occasionally until the greens have collapsed and their moisture has fused into the roux. Finish with freshly grated nutmeg if desired. If using ruby chard or beetroot greens here, the sauce will turn a lovely shade of pink.

SERVE THIS FOR BREAKFAST (or any time of day) with a runny poached or fried egg on top and toast underneath, if desired. You could also wrap it up in a warm tortilla, fold it into an omelette or enjoy it in solitary splendour as a sort of savoury spinach pudding. However you have it, this spinach sensation will do a star turn on the plate.

The addition of a spoonful of uncooked rice may seem a little odd, but its purpose is to absorb the excess liquid as it bakes – the rice virtually disappears. Chard can be used in place of spinach.

Baked spinach with herbs and cheese

SERVES 4–6 | **PREP** 20 MINS | **COOK** 45 MINS

GOOD SOURCE OF PROTEIN | GLUTEN FREE

3 tablespoons ground almonds

1 tablespoon extra virgin olive oil

3 spring onions (scallions), chopped

350 g (12 oz) fresh English spinach, washed and trimmed, or frozen leaf spinach

200 g (7 oz/^{3}/$_4$ cup) cottage cheese, drained of any excess whey

200 g (7 oz) feta cheese, crumbled

2 tablespoons chopped dill

2 tablespoons chopped parsley

sea salt and freshly ground black pepper

1 tablespoon uncooked rice (ideally basmati)

OPTIONS
Serve with poached or fried eggs or any savoury breakfast food.

SPECIAL EQUIPMENT
Casserole or gratin dish approx. 20 x 30 cm (8 x 12 inches) and foil.

1 Preheat the oven to 200°C (400°F) and brush a casserole dish liberally with oil. Sprinkle 1 tablespoon ground almonds over the bottom of the dish.

2 Heat a large lidded saucepan over a low–medium heat and add the oil. Cook the spring onions until soft. Stir in the spinach and cook until just wilted. (If using frozen spinach, cook until heated through.) Drain in a colander and leave to cool for a few minutes, then return to the saucepan.

3 Stir in all the remaining ingredients except the rice and taste for seasoning, then add the rice and stir very thoroughly. Spread the mixture into the prepared casserole dish and smooth the surface.

4 Cover with foil and bake for 20 minutes.

5 Remove the foil and discard. Sprinkle the remaining 2 tablespoons ground almonds over the surface. Return it to the oven for a further 15–20 minutes, until light golden and bubbling. Serve hot or warm.

NOTE
This reheats well and will keep in the fridge for up to 3 days. If making for breakfast, it can be prepared the night before up to the end of step 3 and refrigerated overnight, then baked. Ideally return it to room temperature before baking or add 5–10 minutes to the baking time if chilled.

HERE'S AN IMPRESSIVE Japanese-inspired presentation of spinach. The cooked spinach is rolled up and sliced like sushi and served with a delectable dipping sauce. If you're not fussed over the presentation, just serve the cooked and cooled or chilled spinach in a heap with the sauce drizzled over it – it's a match made in heaven.

Rolled English spinach with sweet sesame sauce

SERVES 4 AS A SIDE | **PREP** 20 MINS + CHILLING | **COOK** 5 MINS

FEAST DISH | LOW CALORIE | GLUTEN FREE (IF TAMARI IS USED) | DAIRY FREE | VEGAN (IF MAPLE SYRUP IS USED)

600 g (1 lb 5 oz) fresh English spinach, washed and drained

sea salt and freshly ground black pepper

For the sauce

5 tablespoons raw sesame seeds

2 tablespoons dark soy sauce or tamari

2 teaspoons maple syrup or runny honey

2 teaspoons sesame oil

OPTIONS
Serve with a noodle dish or with a spread of salad and veg dishes such as *Asparagus with Polenta Crumb* (page 96) and *Mushroom Ceviche* (page 173) or with *Smothered Sweet Potatoes with Tangy Mushrooms and Mozzarella* (page 84).

SPECIAL EQUIPMENT
Sushi mat or aluminium foil and chopsticks, to serve (optional).

1 Place the spinach in a large lidded pan and season with a little salt and pepper. Cook, covered, over a medium–high heat, stirring frequently, until wilted. Drain and leave to cool completely.

2 Press any remaining moisture out of the cooled spinach. Using a sushi mat or a double layer of foil measuring approx. 30 cm (12 inches) square, place half the spinach near the bottom of the mat or foil and press firmly, then roll the mat or foil around the spinach tightly into a tube, forming a firm sausage shape. Unroll, wrap in plastic wrap and chill until needed. Repeat with the other half of the spinach. Chill for about 30 minutes or more.

3 Once chilled, unwrap and use a very sharp knife to cut each roll into about five to six sections, each about 3 cm (1^1/4 inches) long, and stand them upright on a serving plate or four individual plates.

4 To make the sauce, heat a small frying pan without oil over a medium heat and add the sesame seeds. Toast, stirring frequently, until golden and popping. Remove from the pan and transfer to a plate to cool. Reserve 1 tablespoon sesame seeds for sprinkling over the spinach. Mix the remaining sesame seeds with the remaining ingredients and transfer to a dipping bowl or four individual dipping bowls.

5 Sprinkle the reserved sesame seeds over the spinach rolls and serve with the dipping sauce and chopsticks, if desired.

GOLDEN GARLIC, CHILLI, LEMON and heaps of wilted fresh greens suspended in a light yoghurt-based sauce enrobe your pasta of choice – ideally wholemeal (whole-wheat) spaghetti or linguini. Alternatively, wholegrain rice or quinoa make a satisfying vehicle for this vitamin-packed deliciousness.

Baby spinach is ideal, though you can use regular English spinach or young chard, both stripped from the stems and chopped. If using a bag of pre-washed baby spinach, it's super simple to chop it roughly by leaving it in the bag and attacking it with a pair of kitchen scissors in intervals.

Spiked lemon spinach with pasta

SERVES 4　|　**PREP** 10 MINS　|　**COOK** 15 MINS

30 MINUTES OR LESS　|　GLUTEN FREE (IF GLUTEN-FREE PASTA IS USED)

cooking salt

400 g (14 oz) pasta of choice (see above)

450 g (1 lb/1²/₃ cups) plain yoghurt

6 teaspoons cornflour (cornstarch)

sea salt and freshly ground black pepper

1 tablespoon extra virgin olive oil

5–6 garlic cloves, thinly sliced

1 teaspoon chilli flakes, or to taste

300 g (10¹/₂ oz) baby spinach, roughly chopped (see tip above)

1 teaspoon grated lemon zest

2 teaspoons lemon juice

OPTIONS
Add toasted flaked almonds or crumbled feta on top for extra protein.

Substitute crème fraîche or Greek-style yoghurt to get a richer sauce, though low-fat yoghurt (5% fat) works a treat.

SPECIAL EQUIPMENT
Large frying pan

1 Bring a large pan of salted water to the boil and cook the pasta according to package directions.

2 Place the yoghurt in a bowl, add the cornflour and a generous seasoning of sea salt and pepper and stir until smooth. Set aside.

3 Heat a large frying pan over a medium heat. Add the oil, then add the garlic and fry until the garlic is fragrant and just barely tinged with gold.

4 Add the chilli flakes and pour in the yoghurt mixture. Stir constantly, and as soon as it starts to bubble, start stirring in the chopped spinach a handful at a time, letting it collapse into the sauce. As soon as all the spinach is incorporated, take the pan off the heat and stir in the lemon zest and juice. Taste for seasoning.

5 Drain the cooked pasta well, then return it to the pan and stir in the sauce very thoroughly. Serve right away. Alternatively, serve the sauce on top of your chosen pasta or grains.

NOTE
The sauce may separate if left to stand – simply stir until smooth. The sauce can be saved if necessary and will reheat successfully in a pan or microwave.

Watercress

... a study ranking all vegetables by nutrient density rated watercress at the very top of the list. Watercress might just be the mightiest SuperVeg of them all – El Número Uno.

Watercress

You might be wondering why watercress gets the honour of a whole chapter and doesn't just fall under the lettuce category, since most people just eat it as part of a salad mix or as a thoughtless side garnish. I have bestowed it with its own SuperVeg status mainly because of its superlative nutrition content, but also because there's much more to watercress than being relegated to a bit on the side – it deserves more of a chance to shine, plus the more you eat, the more you are supporting your health.

Just about anything you can do with English spinach or chard or cabbage or kale, you can do with watercress (except oven-baked crisps, though watercress does make excellent tempura!). Watercress is classified as an aquatic herb; it is grown in water and occurs in the wild in streams and brooks. Its peppery, mustard-hot flavour is a genetic trait pointing to its membership of the brassica family like cabbages, kale and broccoli, so it shares that family's wealth of nutrients. The US Department of Agriculture produced a study ranking all vegetables by nutrient density, and it rated watercress at the very top of the list. Watercress might just be the mightiest SuperVeg of them all – El Número Uno.

THE NUTRITIONAL SUPERPOWER

Contains gluconasturtiin, its peppery compound; a powerful anti-cancer chemical.

OTHER HIGH LEVELS OF NUTRITIONAL EXCELLENCE

▮ Antioxidant flavonoids beta-carotene, zeaxanthin and lutein, for eye health.

▮ Multiple antioxidant phytochemicals, which prevent disease.

▮ Vitamin C, for healthy tissues and immunity.

▮ Vitamin K, for brain health.

▮ B-complex vitamins, for converting food into fuel and giving us energy.

▮ Multiple minerals including calcium, for bone and tissue health.

SEASON

Spring; available year-round.

VARIETIES

Seek out full-grown, thick-stemmed bunches of watercress for the best flavour and texture. Baby watercress is available in pre-washed salad leaf bags. Land cress is a soil-grown variety, which has an especially assertive spicy oomph.

CHOOSE AND STORE

Use conventional salad leaf wisdom and choose bunches with perky, lively leaves and rigid stems; avoid yellowing or crushed-looking leaves. As it's grown in water, watercress can sometimes appear wetter than other salad leaves when wrapped in plastic; this shouldn't be a problem, but you won't really know until you get it out of the packet and give it a good sniff – it should smell fresh. Store in a sealed plastic bag in the fridge veg crisper drawer.

PROCESSED AND PRESERVED

Fresh is the only watercress.

PREP

Any spindly roots should be snipped off with scissors, but keep as much stem intact as possible. Rinse under cold running water and drain; spin dry if using for a salad.

Watercress's best mates

Eggs any style | Cream, crème fraîche, yoghurt | Butter | Blue cheese, goat's cheese, soft-rinded cheese, Parmesan | Cottage cheese | White and sweet potato | Apple | Pear | Orange | Mushroom | Cucumber | All good vinegars | Lemon | All good oils, nut oils | Walnuts, pine nuts, pecans, almonds | Lentils | White beans

Cook and eat

Watercress sandwiches

A thick layer of watercress, stem and all, whole or roughly chopped, tastes beautiful between two slices of really good fresh crusty bread. Anoint the bread with good salty butter (or unsalted, which tastes creamier, but then lightly salt the watercress), and that is quite satisfying enough on its own. Or try butter and a slick of Marmite or Vegemite or another yeast spread, or butter and miso (dark miso on toast is a revelation – try it), or cream cheese and black pepper, or a really nice thick smear or slice of ripe blue cheese such as Stilton.

Watercress potato salad

Cook new potatoes or potato chunks in well-salted boiling water. Drain, and while still hot, place in a bowl and sprinkle quite liberally with white wine vinegar and extra virgin olive oil and leave to cool and absorb the flavours. Stir together with lots of roughly chopped watercress leaves and stems and serve, adding a little extra splash of oil if you wish.

Creamy watercress and egg salad

For four servings, blend 125 g ($4^1/_2$ oz/$^1/_2$ cup) crème fraîche with 125 g ($4^1/_2$ oz/$^1/_2$ cup) yoghurt. Season with sea salt and pepper and stir in a chopped pickled cucumber, chopped spring onion (scallion), 1 teaspoon white wine vinegar and 1 teaspoon Dijon mustard. Finally, add 2 large handfuls (about 100 g/$3^1/_2$ oz) of finely chopped watercress. Serve with halved boiled eggs (1–2 per person).

FRESH, PEPPERY AND UBER-HEALTHY, watercress lends itself happily to form the body of a bright and tangy pesto-style sauce. Stir it through freshly cooked pasta or a 50/50 blend of spaghetti/'courgetti' (see page 222), serve with baked potatoes or even use as a dipping sauce for bread or crudités. Here it makes a saucy green spaghetti, topped with ripe cherry tomatoes in tandem with their best friends balsamic and basil for a summery Italian flourish.

Watercress pesto spaghetti with marinated tomatoes

SERVES 4 | **PREP** 15 MINS | **COOK** 12 MINS

30 MINUTES OR LESS | GOOD SOURCE OF PROTEIN | GLUTEN FREE (IF GLUTEN-FREE PASTA IS USED)

For the spaghetti and tomatoes

16 cherry tomatoes, halved

2 teaspoons best balsamic vinegar

sea salt and freshly ground black pepper

handful of basil leaves

400 g (14 oz) spaghetti or other pasta

drizzle of extra virgin olive oil

For the pesto

2 small garlic cloves, any sprouts removed

100 g (3$\frac{1}{2}$ oz) watercress, leaves and stems, washed and drained, roughly chopped

$\frac{1}{2}$ teaspoon finely grated lemon zest

1 tablespoon lemon juice

50 g (1$\frac{3}{4}$ oz/$\frac{1}{3}$ cup) pine nuts

20 g ($\frac{3}{4}$ oz/$\frac{1}{4}$ cup) finely grated Parmesan cheese or vegetarian alternative

60 ml (2 fl oz/$\frac{1}{4}$ cup) extra virgin olive oil + more for drizzling

OPTIONS
Substitute 10 g ($\frac{1}{4}$ oz) nutritional yeast flakes for the Parmesan to make this vegan.

SPECIAL EQUIPMENT
Food processor or blender.

1 Put a large pan of well-salted water on to boil.

2 Place the tomatoes in a small bowl and sprinkle with the balsamic vinegar, sea salt and pepper. Tear in the basil leaves and stir.

3 Make the pesto. In a food processor or blender, whizz the garlic cloves until finely chopped, then add the remaining ingredients and blend to a paste. Taste for seasoning.

4 Cook the spaghetti until done to your liking. Drain quickly but do not let it drain too dry – a little moisture will help distribute the pesto. Return the pasta to the hot pan and stir through the pesto until evenly mixed.

5 Divide the spaghetti amongst four warmed bowls and top with the marinated tomatoes and a light drizzle of olive oil. Eat right away.

THESE LIGHT AND FLUFFY crustless quiches are baked in a muffin or cupcake tin. Serve hot or warm for breakfast, or with a salad for lunch. They taste good cold too, and their compact form makes them handy for packed lunches and picnics.

Watercress and pine nut egg cups

SERVES 4–6 | **PREP** 15 MINS | **COOK** 20 MINS

GOOD SOURCE OF PROTEIN | GLUTEN FREE (IF RICE FLOUR IS USED)

2 tablespoons polenta (optional)

6 eggs

1 tablespoon plain (all-purpose) flour or rice flour

$^1\!/_2$ teaspoon baking powder

100 g ($3^1\!/_2$ oz) watercress, washed and drained, chopped

2 spring onions (scallions), chopped

150 g ($5^1\!/_2$ oz) cottage cheese

sea salt and freshly ground black pepper

60 g ($2^1\!/_4$ oz) pine nuts

Greek-style yoghurt, to serve (optional)

OPTIONS
Serve with a tomato salad dressed in a balsamic vinaigrette.

SPECIAL EQUIPMENT
12-hole muffin tin, baking tray that fits the tin (optional).

1   Preheat the oven to 200°C (400°F). Generously oil a 12-hole muffin tin. Sprinkle the polenta to coat the bottom of each hole, plus a little around the sides. (This is not essential, but goes a long way to preventing the egg cups from sticking to the tin and also adds a nice texture.) Place the tin on a baking tray, if using (this helps distribute the heat evenly).

2   In a pouring jug, beat together the eggs, flour and baking powder with a fork until well combined. Next beat in the watercress, spring onions and cottage cheese. Season well with salt and pepper.

3   Start by using a large spoon to distribute the mixture equally amongst the 12 muffin holes, finishing by pouring in the remaining mixture. The holes should be about two-thirds to three-quarters full. Sprinkle the pine nuts on top and gently press them in so they are not submerged but are in contact with the mixture.

4   Bake on the middle shelf of the oven for 15–20 minutes until puffed and golden. The pine nuts should be golden brown – cover with foil if they seem to be darkening too much early on. Test for doneness as you would a cake – stick a sharp knife in the centre of one of them and it should come out clean. They will set further as they cool.

5   Cool for 5 minutes, then run a knife around the edges and gently release from the tin. Serve hot or at room temperature. A dollop of Greek yoghurt is a nice accompaniment.

FATTOUSH IS AN ICONIC SALAD from the Levant and varies from region to region. Its core element is broken shards of toasted flatbread, combined with lettuce, herbs, crunchy raw veg and an assertive lemon dressing, usually enhanced and authenticated with the addition of sumac. Sumac, to the uninitiated, is a dark red spice with a citrus zing. If you can't find it, don't let that stop you making this refreshing and filling salad – it can be omitted, though sumac is an ingredient worth discovering if you haven't already.

Green fattoush

SERVES 4–6 | **PREP** 20 MINS | **COOK** 10 MINS

30 MINUTES OR LESS | FEAST DISH | LOW CALORIE | DAIRY FREE | VEGAN

2 large or 4 small wholemeal (whole-wheat) pita breads

2 tablespoons extra virgin olive oil

4 spring onions (scallions), diagonally sliced

1 green capsicum (pepper), cut in small chunks

1/2 cucumber, halved lengthways, deseeded and medium sliced

100 g (3 1/2 oz) sugar snap peas, diagonally sliced

200 g (7 oz) watercress, washed and drained, roughly chopped

2 handfuls of mint sprigs, leaves stripped

2 handfuls of flat-leaf (Italian) parsley sprigs, leaves stripped

handful of pomegranate seeds

For the dressing

1 garlic clove, any sprout removed

coarse sea salt

60 ml (2 fl oz/1/4 cup) lemon juice

1 1/2 tablespoons sumac

freshly ground black pepper

60 ml (2 fl oz/1/4 cup) extra virgin olive oil

OPTIONS
Add crumbled feta, fried halloumi or quartered boiled eggs to make this a main course salad.

SPECIAL EQUIPMENT
Large baking tray and a mortar and pestle (optional).

1   Preheat the oven to 200°C (400°F). Divide the pita pockets and separate as best you can, tearing each into two thin layers – the pieces will be crumbled later. Lay them on a large baking tray and drizzle olive oil over them. Toast in the oven until crisp and golden, then cool.

2   For the dressing, place the garlic and a large pinch of coarse sea salt in a mortar and crush to a paste with a pestle, or use a garlic crusher. Beat together with the remaining dressing ingredients, directly in the mortar, a bowl or in a screw-top jar. Taste for seasoning.

3   Mix together all the salad ingredients (except the bread and pomegranate seeds) in a large bowl. Toss the dressing through the salad. Finally, crush the toasted bread into bite-sized pieces, toss into the salad and mix well, then scatter over the pomegranate seeds. Serve immediately.

NOTE
The salad can be prepared in advance, keeping the toasted bread, veg and dressing separate. Toss together immediately before serving.

Veggie Fruits

Eggplant
Avocado
Zucchini and Summer Squash
Peas
Pumpkin and Winter Squash
Capsicum and Chilli Pepper
Tomato

Eggplant

... even steaming in the microwave transforms the watery cells in its spongy structure to reveal its smoothly pulpy and flavourful character.

Eggplant

This vegetable's name is the source of much confusion in the English-speaking world – in the UK it's called by its French name, aubergine; in the US, Canada, Australia and NZ it's eggplant. In West Africa it's garden egg; in parts of the Caribbean it's brown jolly. The egg part comes from a certain variety that is an ivory oval about the size of an egg – a rare find these days compared to the common deep purple truncheon we know and love – but this was the first variety to reach Europe from its origin in India. Brown jolly is a name I adore; quite descriptive of this sometimes brownish and fun-shaped veggie fruit; it's derived from the Indian name, *brinjal*. The Italian name *melanzana* comes from the Latin *mala insana* or 'apple of madness' – as a member of the nightshade family, it was originally suspected of being poisonous by medieval Europeans.

I'm convinced that anyone who does not like eggplants must have eaten one that was undercooked, then banished it for life. Eggplants simply must, absolutely, categorically be thoroughly cooked or else they are quite horrible tasting and so tough they're impossible to cut with a knife and fork, let alone chew. I'd just as soon serve someone a raw potato as I would a raw or even slightly undercooked eggplant – i.e. never. If I taste an undercooked eggplant in a restaurant, I am immediately suspicious of the kitchen staff and the rest of the food on my plate. That said, it responds well to most cooking methods with finesse: roasting, barbecuing, chargrilling and frying, of course, but even steaming in the microwave transforms the watery cells in its spongy structure to reveal its smoothly pulpy and flavourful character.

THE NUTRITIONAL SUPERPOWER
Phytochemicals, which lower cholesterol and are cardioprotective.

OTHER HIGH LEVELS OF NUTRITIONAL EXCELLENCE

▌ Anthocyanins (in the eggplant skin) are anti-inflammatory, anti-cancer and anti-viral.

▌ Potassium, for heart and kidney health.

▌ B-complex vitamins, for converting food into fuel and giving us energy.

▌ Copper, for bone and tissue health.

▌ Manganese, for skin and bone health, which is made easily available to the body by another antioxidant in the eggplant.

SEASON
Best in summer through autumn; available year-round.

VARIETIES
Other than the common purple/black eggplant, more unusual varieties with different colour skins and mixed shapes tend to be very tasty and are worth seeking out in season. You might find the common shape in white, mottled purple or light green. A teardrop-shaped miniature version, sometimes called Indian, is good for slicing, keeping the top intact, then marinating in oil and spices and cooking in a small amount of stock or liquor; the same treatment can be used with the original creamy coloured or light yellow one with the size and shape of a hen's egg. Japanese eggplants are long and slender, and bright purple, lavender or white. An Italian variety (of numerous names) is fat, round and deep purple with a white star-shaped patch under its stem – these are wonderfully dense-textured and the skin gets lighter purple as it cooks. Thai eggplants and pea eggplants are small and round, sometimes looking like large peas – they are more seeds than flesh and are best halved or sliced and fiercely fried before adding to a curry or other dish.

CHOOSE AND STORE
Common purple/black eggplants should be firm, bouncy and heavy for their size, with a sheen almost as shiny as a patent leather shoe, and the stem should be bright green and rigid. Avoid anything remotely soft or dull. Eggplants are sun-loving fruits and don't take kindly to being put in the fridge, so once you get them home, store in a cool, dark place.

PROCESSED AND PRESERVED
Pickled eggplants and eggplants in oil make delicious accompaniments, salad additions or sandwich fillings.

PREP
To salt or not to salt? I have experimented with this hundreds of times over the years and my conclusion is firm. You only need to salt first if you are frying in oil. Firstly, any 'bitter' juices that eggplants may have contained in the past – a compound that also makes some people's mouths tickle – has been bred out of the modern eggplant, so traditionally the salting was essential to draw this element out, but not anymore. Secondly, the salting does change the texture of the flesh, collapsing its watery cells, which has the effect of preventing them from absorbing too much oil. So if, and only if, you are frying eggplants, do salt them first, using either of the methods below. Roasting, chargrilling, steaming etc. do not require you to perform this step. But do add a little salt during other cooking methods or to the final result to enhance the flavour.

There are two effective salting methods – dry salting and soaking. If frying chunks or slices of eggplant, cut them to the desired shape and size and do one of the following:

DRY SALTING METHOD Place in a colander and sprinkle lightly with salt all over. Leave perched over a bowl or sink for 30 minutes, then pat dry with a paper towel before frying.

SALT BATH METHOD Especially good results when deep frying. Prepare a bowl of cold water and stir in enough salt to make it taste distinctly saline. Add the cut eggplant and soak for a minimum of 30 minutes or up to several hours. Drain and pat dry with paper towel before frying.

If you are baking an eggplant whole in the oven in order to extract its soft pulpy flesh, always stab small holes in it first, or you risk it exploding in the oven.

Smoking eggplant over a naked flame or directly on hot coals is an incredible way to cook the flesh.

Eggplant's best mates

Salt | Olive oil | Garlic | Paprika, smoked paprika | Ground cumin, cinnamon | Chilli | Capsicum (pepper) | Tomato, tomato sauce, tomato purée | Lemon | Coconut | Caramelised onions | Soy sauce | Miso | Tahini | Toasted sesame seeds | Yoghurt | Dill, mint, parsley | Thyme, rosemary, sage | Honey, treacle, date syrup | Pomegranate molasses

Cook and eat

Microwave-steamed eggplant

Eggplants used in classic casserole dishes like moussaka or parmigiana are usually pan-fried or deep-fried first. If you wish to cut down on the fat content of the dish or save time, you can steam in a microwave before layering up with the sauce/cheese/etc. Cut the eggplant as needed, place in a microwave-safe container, and salt lightly (for flavour); no need to add extra water. Cover and cook at high power until completely soft and steamed through, then drain, cool and use in your recipe.

Baba ghanoush

Cook, cool and peel an eggplant as for *Smoked Eggplant Dal* (opposite). Blend the flesh (either briskly by hand or in a food processor) with a little yoghurt, lemon juice, crushed garlic and salt, adding extra virgin olive oil and tahini, if desired, for extra richness.

Eggplants in yoghurt

A simple and classic Middle Eastern-style salad. Cut eggplants into thin rounds and salt for 30 minutes. Pat dry, then batch fry in olive oil until golden. Cool and cover with a sauce of thick yoghurt mixed with crushed garlic, a little lemon juice, salt and pepper. Finish with fresh mint leaves.

Honeyed eggplants

Cut eggplants into 1 cm (½ inch) thick rounds and salt for 30 minutes. Pat dry, then batch fry in olive oil until golden. Serve drizzled with honey, cane molasses or, my favourite, date nectar.

THE EGGPLANT (AUBERGINE) HAS A UNIQUE TALENT – it can be transformed into a hero ingredient that imparts a deep smoke flavour to a dish. Put directly into scorching flames and, as its skin blisters and burns, it produces smoke, which permeates its interior with flavour, while simultaneously steaming it in its own juices. It then becomes a different thing altogether: a mound of silky flesh full of delicious smoky juice.

Rules of smoking eggplants:

1   You need actual flames. It only works on gas burners. (Alternatively, use a gas BBQ if you can access the flames directly, or an open fire or coal BBQ.)

2   If doing this indoors, it will fill your home with strong aromas and possibly smoke for a while. Have a tea towel at the ready to fan the smoke detector if it starts beeping.

Smoked eggplant dal

SERVES 4 | **PREP** 15 MINS | **COOK** 1 HOUR

GOOD SOURCE OF PROTEIN | GLUTEN FREE | DAIRY FREE (IF YOGHURT IS OMITTED) |
VEGAN (IF MAPLE SYRUP IS USED AND YOGHURT IS OMITTED)

1 eggplant (aubergine), ideally long and slim

For the dal

200 g (7 oz/1 cup) red split lentils

3 garlic cloves, crushed

3 cm (1¼ inch) piece fresh ginger, grated

1 teaspoon ground turmeric

¼ teaspoon chilli flakes, or to taste

1 teaspoon lemon juice

1 teaspoon maple syrup or honey

1 teaspoon salt

For the tempering oil garnish

1 tablespoon coconut oil or olive oil

1 teaspoon black or brown mustard seeds

1 teaspoon cumin seeds

To serve

thick and creamy yoghurt (optional)

handful of fresh coriander (cilantro) leaves and stems (optional)

OPTIONS
Serve with wholemeal pita or rice.

SPECIAL EQUIPMENT
All-metal dinner fork you don't mind damaging and a hand blender (optional).

1   First, smoke the eggplant. Push a metal fork firmly into the stem to use as a turning tool and place the eggplant directly onto a high gas flame on the cooker. Turn with the fork occasionally, moving it slightly every 4–5 minutes to cook all parts, until completely soft and collapsed. The skin should be blackened to the point of ash in places, and steam should be escaping through the holes. Remove it to a plate and leave to cool completely. Chop off the stem, then scrape off as much of the charred skin as you can – a few black specks left on are inevitable.

2   Meanwhile, make the dal. Rinse the lentils under cold running water, then put in a medium saucepan with 1.2 litres (42 fl oz) water. Bring to the boil, then lower to a medium simmer for 10 minutes. Skim off any foam with a slotted spoon.

3   After 10 minutes, add the remaining ingredients for the dal. Cook on a low simmer, stirring occasionally, for about 30 minutes, or longer if you prefer it thicker. Taste for seasoning.

4   If you want chunks of eggplant in the dal, chop it into chunks and add to the dal. If you want a smooth, smoky dal with added silkiness, chop it roughly, add and purée with a hand blender.

5   To make the tempering oil garnish, heat the oil in a frying pan over a medium–high heat. Add the mustard seeds and as soon as they start popping, add the cumin seeds, then remove the pan from the heat and pour the oil and spices into a heatproof bowl.

6   Reheat the dal if necessary and ladle into warm bowls. Top with a dollop of yoghurt, if using. Use a teaspoon to drizzle the warm oil and spices on top. Finally, chop the coriander, if using, and scatter it over each bowl.

EGGPLANTS (AUBERGINES) ARE LIKE SPONGES; they are fabulous for soaking up flavours. Here they are first chargrilled to impart a smoky tone, then they drink up a dousing of wine and honey. This main-course salad is a festival of taste and texture. It can be plated individually or artfully arranged on a platter for sharing.

Warm salad of sweet and sour eggplants with cheese and pistachios

SERVES 4–6 | **PREP** 10 MINS | **COOK** 20 MINS

30 MINUTES OR LESS | FEAST DISH | GOOD SOURCE OF PROTEIN | GLUTEN FREE

2 large or 3 medium eggplants (aubergines)

60–90 ml (2–3 fl oz) extra virgin olive oil

100 ml (3^1/2 fl oz) dry vermouth or white wine

3 tablespoons wine vinegar

1^1/2 tablespoons runny honey

sea salt and freshly ground black pepper

2 large handfuls of baby spinach leaves

200 g (7 oz) crumbly or soft cheese, such as feta or goat's cheese, broken into chunks

4 teaspoons pomegranate molasses

handful of mint leaves, chopped

75 g (2^1/2 oz/^{1}/2 cup) shelled pistachio nuts, roughly chopped

OPTIONS
Substitute an aged balsamic or balsamic glaze/syrup if pomegranate molasses is unavailable.

SPECIAL EQUIPMENT
Chargrill pan (alternatively fry the eggplants in a large frying pan).

1   Slice the stem off the eggplants. Stand them on the severed end and slice downwards, shaving off and discarding the first and last bit of skin. Make slices 1 cm (^{1}/2 inch) thick. Brush each slice on both sides with olive oil.

2   Cook the eggplant in batches. Heat a chargrill pan until very hot. Lay the eggplant slices in the pan and cook each side until translucent and striped with black. Allow to cool slightly, then cut the cooked eggplants into long strips about 2 cm (^{3}/4 inch) wide.

3   Heat the remaining oil in a large frying pan over a medium heat. (If you have used up all the oil, add a couple of tablespoons to the pan.) When hot, add the eggplants and spread them out evenly in the pan. Add the vermouth or wine all at once – stand back as it may splutter at first. Season well with salt and pepper and cook, stirring gently, until the wine has almost completely evaporated. Add the vinegar and honey to the pan and stir. Cook for a couple more minutes, while the juices thicken and caramelise, then remove the pan from the heat.

4   Make a bed of baby spinach leaves on each plate and pile the eggplants on top. Scatter the cheese over them. Drizzle with pomegranate molasses, sprinkle with the chopped mint and pistachios and serve.

SWEET CUMIN-SPIKED EGGPLANTS (AUBERGINES), roasted to a silky texture, take centre stage in this impressive and generous set of components to share.

Candied cumin eggplant and noodle platter

SERVES 4–6 | **PREP** 30 MINS | **COOK** 30 MINS

FEAST DISH | GOOD SOURCE OF PROTEIN | GLUTEN FREE (IF TAMARI AND GLUTEN-FREE NOODLES ARE USED) | DAIRY FREE | VEGAN (IF MAPLE SYRUP IS USED)

For the platter

2 eggplants (aubergines)

90 ml (3 fl oz) extra virgin olive oil or melted coconut oil

sea salt and freshly ground black pepper

1 teaspoon cumin seeds

3 teaspoons maple syrup or runny honey

300 g (10^1/2 oz) black rice or soba noodles

2 tablespoons dark soy sauce or tamari

25 g (1 oz) raw sesame seeds

25 g (1 oz) unsweetened desiccated (grated dried) coconut

50 g (1^3/4 oz/^{1}/3 cup) raw cashew nuts

1 large mango, peeled, cut into thin strips

1 capsicum (pepper), deseeded and sliced

^{1}/2 cucumber, cut into thin strips

3 spring onions (scallions), sliced diagonally

50 g (1^3/4 oz) mung bean sprouts

handful of mint, leaves stripped

handful of coriander (cilantro), leaves stripped

For the dressing

90 ml (3 fl oz) lime juice

90 ml (3 fl oz) tamari or dark soy sauce

60 ml (2 fl oz/^{1}/4 cup) maple syrup or honey

1 large garlic clove, sprout removed, crushed

1–2 small red chillies, finely sliced

OPTION
Add tofu or boiled eggs for extra protein.

SPECIAL EQUIPMENT
Large baking tray, non-stick foil or baking paper, mortar and pestle (optional).

1   Preheat the oven to 220°C (425°F) and line a baking tray.

2   Cut the stem end off the eggplants and discard. Cut each one into four or six long wedges. Score the flesh in one diagonal direction, without piercing the skin. Lay the wedges on the lined baking tray. Brush thoroughly with about 60 ml (2 fl oz/^{1}/4 cup) of the oil and season with salt and pepper. In a small bowl, mix together the cumin seeds and syrup, then brush over the eggplants. Roast in the oven for 20–25 minutes until soft and golden. Keep warm.

3   To make the dressing, combine all the ingredients, mix well and set aside. If desired, prepare it using a mortar and pestle by pounding the garlic and chillies with a pinch of sea salt, then whisk in the remaining ingredients. It can then be served straight from the mortar, if desired.

4   Cook the noodles according to the package instructions. Drain well and place in a bowl. Toss with the soy or tamari and the remaining oil, cover and set aside.

5   Heat a frying pan over a medium heat and add the sesame seeds. Cook, stirring occasionally, until golden and popping. Remove to a plate and set aside to cool, then repeat with the coconut until light golden and set aside.

6   Just before serving, assemble on a large platter or two large plates. Spread the noodles out on one side of the platter and sprinkle with the sesame seeds and coconut. Arrange the eggplants on top and sprinkle with cashews. Toss together the mango, capsicum, cucumber and spring onion and arrange a bowl on the other side of the platter, then top with the bean sprouts. Tear the mint leaves and scatter, along with the coriander leaves. Place the dressing in a serving bowl and serve on the side.

Avocado

... Mexicans have used them as a butter replacement for centuries, long before they appeared on every hipster café menu smashed on toast.

Avocado

Each avocado has one prime moment in its lifetime to shine. That perfectly ripe window lasts no more than a day or possibly two. If you try to make them shine too soon (or too late), sadly they go to waste – once opened, they do not keep. If I am served an unripe avocado at a restaurant, I get peeved. I would hope they wouldn't serve me one that's gone past its best, so why is it OK to serve an unripe one? Both are inedible.

Determining that magic moment is key, and I've offered some tips opposite to help you do that. Embracing that magic moment is one of the greatest eating pleasures to be had from plant foods. Avocados are uniquely buttery – they have the highest fat and protein content of all fruits. Mexicans have used them as a butter replacement for centuries, long before they appeared on every hipster café menu smashed on toast. Fun fact: the avocado's name comes from the Aztec word *ahuacatl*, meaning testicle.

THE NUTRITIONAL SUPERPOWER

Monounsaturated fats, which lower cholesterol and promote heart health.

OTHER HIGH LEVELS OF NUTRITIONAL EXCELLENCE

- Antioxidants including tannin, which protects against ulcers and inflammation.

- Vitamin E, another potent antioxidant, which protects against disease.

- Vitamin K, for brain health.

- Folate, for cell vitality.

- Copper, for bone and tissue health.

- Potassium, for heart and kidney health.

SEASON

Available year-round.

VARIETIES

Hass avocados have the creamiest flesh and are simply the best ones to choose, if you have a choice. Hass avocados are easily identifiable by their blackish purple, crinkly, knobbly skin and tend to be either pear shaped or oval. Smooth green-skinned avocados with a long, slender top are usually the Fuerte variety. There is also a giant, round, green-skinned variety from the West Indies. Both of the latter can be slightly watery and less flavourful than the Hass. There are many types, but a good rule of thumb is the darker and 'wartier' the skin, the better.

CHOOSE AND STORE

Hard, unripe avocados are fine to buy if you have time to let them ripen at home. If you need them right away, don't always trust pre-packaged avocados labelled 'ripe and ready to eat'. Have a feel for yourself by using your thumb to gently press the surface of the fruit – you should feel the flesh just barely give underneath. Try this in a few spots. The stem end will most likely be softer than the round bottom. If both ends respond with a nod to your pressing, without yelling 'too soft!' then it's probably just right. Another indicator is the stem. Try pulling it off. If it doesn't budge, the avocado is not ripe. If it comes off easily and looks dark brown underneath, it's past it. If it's green underneath, it's probably just right. Do not store avocados in the fridge unless you need to slow down the ripening process – just store in a cool place. Storing them close to bananas will hasten the avocados' ripening; so will putting them in a paper bag.

PROCESSED AND PRESERVED

Frozen avocado halves are available. Not recommended except to put in smoothies as a texture enhancer/nutrition boost.

PREP

- Pop off any remnants of a stem. Cut downwards from the stem until you hit the stone, and work your knife around the stone, then twist to release the halves. To get the stone out, protect your hand with a folded thick cloth and hold the stoned half in that hand, then gently whack your sharp chef's knife into the stone so it lodges in it, then twist gently to pop it out. You may also succeed in doing this with the avocado half still on the board, but it has a tendency to slither away when you whack it. Beware – 'avocado hand' is a modern-day affliction frequently reported by hospitals!

- If you are going to mash it, just use a small spoon to scoop out the flesh in chunky spoonfuls. The darker green flesh right against the inside of the skin is super sweet, so make sure you scrape it all out, rejecting any brown parts and stringy bits.

- If you want quarters or slices, you'll need to get the skin off cleanly. Cut each half in half again lengthways and peel back the skin – if it is perfectly ripe it should come right off.

- For neatly cut small pieces, you can use the scoring method – see step 2 for *Avocado Gazpacho* on page 218.

- If you want complete skinless halves, use a large metal spoon. Heat it up by resting it in a mug of very hot water for a few seconds, then slide it in between the skin and flesh starting at the wide end, and scoop out.

- Always be ready with a cut lemon or lime to squeeze over the avocado flesh immediately after preparation to stop it turning brown. If you are using just half the avocado, leave the stone in the other half, wrap in plastic wrap and refrigerate. Use it ASAP.

Avocado's best mates

Salt | Lime, lemon | Sushi vinegar, balsamic vinegar | Fresh coriander (cilantro), basil, parsley, mint | Chilli | Garlic | Tomato | Sweetcorn | Coconut | Honey | Cumin, coriander seed | Ginger | Soy sauce | Miso | Toasted sesame seeds

Cook and eat

Quick and simple guacamole

Scoop out the flesh into a bowl and add a good squeeze of fresh lime juice. Mash with a fork or potato masher to a lumpy mash. Season it with sea salt and small amounts of cayenne pepper, ground cumin and garlic powder/granules. Stir well and eat right away.

Avocado ginger salad

A fab five-ingredient flavour combo. Toss chunks of avocado in lemon or lime juice. Make a dressing by mixing together 2 teaspoons freshly grated ginger, 2 tablespoons dark soy sauce and 1 tablespoon balsamic vinegar. Serve the avocado with the dressing drizzled over, but don't toss with the dressing; it's too dark and hides the avocado's lovely greenness.

Avocado omelette

Prepare 1 sliced or chunked avocado and 2 tablespoons freshly grated Parmesan or vegetarian alternative. Make the omelette as for *Creamed Pea Omelette* (page 238), steps 2 and 3. Substitute the avocado and Parmesan for the peas, piling them on one half of the cooked eggs. Pop the pan back under the grill for 1 minute before folding over the omelette.

I AM RATHER ADAMANT that avocados should NEVER be cooked – their delicate healthy fats become unpalatable under the stress of too much heat, but a slight warming enhances them deliciously. These avocado wedges are simply rolled in a sesame mixture spiked with tangy sumac and salt, then warmed through. They can also be served cold once coated in the sesame mixture – a lovely addition to a salad. If sumac is unavailable, serve with lemon or lime wedges.

Warm sesame avocado fillets

SERVES 4 | **PREP** 10 MINS | **COOK** 10 MINS

30 MINUTES OR LESS | GLUTEN FREE | DAIRY FREE | VEGAN

4 heaped tablespoons raw sesame seeds

large pinch of sea salt

1 teaspoon sumac (see intro for *Green Fattoush*, page 196)

2 large perfectly ripe avocados

spray coconut oil or other spray oil

OPTIONS
Substitute sumac with lemon or lime wedges for squirting.

Serve with scrambled eggs on toast, or on top of a bowl of noodles seasoned with soy and sesame oil.

SPECIAL EQUIPMENT
Large baking tray, non-stick foil or baking paper.

1   Preheat the oven to 200°C (400°F). Line a baking tray.

2   Heat a small frying pan without oil over a medium heat and add the sesame seeds. Toast, stirring frequently, until golden and popping. Remove from the pan and transfer to a plate to cool.

3   Once the sesame seeds are cool, use a mortar and pestle to grind them with the salt and sumac. Grind until it's slightly powdery and smells fragrant. Transfer the mixture to a plate and spread out.

4   Cut the avocados in half from stem to base and remove the stones. Cut each half in half again, then peel off the skin. Roll the avocado quarters in the sesame mixture, using your fingertips to help sprinkle so that all the surfaces are covered. Place the coated avocados on the baking tray. Spray lightly with oil.

5   Bake the avocados for 5 minutes. Remove from the heat and serve immediately.

USE REAL CORN TORTILLAS (soft or crisp shells), little gem or romaine (cos) lettuce leaves or Chinese leaf (Napa cabbage) – or all three – to function as little taco trucks for delivering all this gorgeousness to the mouth. This is a wonderfully messy sharing affair at the table. The black bean mixture can be served hot if desired, though not essential – warm through in a small saucepan or microwave just before serving.

Smashed avocado, sweetcorn and black bean tacos

SERVES 4–6 | **PREP** 20 MINS | **COOK** 0 MINS

30 MINUTES OR LESS | FEAST DISH | GOOD SOURCE OF PROTEIN | GLUTEN FREE (IF GLUTEN-FREE TORTILLAS ARE USED) | DAIRY FREE (IF OMITTING SOUR CREAM) | VEGAN (IF OMITTING SOUR CREAM)

400 g (14 oz) tin black beans, drained and rinsed

2 tablespoons lime juice + 2 teaspoons for dressing avocados

2 tablespoons extra virgin olive oil

$1/2$ teaspoon ground cumin

sea salt

cayenne pepper, to taste

3 large or 4 medium perfectly ripe avocados

150 g ($5^1/2$ oz/1 cup) frozen sweetcorn, thawed in boiling water (or use tinned or fresh)

2 spring onions (scallions), chopped

1–2 small red chillies, chopped

about 20 basil leaves, shredded

To serve

sour cream, crème fraîche or Greek-style yoghurt (optional)

taco options for 8–12 tacos (see intro)

bottled hot sauce (optional)

OPTIONS

Substitute fresh coriander (cilantro) for the basil if desired, though basil, avocado and sweetcorn are great pals.

Kidney beans can be used instead of black beans.

Add a bowl of grated sharp cheddar or crumbled feta cheese to the table if desired.

SPECIAL EQUIPMENT
None

1   Place the black beans in a bowl and stir through 2 tablespoons of the lime juice, the oil and cumin, then season with salt and cayenne pepper to taste. Set aside.

2   Scoop the avocado flesh into a large bowl and add the remaining lime juice and a good pinch of salt. Mash together until it's the consistency of guacamole, with a few lumps. Stir in the sweetcorn, spring onions, chillies and basil. Set aside.

3   To serve, place the bean mixture (hot or cold), avocado mixture and sour cream in separate serving bowls and the taco shells/tortillas/leaves on a platter. Allow diners to assemble their own tacos – start with the avocado as the first filling; the beans cling to it well. Finish with extra hot sauce for the brave!

THIS IS AN EXCEPTIONALLY PRETTY AND QUITE FANCY LITTLE DISH, which is also deceptively simple. A mound of avocado chunks is the hero, framed by a salmon-pink moat of delicate chilled tomato-yoghurt broth studded with crisp sweet capsicum (pepper) and cucumber dice and shiny green beads of olive oil. If you really want to go to town, this is a perfect opportunity to use a finishing salt for the final flourish (see NOTE). Serve in shallow soup bowls so you have a flat canvas for composing the artwork. This is a perfect first course for a summer dinner party. And it's all about the avocado, so make sure you get good ones that are at their prime eating moment, as always.

Avocado gazpacho

SERVES 4 | **PREP** 25 MINS + CHILLING | **COOK** 0 MINS

FEAST DISH | LOW CALORIE | GLUTEN FREE

For the chilled broth

300 g (10^1/$_2$ oz) ripe vine tomatoes, quartered

150 g (5^1/$_2$ oz) plain yoghurt

1 tablespoon tomato paste (concentrated purée)

1 tablespoon lemon juice

sea salt

To serve

2 perfectly ripe avocados, at room temperature

^{1}/$_4$ sweet yellow or orange capsicum (pepper), cut into small dice

3 cm (1^1/$_4$ inch) piece cucumber, seeds removed, cut in small dice

4 teaspoons extra virgin olive oil

freshly ground black pepper

finishing salt (optional – see NOTE)

OPTIONS
Serve with crusty bread.

SPECIAL EQUIPMENT
Blender or food processor, sieve and pouring jug and shallow bowls for serving (optional, but best for presentation).

1   Whizz all the broth ingredients in a blender or food processor with 60 ml (2 fl oz/^{1}/$_4$ cup) water until smooth. Push it through a sieve, ideally over a pouring jug – or transfer the sieved broth to a pouring jug. Cover with plastic wrap and refrigerate. It needs to chill for at least 1 hour, but it can stay chilled for up to 24 hours if necessary.

2   Shortly before serving, get all your remaining ingredients ready, then prepare the avocados. Cut each in half, remove the stone, then use the tip of a knife to score 1 cm (^{1}/$_2$ inch) chunks, cutting a grid pattern in the flesh of each half without cutting through the skin. Now use a dessertspoon to scoop out the chunks into a bowl. If the avocado needs to stand for more than 10 minutes, dress with a little lime or lemon juice to stop it browning. Otherwise, assemble the gazpacho bowls.

3   Using light fingers and a spoon, gently place an elevated mound of avocado pieces in the centre of each bowl. Gently pour a shallow pool of tomato broth around the avocado. Scatter the capsicum and cucumber pieces on the surface of the broth. Use a teaspoon to drizzle droplets of olive oil across the surface. Grind a little pepper in too, and finish with either a pinch of sea salt flakes on the avocado or a special finishing salt, if using (see NOTE). Transport steadily to the table and eat right away.

NOTE
Use a finishing salt here for crunch and flavour – just a pinch or two on the avocado or the broth edge would do the trick. Here are three of my favourites, which would be ideal with the flavours here:

Smoked salt flakes – light brown and assertively smoky flakes.

Hawaiian black lava salt – jet-black mini crystals.

Hibiscus salt – fine crystals blended with crushed pink hibiscus petals, giving a citrus flavour and a pink pigment that releases in contact with liquid.

Zucchini and Summer Squash

... these plants produce such an abundance of juicy fruits that it's nearly impossible to keep up with eating the harvest.

Zucchini and Summer Squash

Zucchini (courgettes) and summer squashes are an embarrassment of riches in the summer garden, as anyone who grows their own knows. These plants produce such an abundance of juicy fruits that it's nearly impossible to keep up with eating the harvest. They don't lend themselves particularly well to preserving, so every possible cooking method is employed during the days of their endless supply. They taste best when harvested young and small, and their blossoms are a lauded delicacy. The plants' spiky leaves are also incredibly delicious cooked, but that's a secret treat exclusively for the gardener – see *Fried Pumpkin Leaves* (page 244).

Zucchini lend themselves better than any other vegetable to being turned into zucchini spaghetti, or 'courgetti', long spaghetti-like tendrils produced by a spiralizer or julienne tool. Their long, straight shape and easy-to-carve texture make them perfect for this treatment. While I would never suggest that zucchini spaghetti is comparable to real pasta, it can be a useful substitute for people who are cutting out carbs or reducing calories. When my partner and I share the occasional comforting spaghetti dinner at home, sometimes I will make a mix of half real spaghetti/half microwave-steamed zucchini spaghetti for myself (my partner isn't a fan). It lightens my meal and gets some extra nutrients into me when I don't fancy the heaviness of just pasta and sauce.

THE NUTRITIONAL SUPERPOWER

Extremely rich in lutein and zeaxanthin, two antioxidant carotenoids, which are hugely beneficial for eye health and are concentrated in the squashes' skin.

OTHER HIGH LEVELS OF NUTRITIONAL EXCELLENCE

▌ Multiple anti-inflammatory nutrients, for disease prevention.

▌ B-complex vitamins, for converting food into fuel and giving us energy.

▌ Manganese, for skin and bone health.

▌ Copper, for bone and tissue health.

▌ Potassium, for heart and kidney health and regulating blood pressure.

SEASON

Best in summer through late autumn.

VARIETIES

COMMON DARK GREEN ZUCCHINI Grown to a fairly standard size of about 20 cm (8 inches) for general selling. Anything larger will start to have fully formed seeds and watery flesh and should be avoided.

BABY ZUCCHINI Not much bigger than an average lipstick and beautifully sweet and dense yet tender; they tend to be expensive, but superior in flavour for sure. Fresh blossoms attached to baby fruits are females; they are not as tasty or robust as the larger male flowers, which grow on the same plant on a stem, so opt for the boys (a small stem attached) if you are seeking the best blossoms for cooking.

ANY ZUCCHINI WITH AN UNUSUAL COLOUR Zucchini that are pale green, bright yellow or with stripes are likely to have a more interesting flavour than the dark green ones.

MARROW Overgrown zucchini the size of a puppy that do sport stripes, but don't let that fool you – they are not worth eating in my opinion. Oddly they still appear for sale in the UK for people who like to stuff and bake them. There are far tastier squashes to stuff.

SUMMER SQUASH The term covers a plethora of shapes and sizes, ranging from perfect globes and pear shapes to elongated squiggles. Mostly their colours range from pale yellows to deep greens. One of my all-time favourites is the flying saucer-shaped variety called patty pan.

CHOOSE AND STORE

Select firm, heavy, unblemished specimens with no soft spots. Inspect the skin all over and make sure there are no slimy patches. Minor nicks are OK. Store in a loose plastic bag in the fridge crisper drawer. Use blossoms as soon as you get them home if possible; they may keep for a day or so if gently wrapped in paper towels in the fridge.

PROCESSED AND PRESERVED

You might come across pickled zucchini or dried slices, but fresh is your best bet. Definitely avoid frozen.

PREP

▌ Most zucchini and squashes should be topped and tailed before cutting. Any fully formed seeds need to be scooped out from the interior and discarded (also a sign that it has matured past its best and will be watery). Don't peel unless the specimen is large and the skin seems tough.

▌ The best cutting methods for classic club-shaped zucchini and summer squash are numerous. For raw or steamed, slice thinly or use a veg peeler to shave long ribbons (see also *Zucchini Parchment*, page 224).

▌ For sautéeing or shallow frying, cut into little dice, slim batons or medium slices. Slices can be cut lengthways as long tongues, crossways as coins, or on the diagonal. Cutting first in half lengthways, then across on the diagonal makes pretty angular shapes. For stir-frying, cut into thin slices (I prefer the angular/diagonal cut ones as just described).

▌ For roasting, cut into chunky spools or wedges.

▌ For the BBQ, cut diagonally into thick ovals, tongues or long wedges, or thread chunky spools onto skewers through the skin.

▌ Grate zucchini for making pancakes and fritters – see *Zucchini and Dill Pancakes* (page 224).

▌ For zucchini spaghetti (courgetti), see the intro opposite.

Zucchini and Summer Squash's best mates

Salt | Lemon | All good vinegars | All good oils, nut oils | Mint, basil, parsley, dill | Oregano | Garlic | Chilli | Honey | Pomegranate molasses | Yoghurt | Most cheeses | Pine nuts, almonds, walnuts

Cook and eat

Zucchini parchment

Thin slices oven-dried to a crisp. These are truly sublime – it's difficult to make enough; they shrink a lot, and when ready to eat they disappear in seconds! Slice lengthways as thinly as possible, either with a knife, mandoline or veg peeler. Place in a large bowl and add a smidgeon of olive oil – just enough to coat each piece with a light slick when you toss with your hands. Season very lightly with sea salt and pepper and toss to coat. Line one or two large baking trays with non-stick foil or baking paper and lay the slices out in one layer. Bake at 170°C (325°F) for 30 minutes, rotating the tray(s) once during cooking, until golden and crisp. Some slices may not get completely crisp but still taste wonderful.

Zucchini and dill pancakes

Fresh, light fritters to accompany salad or meze. Coarsely grate 150 g (5$\frac{1}{2}$ oz) zucchini in a bowl, mix in some salt and set aside for 10 minutes, then squeeze out the moisture. Combine with 100 g (3$\frac{1}{2}$ oz) drained cottage cheese, a handful of chopped dill, a chopped spring onion (scallion), 1 tablespoon plain (all-purpose) flour, $\frac{1}{4}$ teaspoon baking powder and 1 beaten egg. Mix well, then fry flattened dessertspoonfuls in a small amount of olive oil until golden.

EACH OF THE VEGETABLE TREASURES in this fry-up reaches its peak in late summer in the garden. Here each one is introduced to the pan at a stage that lets its talents shine: first the green capsicum (pepper) is charred, then onions and garlic are browned, chunky zucchini (courgettes) then exude juices and get glazed in the pan flavours, and next sweetcorn and tomatoes sweeten it up and get saucy. Finally, a little cream cheese is stirred in to create a luscious sauce (this could be omitted, or replaced with sour cream or yoghurt). This is a great opportunity to use a mixture of some of the more unusual zucchini and summer squash varieties available in season, and invite them to party with their summery chums. Complete the plate with an egg on top and toast or potatoes, for breakfast, brunch or lunch.

Summer garden fry-up

SERVES 4 | **PREP** 15 MINS | **COOK** 30 MINS

GOOD SOURCE OF PROTEIN | GLUTEN FREE

4 teaspoons extra virgin olive oil

1 green capsicum (pepper), chopped into 1 cm ($1/2$ inch) dice

sea salt

1 onion, chopped

2 garlic cloves, sliced

1 or $1/2$ fleshy red chilli, sliced

350 g (12 oz) young (small) zucchini (courgettes) or summer squashes, cut into bite-sized chunks

80 g ($2^3/4$ oz) fresh sweetcorn kernels stripped from the cob, or frozen and defrosted (see NOTE)

1 large ripe tomato (approx. 150 g/$5^1/2$ oz), chopped

80 g ($2^3/4$ oz/$1/3$ cup) cream cheese

4 eggs (optional)

small handful of parsley, chopped (optional)

freshly ground black pepper

OPTIONS
Serve with toast, or potatoes – sweet or regular – baked, boiled, mashed or pan-fried.

SPECIAL EQUIPMENT
Large non-stick frying pan

1 Heat a frying pan over a high heat and add 2 teaspoons of the oil. Add the green capsicum and cook, stirring occasionally, until nicely charred and soft, about 7–10 minutes.

2 Reduce the heat to medium and add the remaining 2 teaspoons oil and the onion. Cook until soft and starting to brown, then add the garlic and chilli and cook until the garlic starts to brown.

3 Stir in the zucchini. Cook, stirring frequently, until they have softened and are starting to turn golden, about 5 minutes.

4 Stir in the sweetcorn, and then the tomatoes. Stir for a couple of minutes, until the tomatoes just start to collapse, then make a space in the centre of the pan and plop in the cream cheese. Gently stir it through all the pan contents, letting it melt into an evenly distributed sauce, until bubbling. Remove from the heat. Either serve right away, or cook your eggs, if using.

5 Cook your eggs to your liking in a separate pan – poached, fried or scrambled. Reheat the fry-up and serve on warm plates with the eggs on top. Finish with chopped parsley, if using, and a few twists of pepper.

NOTE
To defrost frozen corn, place in a bowl and pour boiling water over to cover. Wait a minute or two, then drain thoroughly.

HERE I'VE TAKEN THE AUSTRALIAN HOUSEWIVES' VINTAGE CLASSIC – *Zucchini Slice* – enriched with cheddar cheese, bacon and wheat flour, and Med-ified it with feta, fresh dill, oregano and peppery olive oil. Brown rice flour makes it lovely and light as well as gluten free. It couldn't be easier – just mix and bake! This can be eaten hot, warm or cold and keeps well in the fridge – a really handy and delicious recipe.

Greek-style zucchini slice

SERVES 4–6 | **PREP** 15 MINS | **COOK** 40 MINS

GOOD SOURCE OF PROTEIN | GLUTEN FREE

400 g (14 oz) zucchini (courgettes) (trimmed weight – about 2 medium), coarsely grated

1 onion, finely chopped

5 eggs, beaten

100 g (3^1/2 oz) feta, crumbled small

130 g (4^1/2 oz) brown rice flour

^{1}/2 teaspoon baking powder

generous handful or 7–8 sprigs dill, finely chopped (about 4 heaped tablespoons)

1 teaspoon dried oregano

125 ml (4 fl oz/^{1}/2 cup) extra virgin olive oil

sea salt and freshly ground black pepper

OPTIONS

White rice flour or wheat flour can be used if brown rice flour is unavailable.

Serve with a leafy salad dressed with a mustardy vinaigrette.

SPECIAL EQUIPMENT

Baking tin or casserole dish 20 x 30 cm (8 x 12 inches) – avoid using anything larger in order to achieve the right thickness.

1 Preheat the oven to 180°C (350°F). Brush a 20 x 30 cm (8 x 12 inch) baking tin or casserole dish generously with olive oil.

2 In a large bowl, combine all the ingredients and mix thoroughly. Season well.

3 Pour into the prepared dish and bake for 40 minutes or until well browned on top and nice and firm.

4 Remove from the oven and loosen the edges with a knife. Cool briefly before cutting into squares and serving, using a bendy spatula to dislodge it from the bottom of the dish.

NOTE

Keeps well, cooled and refrigerated, for up to 3 days. Perfect for picnics and lunchboxes.

THIS SOUP IS PRACTICALLY EFFORTLESS and delivers a huge flavour reward. It's so simple that I can sum up how to make it in a few words, and I have many times. People often ask me what to do with an over-abundance of zucchini (courgettes) and summer squashes. This is the first thing I describe to them: take lots of chunks of zucchini and whole garlic cloves and roast in the oven with oil, salt, pepper and a smidgeon of vinegar until deep golden and shrunken – this is the key to the rich flavour. Then just scrape it all into a saucepan, pour over a little boiling water, purée and serve. That's it!

Roasted zucchini soup

SERVES 4 | **PREP** 10 MINS | **COOK** 50 MINS

GLUTEN FREE | DAIRY FREE | VEGAN

800 g (1 lb 12 oz) zucchini (courgettes) (about 4 medium), halved lengthways and cut into thick chunks

8 garlic cloves, peeled, left whole

2 tablespoons extra virgin olive oil

2 teaspoons apple cider vinegar or white wine vinegar

sea salt and freshly ground black pepper

OPTIONS

I love the naked simplicity of this soup on its own. But you could pretty it up by adding a blob of yoghurt or crème fraîche to each bowl, and a little chopped parsley.

Serve with crusty bread or crisped flatbread strips, if desired.

SPECIAL EQUIPMENT

Large baking tray, non-stick foil or baking paper, hand blender, blender or food processor.

1 Preheat the oven to 200°C (400°F) and line a baking tray.

2 Place the zucchini and garlic on the tray. Add the oil and toss with your hands to coat evenly. Spread out in a single even layer. Sprinkle over the vinegar, then season well with salt and pepper.

3 Roast in the middle of the oven for 40–45 minutes, stirring once or twice during cooking. The zucchini should be thoroughly deep golden – cook longer if necessary. Towards the end of cooking, the garlic may be getting very dark brown – this is good, but do not let the garlic burn. If it looks in danger of burning, either pluck it out with tongs and reserve, or nestle it in a cluster of zucchini to stunt further cooking.

4 Remove the tray from the oven and leave to cool for a couple of minutes. Boil the kettle. Now scrape all the pan's contents including any remaining oil into a medium saucepan. Pour enough boiling water in to just cover the mixture.

5 Use a hand blender to purée until smooth. (Or transfer the mixture to another machine for puréeing.) Taste for seasoning. Ladle into warm bowls and serve.

NOTE

This is super easy for cooking for a crowd if you have the oven space – multiply as necessary.

Peas

... they are incredibly nutritious, delicious, versatile and,
no doubt, the most convenient of all because all you need to do
is grab them out of a bag in the freezer.

Peas

Peas themselves are not veggie fruits, but the whole pod, containing the peas as seeds, is classed as a fruit. By featuring green peas here, I dip my toe into the wonderful world of legumes and beans, which is a whole separate SuperVeg dimension. But we treat green peas much like the other stars of this book, and they are incredibly nutritious, delicious, versatile and, no doubt, the most convenient of all because all you need to do is grab them out of a bag in the freezer. No other pre-cooking effort is necessary at all, not even shopping, if you keep them in stock!

To get a decent quantity of fresh peas, you need a ridiculously large volume of pods, and the patience of a saint to get them removed from the stringy pods (the pods are good for flavouring veg stock, but not much else). Like certain other veg (e.g. asparagus and sweetcorn), as soon as the peas are harvested, they start to lose flavour, so getting fresh peas that are fresh enough is not easy. I grow just a couple of plants on my allotment, only for the rare seasonal pleasure of plucking and shucking the odd pod in passing, popping the candy-sweet peas in my mouth raw in between gardening chores. Commercial frozen peas are flash-frozen shortly after harvesting and all their flavour and goodness is captured and preserved, so this is the one veg I actually prefer and recommend using frozen not fresh. Apologies to any adamant fresh pea purists out there!

THE NUTRITIONAL SUPERPOWER

Unique phytonutrients including coumestrol, which protects against stomach cancer, and saponins, which are anti-inflammatory and antioxidant, as well as reducing the risk of Type 2 diabetes.

OTHER HIGH LEVELS OF NUTRITIONAL EXCELLENCE

- Plant sterols, for lowering cholesterol.
- B-complex vitamins, for converting food into fuel and giving us energy.
- Omega-3 and omega-6 fatty acids, for cardiovascular health.
- Vitamin C, for healthy tissues and immunity.
- Folate, for cell vitality.

SEASON

Year-round; fresh peas in early spring through summer.

VARIETIES

PEA SHOOTS These deserve a mention here – grab them whenever you can as a salad leaf and decoration for the plate. They taste wonderfully herbal and sweet like peas, and look precious with their curly tendrils and delicate petal-like leaves.

SNOW PEAS (MANGETOUT) AND SUGAR SNAP PEAS These are young types of peas grown for the edible pod alone.

CHOOSE AND STORE

Some supermarkets stock fresh peas in bags, removed from the pod. These are delicious but must be used immediately after purchase as peas' flavour deteriorates rapidly once harvested. Frozen peas are available in two types: garden peas/green peas or petits pois. The latter are slightly younger versions of the former and may be sweeter, but not always. Supermarkets may have numerous brands with confusingly varying prices. If you pay more, you are likely to get better peas, but try for yourself by comparing cheap ones against dear ones. In my experience, cheap ones are less flavourful. Frozen peas will not keep forever, so mind the use-by date, and while it's OK to go past it by a couple of months, they will deteriorate eventually. Be sure to seal the bag well after opening with a tight clasp and don't allow peas to thaw slowly and then re-freeze.

PROCESSED AND PRESERVED

Frozen peas are preferable even to fresh, as discussed earlier. Tinned are not to be touched. Dried peas take on a different personality altogether, becoming starchy like other dried beans and pulses.

PREP

Frozen peas only need brief boiling or steaming direct from frozen. Boil for just 3–4 minutes in a small amount of salted water, or steam in a microwave with a splash of water and a little salt for 3 minutes, or until hot and tender throughout. Drain and eat right away or refresh in cold water. Frozen peas can also simply be defrosted by pouring boiling water over them for certain recipes, such as the *Pea Fritters* (page 237).

Peas' best mates

Lemon | Mint, basil, dill, oregano | Eggs any style | Cream, crème fraîche, yoghurt | Butter | Parmesan, paneer | Cream cheese | White potato | Rice, barley | Lettuce | Asparagus

Cook and eat

Peas cooked in lettuce

One of the best ways to cook a small amount of very fresh peas (see page 162).

Green pea soup

Super green and super quick! Sweat chopped spring onions (scallions) in a little butter or olive oil. Add frozen peas and enough stock just to cover the peas. Bring to the boil and simmer until the peas are tender, then purée. Adjust the seasoning with sea salt and black pepper or white pepper. You can add a touch of fresh lemon juice and/or zest or some chopped fresh dill, mint or parsley for a lift if you wish. Finish each bowl with a blob of crème fraîche or creamy yoghurt.

Crunchy pea salad

Cook frozen peas, refresh in cold water and drain well. Combine with thickly sliced raw sugar snap peas and snow peas (mangetout), making the quantities approximately equal parts of all three. Arrange on a platter and drizzle with *Tangy Lemon Dressing* (page 163). Top with a tangle of young pea shoots.

BARLEY IN PLACE OF RICE and cooked in the style of a risotto, this is called *orzotto* in Italy, but I'm fond of this English hybrid name. The result is very different from its famous refined white rice alter ego. It has a sort of peasant charm, plus it's cheap! Pearl barley expands into wonderfully chewy, rugged grains, and peas are a lovely pairing, as their green sweetness sets off the nutty barley. Comforting winter bowl food that clings to the bones and, like risotto, doesn't necessarily need any side dishes.

Pearl barley is used here, and will cook more quickly than wholegrain pot barley. Extend the cooking time in step 2 if necessary, to reach that creamy threshold.

Pea barlotto

SERVES 4 AS A MAIN | **PREP** 20 MINS | **COOK** 45 MINS

GOOD SOURCE OF PROTEIN | DAIRY FREE (IF CHEESE IS OMITTED) | VEGAN (IF CHEESE IS OMITTED AND VEGAN WINE USED)

1 tablespoon extra virgin olive oil

1 onion, chopped

3 garlic cloves, chopped

150 g (5^1/$_2$ oz/^{3}/$_4$ cup) pearl barley

150 ml (5 fl oz) dry vermouth or white wine

500 ml (17 fl oz/2 cups) vegetable stock

^{1}/$_2$ teaspoon lemon zest

sea salt

300 g (10^1/$_2$ oz) frozen peas

To serve

extra virgin olive oil

freshly ground black pepper

freshly grated Parmesan cheese or vegetarian alternative, to serve (optional)

SPECIAL EQUIPMENT
Hand blender or regular blender.

1   Heat a medium saucepan over a medium–low heat and add the oil. Add the chopped onion and cook until soft and translucent. Add the garlic and barley and cook for 2–3 minutes, stirring frequently to toast the barley. Pour in the vermouth or wine all at once. Simmer until it is completely absorbed, stirring occasionally.

2   Add the stock and lemon zest and stir. Bring to the boil and simmer for about 15–20 minutes, stirring occasionally, until the barley is cooked and the liquid is absorbed. Taste the liquid as it nears the end of cooking and season with more salt if necessary. The grains will reach a point somewhere after 15 minutes where they surrender to the broth and start to expand rapidly, making the mixture creamy and thick.

3   Meanwhile, get the peas and pea purée ready. Bring about 300 ml (10^1/$_2$ fl oz) salted water to the boil in a small saucepan. Add the frozen peas, return to the boil and cook for 3 minutes. Strain the peas over a bowl or measuring jug to catch the water. Cool for a couple of minutes.

4   Place half the peas in a bowl with 125 ml (4 fl oz/^{1}/$_2$ cup) of the cooking water and whizz to a smooth purée with a hand blender (or whizz in a regular blender). Reserve the remaining peas.

5   When the barlotto reaches that creamy threshold (and just before serving to preserve the bright colour and perfect texture), stir the pea purée and the peas into it quickly. Return to the heat and warm through. Serve immediately in warm bowls topped with a drizzle of olive oil, black pepper and grated cheese, if desired.

NOTE
As it cools, the barley continues to expand. Any leftovers will have an almost solid character, but it's still delicious reheated if cooled completely, refrigerated and reheated within 24 hours.

I FIRST HEARD OF THE GENIUS TECHNIQUE of using whizzed cornflakes for breading from children's food expert Annabel Karmel, who uses it to make fish fingers. I've adopted it as a superior crunchy coating in place of breadcrumbs for all sorts of things, including halloumi fingers and cauliflower – see *Cauliflower Wings* (page 125). Avoid cheap cornflakes and opt for a natural, additive-free brand. Here the mixture encases a pea purée. It bakes to a perfect crisp golden shell, revealing the bright green pea deliciousness within.

Pea fritters

SERVES 4 | **PREP** 30 MINS + FREEZING | **COOK** 20 MINS
GLUTEN FREE (IF GLUTEN-FREE CORNFLAKES ARE USED) | DAIRY FREE (IF SERVED WITH A DAIRY-FREE SUBSTITUTE FOR CRÈME FRAÎCHE)

250 g (9 oz/1^3/4 cups) frozen peas

sea salt and freshly ground black pepper

^{1}/2 teaspoon finely grated lemon zest

^{1}/2 teaspoon lemon juice

100 g (3^1/2 oz/3^1/3 cups) cornflakes

1 tablespoon raw sesame seeds

coconut oil spray or other oil spray

2 eggs

crème fraîche or Greek-style yoghurt and lemon wedges, to serve

OPTIONS
Serve with pea shoots and/or watercress tossed in a lemon or balsamic dressing.

SPECIAL EQUIPMENT
Food processor or hand blender, small tray that will fit in the freezer, baking tray and non-stick foil or baking paper.

1   Place the frozen peas in a bowl and pour freshly boiled water over them. Leave for 5 minutes, then drain. Run cold water gently over them until cool, then drain thoroughly. Prepare a small tray lined with paper towels and spread the peas out to dry for about 5–10 minutes.

2   Place the peas in a food processor with the salt, pepper, lemon zest and juice and purée until as smooth as possible. Taste for seasoning.

3   Line the small tray with plastic wrap. Divide the purée into four parts, spooning each part separately on to the tray. Use a spoon to even out the amounts if necessary. Gently form each part into a round, flattened patty, about 2 cm (^{3}/4 inch) thick. Drape another piece of plastic wrap on top of the patties. Place the tray in the freezer and freeze for 1 hour, or until very firm (they do not need to be frozen solid, just firm enough to handle easily).

4   Meanwhile, whizz the cornflakes to fine crumbs. Heat a small frying pan without oil over a medium heat and add the sesame seeds. Toast, stirring frequently, until golden and popping. Place in a shallow bowl and stir in the cornflakes and a little salt.

5   Once the freezing time is up, preheat the oven to 200°C (400°F). Line a baking tray, then spritz with spray oil. Beat the eggs in a bowl until frothy. Take the pea cakes from the freezer and work quickly. Dip each one first in crumbs, then in egg, then in crumbs, then once more in egg, then crumbs, making sure each patty is completely covered (see NOTE). Place on the baking tray. (There will be an excess of cornflake mixture, but this makes it much easier to coat the cakes.)

6   Spray the patties several times with spray oil. Bake for 20 minutes until firm, crisp and golden. Serve right away with a generous dollop of crème fraîche or yoghurt on the side and lemon wedges, if desired.

NOTE
If making ahead, the patties can be prepared up to the breaded stage in step 5, covered with plastic wrap and chilled until ready to bake.

ALL HAIL THE MIGHTY FROZEN PEA – the most convenient of all SuperVeg! When there are no other greens in the house, peas come to the rescue. Here's one of the quickest dishes ever for breakfast, lunch or dinner, and one you might be likely to have all the ingredients for without planning.

Omelettes, like all ways with eggs, are subject to personal preference. This one is made American-style – quite thick and capable of transporting a heavy cargo of cream-cheesy peas that gush out on the plate. If a thin, wispy omelette à la française is more your style, make it your way, but wait to add the peas until it's on the plate or it might rip in transit.

Creamed pea omelette

SERVES 2 | **PREP** 15 MINS | **COOK** 10 MINS

30 MINUTES OR LESS | GOOD SOURCE OF PROTEIN | GLUTEN FREE

150 g (5^1/2 oz) frozen peas

sea salt and freshly ground black pepper

60 g (2^1/4 oz/^{1}/4 cup) cream cheese

3 large eggs

2 tablespoons milk

large pinch of dried oregano

1 teaspoon butter or coconut oil

OPTIONS
Serve with buttered toast or potatoes, or a crisp green salad.

SPECIAL EQUIPMENT
Non-stick ovenproof frying pan, ideally 24 cm (9^1/2 inches).

1   Place the peas in a small saucepan and cover with water. Add a pinch of salt and bring to the boil, then simmer for 3 minutes, until tender. Quickly drain and return the peas to the pan. Place it over a low heat and stir in the cream cheese until completely melted and saucy. Add a few twists of black pepper and taste for seasoning. Cover and set aside.

2   Heat the non-stick frying pan over a medium heat. Crack the eggs into a bowl and add the milk, salt, pepper and oregano. Mix with a fork until just combined. Add the butter or coconut oil to the hot pan and spread it around. Pour in the egg mixture and swirl it. Cook, loosening the edges from time to time and filling them again by swirling uncooked egg into them. Lift the omelette to inspect the underside, and when it is just golden, remove from the heat.

3   To set the egg completely, heat the oven grill on high and flash the pan under it for a minute or two to set. Don't forget to use an oven glove to grab out the hot pan!

4   Mound the peas onto one half of the omelette and fold the other side over them. Cleave the omelette into two wedges with your cooking spatula and serve right away on warm plates.

Pumpkin and Winter Squash

... slow and steady maturation ultimately delivers the dense, velvety, ample and sugary flesh of the best eating pumpkins, which often look as beautiful on the outside as they taste within.

Pumpkin and Winter Squash

Pumpkins and winter squashes start producing their fruits around the same time as their zucchini (courgette) plant sisters, during high summer in the garden, but their fruits are less numerous and grow much more slowly. During four to five months of absorbing the sun's energy and the soil's nutrients, and sometimes swelling to a gigantic size, the fruits finally reach ripeness in the cool autumn months. That slow and steady maturation ultimately delivers the dense, velvety, ample and sugary flesh of the best eating pumpkins, which often look as beautiful on the outside as they taste within.

The Halloween tradition of carving pumpkins into jack-o'-lanterns brings a flood of plump, round orange pumpkins gushing to market in October, but these mustn't be mistaken for good eaters. These generic behemoths have a thin skin and spongy flesh, which is easy to carve, but mostly contain tasteless watery cells suspended in stringy sinews. What you want out of a good eating pumpkin is flesh that is so dense that it is quite a task to even get your knife through it (and you must be very careful doing so). Most good eaters also have flesh the colour of a blinding sunset – blazing dark yellow or orange – never pale. The skin colour is no indication of the quality of the flesh, but it will help you identify the variety, which is helpful to know. The skin of some of the tastiest varieties are beige, muddy brown, silver grey or deep forest green, and it's so rigid that you shouldn't be able to pierce it with your thumbnail. The ubiquitous butternut squash is a good case in point – its drab, ecru-coloured skin is tough as an old boot, encasing a sweet bright orange flesh, which is delicious cooked. If in doubt, you can usually depend on good old butternut squash whenever pumpkin is required in a recipe.

THE NUTRITIONAL SUPERPOWER

Beta-carotene, a powerful antioxidant; butternut squash has the highest levels. Pumpkin seeds contain remarkably high levels of zinc, for healthy immunity, and tryptophan, a mood elevator and sleep aid.

OTHER HIGH LEVELS OF NUTRITIONAL EXCELLENCE

▌ Combined antioxidants and anti-inflammatory compounds, which have powerful anti-cancer properties.

▌ Zeaxanthin, for eye health.

▌ B-complex vitamins, for converting food into fuel and giving us energy.

SEASON

Autumn through winter. Butternut squash available year-round.

VARIETIES

Here are just a few of the best varieties to look out for:

KABOCHA Possibly the tastiest of all with a super creamy texture. A Japanese variety, small to medium size, with a slightly flattened round shape and dark green mottled skin.

CROWN PRINCE Large, smooth, flattened round shape with subtle ridges and light silvery grey or pale green skin (see photos pages 12 and 240).

ONION SQUASH/RED KURI Dark orange skin and smallish, shaped like a giant onion.

ACORN SQUASH Dark green and orange mottled skin with deep ridges, smallish and shaped like a giant acorn or a round heart.

SPAGHETTI SQUASH Light yellow and zeppelin-shaped. These unique squashes require a special cooking technique to utilise their spaghetti-strand like flesh (see page 244).

CHOOSE AND STORE

Select a pumpkin/winter squash with the stem intact. If the stem is green and tender looking, the squash is probably freshly harvested, which (for once) is not necessarily a good thing. Most pumpkins need a couple of weeks to harden off to develop flavour, so a dry stem is usually best if you are using it right away. Make sure the spot opposite the stem on the bottom (the blossom end) is firm and not spongy. Inspect the surface for wounds – make sure there are no soft patches, bruises or deep gouges. Store at home in a cool place, away from sunlight. When you come to cut your pumpkin, if you find that the stem end, blossom end or another spot has gone soft or mouldy, don't panic – as long as the rest of the flesh seems good, you can cut away and discard the damaged bits.

PROCESSED AND PRESERVED

Tinned pumpkin is a reliably sweet and smooth purée, which can be very handy for using in baking – it's absolutely fine for a classic pumpkin pie or sweet muffins.

PREP

▌ It is very important to use a very sharp, medium (not large), stiff knife when tackling a pumpkin, as it puts up a lot of resistance. Here's a good process for breaking down a round pumpkin (see note on butternut squash below). First wipe the surface clean with a damp cloth. Cut the pumpkin in half to one side of the stem, working your knife gradually around it. Then cut off the stem a little below where it's attached. Use a large spoon to scoop out all the seeds and strings (save the seeds if you wish to toast them for a yummy snack, see page 244). Place one half cut-side down on the chopping board and cut through the skin into wedges. To remove the skin, cut downwards along the edge of each wedge, then cut the flesh into the desired chunks or slices. If you have more pumpkin than you need to use now, you can wrap the unused portion in a plastic bag, seal, refrigerate and use within 3 days. Or you can freeze it for future use: cut into chunks and freeze raw, or cook and cool before storing in sealed freezer bags.

▌ To tackle a butternut squash, first cut a slice off just below the stem, then a slice off the bottom. Next cut in half across the squash just where the bottom half starts to bulge into a round shape. Stand each piece on the flat cut side and use your knife to pare off the skin, cutting downwards. Cut the round piece in half and scoop out the seeds and strings, then cut all the remaining flesh as required.

Pumpkin and Winter Squash's best mates

Salt | Cinnamon, nutmeg, cloves, cardamom, cumin | Ginger | Garlic | Chilli | Sage, rosemary, thyme, oregano | Black pepper | Olive oil | Coconut | All nuts | Toasted sesame seeds | Soy sauce | Miso | Honey, unrefined sugar

Cook and eat

Pumpkin soup

Prepare and roast the pumpkin with spices as for *Pumpkin, Avocado and Quinoa Salad* (page 248). Place all the baking tray contents in a pan and add vegetable stock to cover, or half stock/half coconut milk. Simmer for 15 minutes, then purée into a smooth soup.

Toasted pumpkin seeds

Wash the seeds under cool running water and remove as many strings as possible. Allow the seeds to dry on paper towels. Toss in a little olive oil and salt in a bowl, then spread out on a lined baking tray and toast in a 200°C (400°F) oven until golden and popping. The shells are edible even though a little tough.

Fried pumpkin leaves

If you grow pumpkins or zucchini (courgette) plants, you can make tasty fried greens – their prickly texture becomes delicious when cooked. Cut young leaves and stems and chop finely. Fry with a little salt in olive oil for 10–15 minutes until very soft, adding chopped garlic and chilli flakes towards the end if desired.

Roasted spaghetti squash

Cut a spaghetti squash in half from stem to base, scoop out the seeds and surrounding fibres. Place cut-side down on a lined baking tray and cook for 45 minutes–1 hour until a skewer pushed through the skin meets no resistance underneath. Leave until cool enough to handle. Use a fork to pull all the spaghetti-like strands of squash away from the skin. Serve hot, seasoned with salt, pepper and plenty of butter; grated cheese optional.

HERE'S A RICH, COLOURFUL AND ELEGANT CELEBRATION of pumpkin, where it takes centre stage in a festival of Asian flavours. If you are feeding very hungry people you might want to supply a steaming bowl of rice or noodles on the table too.

Pumpkin and tofu Malay curry

SERVES 4 | **PREP** 30 MINS | **COOK** 35 MINS

FEAST DISH | GOOD SOURCE OF PROTEIN | GLUTEN FREE (IF TAMARI IS USED) | DAIRY FREE | VEGAN (IF MAPLE SYRUP IS USED)

400 g (14 oz) pumpkin or squash, peeled and cut into 2.5 cm (1 inch) wide wedges or long slices (prepared weight)

1 teaspoon coriander seeds, lightly crushed

1 teaspoon cumin seeds

sea salt

3 tablespoons extra virgin olive oil

250 g (9 oz) fresh firm tofu, drained and patted dry, cut into 1 cm (^{1}/2 inch) cubes

1 tablespoon light soy sauce or tamari

1 tablespoon cornflour (cornstarch)

For the Malay curry paste

2 lemongrass stems, white part only

2 garlic cloves

2 fleshy red chillies, deseeded (if they are very hot use less)

2 cm (^{3}/4 inch) thumb fresh ginger

2 spring onions (scallions)

^{1}/2 teaspoon ground turmeric

1 tablespoon oil

For the remainder

400 g (14 oz) tin coconut milk

2 tablespoons light soy sauce or tamari

1 teaspoon maple syrup or honey

To serve

25 g (1 oz) hulled pumpkin seeds (optional)

handful of mint and/or coriander (cilantro) leaves

lime wedges

SPECIAL EQUIPMENT
Non-stick foil or baking paper, one small and two large baking trays, and a food processor.

1   Preheat the oven to 200°C (400°F). Line two large baking trays.

2   Place the pumpkin pieces on one large tray, scatter over the spices and season with salt. Add 2 tablespoons of the olive oil and toss with your hands to coat evenly. Roast for about 30 minutes on the middle rack of the oven until soft and golden around the edges. (Cooking times may vary depending on the type of pumpkin used.)

3   Place the tofu in a bowl and add the soy sauce. Toss with a spoon gently to coat. Next add the remaining oil and toss again, then the cornflour and toss to coat evenly. Spread it out on the second large baking tray and place in the oven below the pumpkin. The tofu will take about 25–30 minutes to cook until golden brown and crisp. Once the pumpkin is cooked, take it out and wrap up to keep warm. Move the tofu tray up in its place to finish cooking.

4   If using the pumpkin seeds, spread them out on a small baking tray. Once the cooked pumpkin comes out of the oven, pop the seeds in and cook for about 3–5 minutes, or until puffed and light golden.

5   Meanwhile, make the curry paste. Slice the lemongrass fairly thinly and chop everything else coarsely. Whizz it all plus the turmeric and oil in a food processor until very finely chopped. The paste can also be made with a blender or hand blender – add a little water if necessary to help grind it finely.

6   Heat a medium saucepan or a wok over a medium–high heat. Add the paste and cook for about 2 minutes, stirring frequently, until bursting with fragrance. Stir in the coconut milk, soy sauce and syrup. Bring to the boil and simmer for 10 minutes, stirring occasionally. Taste for seasoning.

7   Warm four shallow serving bowls and call your diners to the table. Divide the sauce amongst the bowls. Next add the tofu, then arrange the pumpkin on top. Finish by scattering over torn mint and/or coriander leaves and finally toasted pumpkin seeds. Serve right away with lime wedges, fork and spoon.

CERTAIN TYPES of commonly found winter squashes will lend themselves well to this – it's all in the shape. Basically any good eating squash that is round and about grapefruit sized (such as acorn or onion squash), or is partially that shape and size (such as butternut's bottom half, enclosing the seeds). From this you will cut rings with a natural hole, and fill that hole with a grated halloumi, sweetcorn and pickled chilli mixture that forms a crisp crust on the bottom and binds to the rings when served. It's a satisfying contrast of textures, and the ingredient combo is a nod to the Native American food culture of the southwest USA, where I grew up.

Stuffed squash rings

SERVES 2 AS A MAIN, 4 AS A SIDE OR STARTER | **PREP** 30 MINS | **COOK** 20 MINS

FEAST DISH | GOOD SOURCE OF PROTEIN | GLUTEN FREE | DAIRY FREE | VEGAN

600 g (1 lb 5 oz) round squash or butternut bottom (see intro) (unpeeled, uncored weight)

1 tablespoon extra virgin olive oil + more for brushing the rings

sea salt and freshly ground black pepper

125 g (4^1/$_2$ oz) halloumi cheese, coarsely grated

100 g (3^1/$_2$ oz) sweetcorn (cooked from fresh or frozen or from a tin)

1 garlic clove, crushed

1 tablespoon pickled chilli slices, such as jalapenos or *Quick Pickled Chillies* (page 254), roughly chopped

pinch of cayenne pepper

OPTIONS
Serve with roast or mashed sweet potatoes or quinoa.

Also good with fried slices of *Salt-Baked Celeriac* (page 44).

SPECIAL EQUIPMENT
Large baking tray, non-stick foil or baking paper and your best large knife.

1   Preheat the oven to 250°C (500°F) and line a large baking tray. If using a whole squash such as acorn, cut 2 cm (³/4 inch) off the top and bottom. If using butternut, you should already have cut off the slender top half, so just cut the bottom. Score the skin with your knife to make four equal-sized rings about 1 cm (¹/2 inch) thick. Cut the rings and remove the seeds and strings using the tip of your knife.

2   Place the rings on the baking tray and brush all over with oil. Season with salt and pepper. Bake for 5 minutes, then remove from the oven.

3   To make the stuffing, mix together all the remaining ingredients with a pinch of salt. Divide amongst the holes of the rings. Place back in the oven and cook for a further 10–15 minutes, until the squash is soft and the cheese is golden and melted. Eat right away.

HERE'S A SCRUMPTIOUS MAIN COURSE SALAD of three complementary counterparts. It can be served warm or cold. Red or black quinoa looks particularly pretty with the colour scheme here, but white quinoa is fine too. See the NOTE on cooking quinoa – you may have been doing it wrong all along!

Pumpkin, avocado and quinoa salad

SERVES 4 AS A MAIN | **PREP** 30 MINS | **COOK** 35 MINS + COOLING

FEAST DISH | GOOD SOURCE OF PROTEIN | GLUTEN FREE | DAIRY FREE | VEGAN

For the pumpkin

600 g (1 lb 5 oz) raw pumpkin or winter squash such as butternut, peeled and cut into 2 cm (3/4 inch) chunks (prepared weight)

6 garlic cloves, peeled, left whole

5 cm (2 inch) piece fresh ginger, chopped

1 teaspoon cumin seeds

sea salt

2 tablespoons extra virgin olive oil

For the salad

25 g (1 oz) hulled pumpkin seeds

3 medium or 2 large perfectly ripe avocados

1 tablespoon lime juice

250 g (9 oz) cooked red or black quinoa, cooled

SPECIAL EQUIPMENT
Small and large baking tray, non-stick foil or baking paper.

1　Preheat the oven to 200°C (400°F). Line one small and one large baking tray.

2　Spread the pumpkin seeds out on the small baking tray. Toast in the oven for 3–5 minutes, until golden and puffed. Leave to cool.

3　For the pumpkin, mix everything together thoroughly in a bowl and pour onto the large tray. Spread out in one layer, but keep everything nestled towards the centre of the baking tray to help avoid burning the garlic and ginger. Roast for 30 minutes on the middle rack of the oven until soft, stirring once or twice during cooking and scooping everything back to the centre. (Cooking times may vary depending on the type of pumpkin used.) Once cooked, remove from the oven and let cool to room temperature or just warm.

4　Just before serving, cut the avocados into chunks and place in a bowl. Toss with the lime juice and a little sea salt.

5　Spread out the quinoa in a layer on a serving platter or individual plates. Top with the cooked pumpkin mixture, scraping everything from the baking tray. Arrange the avocado on top, and scatter the toasted pumpkin seeds all over. Eat right away.

NOTE
Packaged pre-cooked quinoa is fine for this recipe. If cooking from dry, don't fall for any recommendation to rinse the quinoa first or you will not get a light and fluffy result. The key is to toast the dry grains before cooking. First get your quantities right. The best ratio of cooking liquid to quinoa is 2:1, so measure the volume of quinoa in a measuring jug (say 100 ml/3 1/2 fl oz) and then be prepared to add twice that amount of stock or water (200 ml/7 fl oz). Heat up a lidded pan over a medium heat, without oil, and toss in the dry quinoa. Stir it around for just a couple of minutes until it pops and emits a bit of a toasty fragrance, then add the liquid. Stir, reduce the heat to a simmer, cover and cook until the liquid is absorbed, about 13–15 minutes, then fluff to perfection.

Capsicum and Chilli Pepper

... the fire on the tongue is immediately perceived by the brain as pain (even if you are enjoying the heat), and it releases endorphins – hormones that induce an opium-like euphoria.

Capsicum and Chilli Pepper

Peppers is the generic word that labels this whole group of two distinct sets of veggie fruits: one mainly large and sweet, the other mostly smaller and fiery. The word *peppers* is at the heart of one of my all-time favourite food history stories. In the time of Christopher Columbus (late 1400s), black pepper, or *pimienta*, was one of the world's most valuable commodities. His famous journey to what he thought would be Asia and during which he accidentally 'discovered' America, was commissioned by the king and queen of Spain. They hoped that he would discover a new source of *pimienta* (among other things) and they would get a big return on their investment. When he arrived in the Caribbean islands early on, he tasted a chilli pepper for the first time. He likened its biting heat to that of black peppercorns, and so he named them *pimiento*, hoping to please the monarchs by declaring he'd found the much anticipated spice goldmine. (Peppercorns, incidentally, are no botanical relation to chilli peppers. The Mexican name chilli became attached to the word pepper much later on.)

Chillies have the power to induce a psychoactive effect: the fire on the tongue is immediately perceived by the brain as pain (even if you are enjoying the heat), and it releases endorphins – hormones that induce an opium-like euphoria. Milk or sugar will help relieve this pain. Some people seem to get addicted to chillies – could it be an addiction to the brain drug their own body produces? Evidence suggests perhaps. Luckily nobody can overdose on chillies, but chillies can be manipulated for harm. The early Mayans used chilli juice grenades in battles, and in modern times we still use pepper spray as a weapon. I sprinkle cayenne powder in my veg patch to keep squirrels off my corn plants though, of course, I wish the little pests no harm, just a warning.

THE NUTRITIONAL SUPERPOWER

Chillies' unique chemical, capsaicin, is anti-cancer, anti-bacterial, anti-inflammatory, reduces cholesterol, dissolves blood clots and induces euphoria! Capsicums (peppers), especially red ones, are one of the best sources of vitamin C, for immune health.

OTHER HIGH LEVELS OF NUTRITIONAL EXCELLENCE

▌ Antioxidants, which resist disease, including vitamin E and vitamin A/beta-carotene.

▌ B-complex vitamins, for converting food into fuel and giving us energy.

▌ Copper and iron, for blood health.

▌ Potassium, for heart health.

▌ Folate, for cell vitality.

SEASON

Best in summer through autumn; greenhouse grown varieties available year-round.

VARIETIES

CAPSICUMS (PEPPERS) Generally vary mostly by colour, but also by size and shape. The classic flat-bottomed heart shape is the most common, and green ones are unripe versions of the warm colours (red, orange, yellow), whose pigment makes them sweet. Special purplish, black and almost white ones taste similar to green – hardly any sweetness but clean tasting. Baby capsicums have a very sugary flavour and are handy for keeping for those occasional moments when you want to have a few slices in a salad without having to borrow a portion of a larger one. Long and slender red capsicums, sometimes called Romano, have thinner walls of flesh than standard ones with few seeds and are good for stuffing and creating attractively shaped slices.

CHILLIES There are countless varieties. What is considered common depends on where you live; in the UK we mostly see green and red versions of jalapenos (thumb-sized, plump and medium hot), cayenne (long, slim and about 1 cm/½ inch wide, medium to hot), bird's eye or Thai chillies (small and hot), and habaneros or Scotch bonnets (lantern-shaped and extremely hot, but with a complex fruit flavour behind the fire).

Definitely seek out more unusual local varieties from farmers' markets in summer – each chilli has a distinct personality. As a very general rule, the smaller the chilli, the hotter it is. There exists a sort of international chilli Olympics that drives fanatics to try to breed the hottest chilli in the world, and every year a new type claims the prize. These chillies are pointless to my mind – they are simply too hot to even attempt to touch, let alone eat – it's pure sport.

Chillies are one of the easiest edible plants to grow at home, even if all you have is a sunny windowsill. It's a great way to experiment with unusual varieties, and they are very ornamental plants too.

CHOOSE AND STORE

With all peppers, choose firm, flawless specimens with a smooth sheen, ideally with even colouring, and no signs of bruising or soft patches. The stem should also be firm and green, not shrivelled or limp. They will last best if kept in a loose plastic bag in the fridge. Small chillies can also be frozen, which is super handy – they are defrosted in a few seconds held under a hot tap. They lose their firmness when frozen (large ones go mushy, so stick with small), but not their fire.

PROCESSED AND PRESERVED

Roasted, skinned capsicums in brine or oil are a fantastic convenience food. Quality varies, but they are usually sold in jars (sometimes tins) and have a soft, creamy texture and a good flavour when used after draining and patting dry, discarding any seeds. Pickled chillies often take on a perky crunch, which is in good company with the pickling vinegar, delivering a high-impact burst of heat and acid. The vinegar itself is spicy and can be used as a seasoning. Dried chillies are great for simmering in stews and soups and you are likely to find interesting and unusual varieties dried. Dried chilli flakes (crushed dried red chillies) are one of my go-to seasonings. Cayenne pepper is powdered dried cayenne chillies. Products labelled 'chilli powder' sometimes have other ingredients added, so check the label.

PREP

Capsicums need to have the stem, seeds and membranes removed. Cut through the stem top to bottom, snap out the stem and its seed cluster. Pull out any large whitish membranes with seeds and 'spank' the outside of the half to release any more seeds clinging on inside. (For stuffing capsicum halves, sometimes the stem is left on to help hold its shape – see *Double Tomato and Lentil-Stuffed Capsicums*, page 260.)

Chilli preparation requires an essential first step in my kitchen: putting on a pair of plastic stretchy examination gloves. I keep a large medic's box in my kitchen drawer (also good for beetroot/beets). If your fingers make contact with the hot chemical in chillies called capsaicin, it stays there, even after thorough washing, for hours. Later when you happen to touch your eye or some other sensitive part of your body (or somebody else's), there will be pain. Wear gloves and everybody's safe.

The membranes clasping the seeds of the chillies possess the main concentration of capsaicin i.e. heat; seeds are spicy too, but removing is optional. In general, small chillies' seeds are soft and compact and don't need to be removed. I do remove the seeds from bigger chillies (jalapeno size and up) because they are large, chewy and hard to digest.

While you can usually rely on tiny chillies being hot, larger ones are harder to assess – sometimes even in the same batch they are mild or scorching. Too much heat can ruin a dish. Here's a good way to test the heat: cut off the top just under the stem. Take the stem end and touch it to the tip of your tongue for 1 second. If you can count a few seconds before you feel anything, it's medium to mild. If it hits you immediately, it's a hot one.

Capsicum and Chilli Pepper's best mates

All good vinegars | Lemon, lime | Garlic | Basil, parsley, dill, mint | Rosemary, sage, thyme, oregano | Olives | Capers | Most cheeses | Coconut | Tomato | Ground cumin, cardamom, coriander | Honey, unrefined sugar | Cream, crème fraîche, yoghurt

Cook and eat

Quick pickled chillies

A handy condiment that keeps in the fridge for ages. Both the chillies and its vinegar can be used to spice up salads, steamed veg, pizza – anything that welcomes a jolt of extra flavour. Slice several chillies thinly, leaving seeds in. Place in a small clean jar (I use one that holds about 200 ml/7 fl oz) to fill it nearly to the top, gently packed in. Pour in apple cider vinegar to cover. Add a generous pinch of salt and about $1/2$ teaspoon maple syrup or honey. Seal tightly and shake. Refrigerate and use after waiting 24 hours, for up to 4 weeks.

THIS COLOURFUL INDO-CHINESE-STYLE FRY-UP is inspired by one of my favourite classic takeaway dishes, improved and simplified with a light and healthy rework. The paneer is baked. The capsicums (peppers) are only briefly cooked so they retain a juicy crunch, but you can cook them longer if you prefer them soft. This can easily be made vegan by substituting tofu for the paneer.

Capsicum paneer fry

SERVES 4 | **PREP** 15 MINS | **COOK** 25 MINS

GOOD SOURCE OF PROTEIN | GLUTEN FREE (IF TAMARI IS USED) | DAIRY FREE (IF TOFU IS SUBSTITUTED FOR PANEER) | VEGAN (IF TOFU IS SUBSTITUTED FOR PANEER, AND MAPLE SYRUP IS USED)

250 g (9 oz) paneer, cut into 1 cm (1/2 inch) cubes

2 tablespoons coconut oil, melted, or extra virgin olive oil

sea salt and freshly ground black pepper

2 red onions, sliced

3 plump garlic cloves, sliced

5 cm (2 inch) piece fresh ginger, peeled and chopped

2 teaspoons ground turmeric

2 teaspoons cumin seeds

1 teaspoon ground coriander

1 red, 1 yellow and 1 green capsicum (pepper), each deseeded and cut into 2 cm (3/4 in) chunks

1–2 small red chillies, slit lengthways

For the sauce

2 tablespoons dark soy sauce or tamari

2 tablespoons tomato paste (concentrated purée)

1 tablespoon maple syrup or honey

2 teaspoons lime juice

OPTIONS
Add fresh coriander (cilantro) to garnish

Substitute tofu for paneer to make it vegan

Serve with cooked wholegrain rice, noodles or quinoa

SPECIAL EQUIPMENT
Small baking tray, non-stick foil or baking paper and a wok or large frying pan.

1   Preheat the oven to 200°C (400°F) and line a small baking tray. Place the paneer cubes in a small bowl with 1 tablespoon of the oil and a couple of pinches of salt and pepper and stir to coat. Spread out in a single layer on the baking tray and bake for 15–20 minutes until golden and crisp.

2   Meanwhile, in a small bowl or jug, mix together all the sauce ingredients and set aside. Prepare all the remaining ingredients and line them up on a board or plate next to the cooker.

3   Once the paneer is cooked, heat a wok or large frying pan over a high heat. Add the remaining oil, followed by the onion, garlic, ginger, turmeric, cumin and coriander and stir-fry for about 3 minutes until the onion starts to soften.

4   Add all the capsicums and chillies and cook, stirring frequently, for about 5 minutes, or until the capsicums are just soft but still crunchy.

5   Add the baked paneer to the pan and stir, then add the sauce mixture. Stir until heated through and bubbling. Serve right away.

NOTE
This dish keeps well and leftovers can easily be reheated in a pan or microwave.

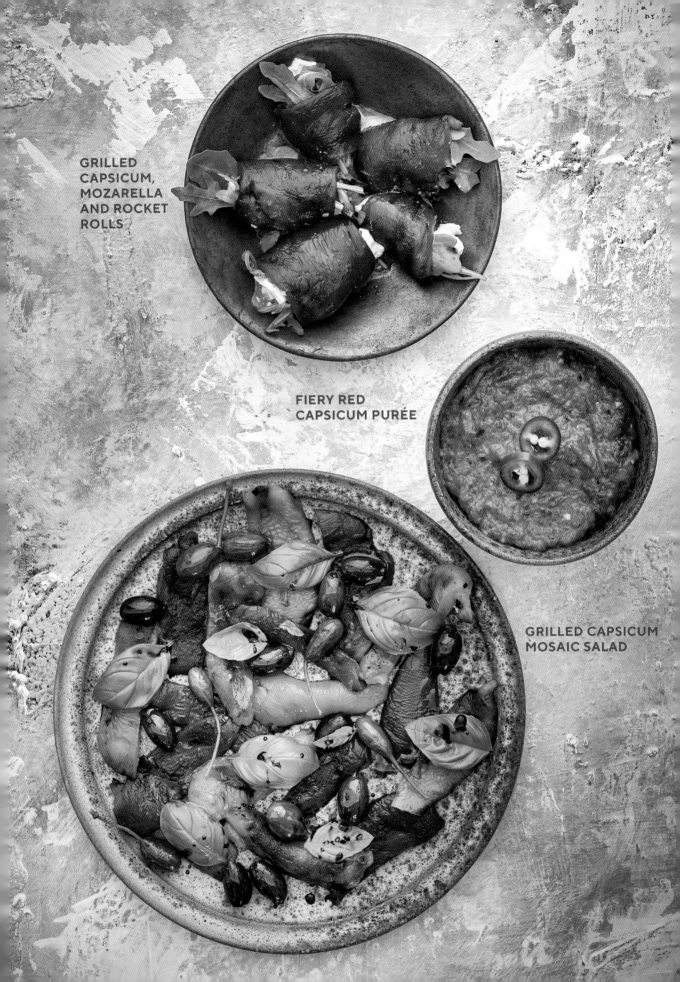

GRILLED CAPSICUM, MOZARELLA AND ROCKET ROLLS

FIERY RED CAPSICUM PURÉE

GRILLED CAPSICUM MOSAIC SALAD

GRILLING CAPSICUMS (PEPPERS) BRINGS OUT THEIR MOST SUPREME FLAVOUR and gives them a sensuous texture to boot. These recipes are all done with an oven grill or broiler, but you could also keep the capsicums whole and turn them over a gas or charcoal barbecue until blackened all over for the same effect.

Grilled capsicums three ways

Grilled capsicum mosaic salad

Capsicums of mixed colours are studded with twinkling olives, caperberries and basil. Add cheese if you like – sizzling fried halloumi slices fresh out of the pan, thickly torn shreds of fresh mozzarella, a whole ball of burrata or crumbled feta all work beautifully.

SERVES 2–4 | **PREP** 20 MINS | **COOK** 20 MINS + COOLING

LOW CALORIE | GLUTEN FREE | DAIRY FREE | VEGAN

2 red capsicums (peppers), halved and deseeded

1 yellow capsicum (pepper), halved and deseeded

1 orange capsicum (pepper), halved and deseeded

handful of oil-cured black olives

handful of pickled caperberries or 1 tablespoon capers in vinegar

8 basil leaves

2 teaspoons best balsamic vinegar

1 tablespoon extra virgin olive oil

sea salt and freshly ground black pepper

SPECIAL EQUIPMENT
Large baking tray, non-stick foil or baking paper, and a large plastic bag (or bowl and plastic wrap) for sweating capsicum.

1 Heat the grill or broiler to high. Place the capsicums cut-side down on a lined baking tray. Grill until blackened all over. (This will take about 20 minutes, but depends on the strength of your grill.)

2 Remove the blackened capsicums from the tray with tongs, place them in a plastic bag and seal (alternatively place in a bowl and cover with plastic wrap). Leave until cool. Peel the papery skin off the capsicums.

3 Cut each capsicum half into four long strips. Arrange in one layer on a flat serving plate.

4 Arrange the olives and caperberries (or capers) on top. Tear over the basil leaves, and drizzle over the balsamic and oil. Finish with a little sea salt and pepper and serve.

Fiery red capsicum purée

Use this as a sauce for pasta, grains or potatoes, or as a dip for chips or crudités. Or think of it as a spicy ketchup (they have a similar consistency) and use it as a condiment to spice up a toasted cheese sandwich, Welsh rarebit, egg on toast, a veggie burger or barbecue fare. It will keep refrigerated for 3 days.

SERVES 4–6 | **PREP** 20 MINS | **COOK** 20 MINS + COOLING

LOW CALORIE | GLUTEN FREE | DAIRY FREE | VEGAN

4 red capsicums (peppers) (approx. 800–900 g/1 lb 12 oz–2 lb), halved and deseeded

1–2 large fleshy red chillies, halved and deseeded

1 garlic clove, crushed

2 teaspoons sushi or rice vinegar

sea salt

SPECIAL EQUIPMENT
Large baking tray, non-stick foil or baking paper, a large plastic bag (or bowl and plastic wrap) for sweating capsicum and a food processor.

pictured page 256

1   Heat the grill or broiler to high. Place the capsicums cut-side down on a lined baking tray. Grill until blackened all over. (This will take about 20 minutes, but depends on the strength of your grill.) When the capsicums are close to being done, place the chillies cut-side down on the tray with them (for the last 5 minutes or so).

2   Remove the blackened capsicums and chillies from the tray with tongs, place them in a plastic bag and seal (alternatively place in a bowl and cover with plastic wrap). Leave until cool. Peel the papery skin off the capsicums.

3   After peeling the capsicums, if the skin of the chillies is loose, peel them too, though this isn't strictly necessary (wearing gloves is advisable if you do).

4   Place the capsicums and chillies in a food processor with the remaining ingredients, along with any grilled capsicum juices. Whizz until completely smooth and taste for seasoning.

Grilled capsicum, mozzarella and rocket rolls

Precious little red, white and green parcels that make a lovely dinner party starter.

SERVES 4 | **PREP** 25 MINS | **COOK** 20 MINS + COOLING

FEAST DISH | GLUTEN FREE

2 red capsicums (peppers), halved and deseeded

sea salt and freshly ground black pepper

250 g (9 oz) fresh buffalo or cow's milk mozzarella ball

handful of baby rocket (arugula) leaves (about 30 g/1 oz)

best balsamic vinegar or balsamic glaze or pomegranate molasses, to finish

SPECIAL EQUIPMENT
Large baking tray, non-stick foil or baking paper and a large plastic bag (or bowl and plastic wrap) for sweating capsicum.

pictured page 256

1   Heat the grill or broiler to high. Place the capsicums cut-side down on a lined baking tray. Grill until blackened all over. (This will take about 20 minutes, but depends on the strength of your grill.)

2   Remove the blackened capsicums from the tray with tongs, place them in a plastic bag and seal (alternatively place in a bowl and cover with plastic wrap). Leave until cool. Peel the papery skin off the capsicums.

3   Cut each capsicum half in two, stem end to base. Lay peeled-side down on a chopping board. Season with salt.

4   Drain the mozzarella and pat dry. Tear into eight equal longish pieces, starting by tearing in half, then in half again, etc. Take a pinch of rocket leaves and place across the narrow end of a capsicum strip, sticking out over the edges. Top with one piece of cheese, then roll up to the top end of the capsicum strip, so that the capsicum is snugly wrapped around them both. Place the capsicum rolls seam-side down as you go on a serving plate or individual plates.

5   Season each roll with a little more sea salt and a few twists of pepper. Use a teaspoon to fling a light splatter of balsamic over them, then serve.

CAPSCIUM (PEPPER) HALVES ACT LIKE MINIATURE EDIBLE ROASTING DISHES, infusing their stuffing contents with their delectable juices. One of the best fillings is simply to tuck in fresh tomato wedges, garlic slices and basil, perhaps a few olives and capers if desired, and a glug of fine olive oil. Here's a variation on that theme, incorporating protein-packed lentils to soak up the nectar. Stock your cupboard with packets of ready-to-eat lentils – Puy, green, brown or black – a great modern invention for speed and convenience.

Double tomato and lentil-stuffed capsicums

SERVES 2 AS A MAIN, 4 AS A SIDE | **PREP** 20 MINS | **COOK** 35 MINS

FEAST DISH | GOOD SOURCE OF PROTEIN | GLUTEN FREE | DAIRY FREE | VEGAN

2 large round red, yellow or orange capsicums (peppers) (or mixed colours)

200 g (7 oz) cooked Puy, green, brown or black lentils

2 garlic cloves, sliced

2 sundried tomatoes in oil, roughly chopped

8 basil leaves, torn

sea salt and freshly ground black pepper

4 tablespoons extra virgin olive oil

4 teaspoons balsamic vinegar

10–12 cherry tomatoes, halved, or 2 roma (plum) or vine tomatoes, sliced 5 mm (1/4 inch) thick

OPTIONS
Serve with crusty bread, wholewheat couscous or other cooked grains or with a pan-fried slab of *Salt-Baked Celeriac* (page 44) as a base.

SPECIAL EQUIPMENT
Baking dish

1   Preheat the oven to 200°C (400°F). Cut the capsicums in half from stem to base, cutting right through the stem, leaving it attached. Carve out the seeds and membranes and discard. Lay the capsicum halves cut-side up in a baking dish.

2   Place the cooked lentils in a bowl. Add the garlic, sundried tomatoes, 4 leaves of torn basil, salt, pepper, 2 tablespoons of the oil and 2 teaspoons of balsamic. Mix very thoroughly, then divide the mixture amongst the capsicum halves, filling them equally. Gently press the surface to compact the filling.

3   Place the cherry tomato halves or tomato slices over the lentils to cover as much as possible. Top with another torn basil leaf, 1/2 tablespoon of oil each and 1/2 teaspoon balsamic, and season with salt and pepper. Arrange the capsicums so they sit as level as possible to keep the juices in while baking – it might help to nestle them together.

4   Bake for 30–35 minutes, until the capsicums are very soft and sizzling. Serve hot, warm or at room temperature, with any pan juices poured over.

NOTE
These are fab for feeding a crowd. The recipe can be easily multiplied, and they look lovely en masse on a serving platter. They also keep well, cooled and refrigerated, for up to 3 days.

Tomato

... ripe, juicy tomatoes plucked straight from the vine, still warm from the sun's rays, are one of the plant world's most delectable summer offerings – but they are fragile creatures.

Tomato

The noble tomato's universal popularity has led to its demise in quality. We can get tomatoes everywhere any day of the year, but they are often tasteless bullets. Ripe, juicy tomatoes plucked straight from the vine, still warm from the sun's rays, are one of the plant world's most delectable summer offerings – but they are fragile creatures. They won't survive the trip to market – especially travelling hundreds of miles. The solution for the commercial farmer is to harvest them unripe, at the 'mature green' stage, while they are still hard and can be stacked in piles and crates without crushing. They will turn red eventually, but they don't gain any more flavour. In fact, commercial tomatoes are usually speed-'ripened' by being gassed with ethylene in warehouses to change their colour. While harmless, it's mostly cosmetic and the flavour never catches up. See opposite for tips on finding and choosing good tomatoes. Or grow your own. A warning to the uninitiated: the flavour of homegrown tomatoes will spoil you, and you might never enjoy a commercial one again.

Green tomatoes are rare to find for sale, but are in abundance for the gardener, and they are fantastic for cooking. They are an entity unto themselves (see cooking suggestions, page 266). The commercial bullets mentioned above can actually be substituted for green tomatoes, though their flavour is not as good.

THE NUTRITIONAL SUPERPOWER

High concentration of lycopene, a potent antioxidant that blocks UV damage and supports bone health. Cooking tomatoes, especially in olive oil, makes lycopene more available to the body; even highly processed tomato products such as ketchup are a source of the lycopene health boost.

OTHER HIGH LEVELS OF NUTRITIONAL EXCELLENCE

- Zeaxanthin, for eye health.
- Multiple phytonutrients, which support heart health, including vitamin A/beta-carotene.
- Vitamin C, for healthy tissues and immunity.
- Potassium, for heart and kidney health.

SEASON

Summer to autumn.

VARIETIES

There are too many varieties and variations in region and availability to specify here. In general, they can be categorised by size, as cherry tomatoes (some as small as peas), medium size, and giant specimens up to the size of a grapefruit. Size does not reflect their flavour profile, but how and where they are grown does. You will generally get a better tomato if you go on a mission to seek them out from a veg specialist, gourmet market or farmers' market where they stock lots of shapes and colours or buy them in season. Some imported tomatoes from warmer climes may be available earlier or later in the year and I'm not ruling them out. If they have actually ripened in the sun of their home country rather than a greenhouse, they will taste better. (See also about commercial harvesting, opposite.)

CHOOSE AND STORE

Tomatoes in packets labelled 'vine ripened' are probably still cut unripe from the mother plant, but I find they are generally better than the commonest loose ones. I judge the quality and ripeness of tomatoes by smell: good tomatoes have a unique perfume – somewhere between herbal and yeasty – it's just plain tomatoey! Sniff the stem end and rate the fragrance. Nothing? Keep looking. A whiff? Probably fine, or just OK. Potent? Yay, you are probably in luck! Once you have chosen a good variety, if you can, then give them a squeeze – they should be firm but not hard, and finally inspect to make sure they are free of mould, cuts or bruises.

As for storage, do not, I repeat DO NOT store tomatoes in the fridge – they absolutely hate it. Their flesh will turn woolly and they will lose flavour fast. If you have to store a partially cut tomato in the fridge, best use it for cooking afterwards. As soon as you get your tomatoes home, remove any packaging and store exposed to the open air at room temperature, and eat them ASAP.

PROCESSED AND PRESERVED

Processed tomatoes are a godsend. Usually they are produced in a country with a good climate for growing lots of good proper tomatoes – in the UK they are usually from Italy. Tinned whole plum tomatoes in juice are tops. Tinned chopped tomatoes have an additive to keep them firm, so they are less desirable and often watery. Passata (puréed tomatoes) and tomato paste (concentrated purée) are essential cupboard items, as are sundried tomatoes in oil. 'Sunblush' tomatoes or semi-dried are delicious – they can be found chilled at deli counters.

PREP

- Remove any stems and the calyx clinging to the fruit (green and star-shaped when fresh, dark and disconcertingly spider-impersonating when dry). Some larger tomatoes will have a tough, tasteless patch underneath where the calyx was attached – if the calyx is hard to pull off, this is probably the case. You can either dig this bit out with a small knife, or cut the tomato in half through the stem end and pare it away along with the scar left by the calyx.

- Before cutting as required, a freshly sharpened knife is paramount when tackling a tomato. Their skins are like a balloon, thin but tough enough to hold in all that juicy flesh. A sharp knife helps to avoid squashing it and sacrificing the flavourful juice all over the chopping board rather than in your food. (A common test for a knife's sharpness is 'The Tomato Test' – a well-sharpened chef's knife will glide through a tomato skin with no applied pressure.) A serrated knife is a last resort for cutting a tomato.

Tomato's best mates

Salt | Basil, oregano, parsley, dill, coriander (cilantro) | Balsamic vinegar, wine vinegar, sushi vinegar | Olive oil | Black pepper | Garlic | Onions | Ginger | Bread | Chilli | Honey | Most cheeses

Cook and eat

Perfect tomato salad

Keep it simple and classic, especially if you have really good or unusual tomatoes. Mix colours and sizes if possible. Slice or cut in wedges (halve cherry tomatoes) and spread over a plate. Drizzle with a little balsamic (optional), some good olive oil and season generously with sea salt and pepper. Tear over some fresh basil leaves. Serve with excellent fresh bread.

Tomatoes and bread

When my homegrown tomatoes are gushing off the vine in late summer, I often rely on this heavenly marriage for a quick meal, usually in a classic Mediterranean style. My favourites are *Pan amb tomàquet* from Catalunya, *Dakos* from Crete, *Panzanella* and the Tuscan *Pappa al pomodoro*. Look them up if you aren't familiar!

Slow-roasted tomatoes

A simple way to glorify good tomatoes, and to make less good tomatoes tastier, by concentrating their natural flavours within their skins. Cut in half and lay cut-side up on a lined baking tray. Tuck a few slices of garlic right into the juicy bits of each, drizzle with olive oil and a few drops of balsamic vinegar, and season with salt and pepper. Add a pinch of brown sugar or a few drops of honey to each if you wish. Roast in the oven at 150°C (300°F) for 1–2 hours (depending on which tomatoes and how many) until shrunken, golden at the edges and brimming with juice.

Green tomatoes

Unripe tomatoes are hard, less juicy and tart, but they have their place. Pan-fry thick slices in olive oil with salt for a fab side dish – great for breakfast. For classic fried green tomatoes, cut thick slices and dredge in seasoned flour, then beaten egg, then coarse polenta or breadcrumbs and pan-fry in olive oil until deep golden.

THIS MAKES A FUN ALTERNATIVE breakfast or brunch dish to serve with poached or fried eggs. It's super easy and filling as a weeknight supper too – on its own or supplemented with some sliced avocado or simply cooked veg and a protein element such as cheese, beans or eggs. It can also be multiplied to feed a crowd, featuring as the carb factor in a spread of salads and bean dishes.

Cooking the polenta in almond milk is a revelation. See also the *Glazed Fennel Polenta with Secret Baked Ricotta* on page 53.

Honey-roast tomato polenta

SERVES 4–6 | **PREP** 30 MINS | **COOK** 30 MINS

GLUTEN FREE | DAIRY FREE | VEGAN (IF MAPLE SYRUP IS USED)

1 litre (35 fl oz/4 cups) almond milk (natural unsweetened)

1 teaspoon cooking salt

250 g (9 oz) quick-cook polenta

500 g (1 lb 2 oz) cherry tomatoes

4 garlic cloves, sliced

1/2 teaspoon chilli flakes

2 teaspoons runny honey or maple syrup

1 rosemary sprig, leaves stripped, roughly chopped

1 tablespoon extra virgin olive oil

sea salt

OPTIONS
Add crumbled feta or goat's cheese for extra protein; add on top for the last 15 minutes of baking.

Substitute soy milk, cow's milk or another nut milk if almond milk is not available, though you may find it tastes bland; stir in butter and/or grated Parmesan at the end of cooking the polenta to enhance the flavour.

Serve with eggs, avocados, salad, steamed asparagus, wilted greens or a bean dish.

SPECIAL EQUIPMENT
Baking dish approx. 20 x 30 cm (8 x 12 inches) or an oval dish.

1   Preheat the oven to 220°C (425°F). Place the almond milk in a large saucepan with the cooking salt and bring to the boil. Brush the baking dish with oil.

2   Once the almond milk has come to the boil, reduce to a simmer. Pour in the polenta in a slow and steady stream, stirring constantly. It will soon start erupting like lava; keep stirring a little longer until it is very thick, then remove from the heat. Transfer it immediately into the baking dish and spread it out to meet the edges of the dish, smoothing the surface.

3   Place the tomatoes in a bowl and mix through the garlic, chilli flakes, honey, rosemary and oil and season well with sea salt. Pour the mixture on top of the polenta, making sure you scrape out every last drop from the bowl. Spread the tomatoes out evenly over the surface.

4   Bake for about 25–30 minutes, until the tomatoes are lightly browned and burst and the whole dish is thoroughly sizzling. Remove from the oven and cool for a few minutes before cutting into squares and serving hot.

I CAME UP WITH THIS FUSS-FREE RECIPE IN AN EMERGENCY SITUATION when the number of dinner guests suddenly doubled at the last minute – and a heap of fresh tomatoes and a few kitchen staples (including a packet of pre-cooked wholegrain rice) saved the day. It's a one-dish saucy pilaf, which makes a rustic meal in itself – sauce, plants, carbs, protein: it's all in there. I've been making variations on this theme ever since, whacking in different grains and beans, sometimes adding olives or capers with the feta. Feta is all too often thought of as a cold salad cheese; roasting it creates a delectable chewy crust giving way to soft creaminess.

Tomato and feta grain roast

SERVES 4 AS A MAIN, 8 AS A SIDE | **PREP** 20 MIN | **COOK** 50 MINS

GOOD SOURCE OF PROTEIN | GLUTEN FREE (IF GLUTEN-FREE GRAINS ARE USED)

800 g (1 lb 12 oz) ripe tomatoes (about 9 medium), quartered or cut into chunks if very large

3 garlic cloves, sliced

1 tablespoon best balsamic vinegar

2 teaspoons runny honey or maple syrup

4 thyme sprigs

4 small rosemary sprigs

4 tablespoons extra virgin olive oil

sea salt and freshly ground black pepper

250 g (9 oz) cooked grains such as quinoa (pictured), wholegrain rice or spelt

400 g (14 oz) tin chickpeas, drained

200 g (7 oz) block feta cheese, drained

OPTIONS
Add good olives or capers with the feta if desired.

Serve with a green salad.

SPECIAL EQUIPMENT
Deep casserole dish approx. 20 x 30 cm (8 x 12 inches)

1   Preheat the oven to 220°C (425°F). Place the tomatoes, garlic, balsamic, honey, herbs and 2 tablespoons of the oil in a casserole dish and season well with salt and pepper. Stir to combine and spread out in an even layer. Place in the middle of the oven and roast for about 30 minutes, until the tomatoes have softened and simmering juices are pooling in the bottom of the dish.

2   Remove from the oven and stir the cooked grains and drained chickpeas into the tomatoes, gently and thoroughly, until evenly mixed. Now take the feta and break it over the surface in several large chunks and crumbles. Pour the remaining 2 tablespoons of oil all over, coating the cheese.

3   Move an oven rack towards the top of the oven. Place the dish on it and roast for a further 15–20 minutes, until the feta shows patches of golden crust.

4   Serve hot at the table, spooned into shallow bowls.

THIS FRESH AND ZINGY BROTH/SOUP was one of the first things I was ever shown how to cook by my original mentor (more on that in a minute). I think this is one of the greatest things you can do with fresh tomatoes ever, and I've never read, tasted or seen anything like it. I'm really keen to share the love here, so I'm calling it a tonic to attract your attention, but also to define it more precisely. It is not just another tomato soup – it is a pure and invigorating liquid food that really makes you feel good when you consume it, ideally sipping it hot from a mug or teacup. This is a perfect low-labour recipe for using a glut of homegrown tomatoes. If it's a hot summer day, you can have this chilled, or even turn it into a sorbet (see NOTE).

My original mentor was artist Christiane Kubrick, wife of Stanley Kubrick, without whom I would not have had a career in food. When she saw how enthusiastically I reacted to her showing me techniques such as this simple kitchen magic, she very generously allowed me to play around in her kitchen for a few years learning and experimenting as their private chef, cooking for her friends, family and quite a number of visitors from Hollywood.

Tomato and ginger tonic

SERVES 4–6 (MAKES ABOUT 1 LITRE/35 FL OZ) | **PREP** 10 MINS | **COOK** 35 MINS

LOW CALORIE | GLUTEN FREE | DAIRY FREE | VEGAN (IF MAPLE SYRUP IS USED)

1 kg (2 lb 4 oz) ripe tomatoes

5 cm (2 inch) piece fresh ginger, peeled and roughly chopped

4 fat garlic cloves, peeled and roughly chopped

2 teaspoons maple syrup or honey

1 teaspoon sea salt

OPTIONS
Enjoy as a comforting snack or serve as a palate cleanser between courses.

SPECIAL EQUIPMENT
Hand blender, sieve and ladle.

1   Place everything in a lidded pot with 200 ml (7 fl oz) water. Cover, bring to the boil, then turn down the heat to a simmer.

2   Cook for about 30 minutes, stirring occasionally and poking the tomatoes from time to time to help break them down. After about 10 minutes, the tomatoes' skins should have burst. By the end of cooking, the tomatoes should have collapsed completely.

3   Remove from the heat and allow to cool for a bit, then purée with a hand blender. (Alternatively, allow to cool nearly to room temperature, then purée in a blender or food processor.)

4   Place a sieve over a large bowl or jug. Pour or ladle the soup into it in parts, rubbing it through with the ladle.

5   Taste for seasoning. You may want to add a touch more salt, or syrup or honey if the tomatoes were not very sweet to begin with. The ginger zing should be assertive.

6   Reheat the soup and serve in mugs, tea cups, espresso cups or heatproof glasses. Alternatively, cool to room temperature and chill, to serve as a cold soup or to make sorbet (see NOTE).

NOTE
To convert this into a savoury sorbet, chill the soup well and put it in an ice cream maker, following the manufacturer's instructions.

If you don't have an ice cream maker, you can make a granita, which has a delicate crystalline texture. Pour about 500 ml (17 fl oz/2 cups) of the tonic into a plastic container with a lid, so it forms a shallow pool about 1 cm (1/2 inch) thick. Freeze solid. Take out of the freezer and set a timer for 15 minutes (in a cool kitchen, less if it's very warm), then start breaking up the ice crystals with a fork around the edges as much as you can. Wait another 15 minutes, fork again, then another, etc., until it's all broken down into tiny ice crystals. Freeze again until serving.

Index

Acknowledgments

Massive thanks to my recipe test team for being so diligent and generous with your time and efforts: Courtney Arnstein, Ali Bainbridge, Elaine Bancroft, Kimberley Banner, Cheryl Cohen, Julia Dunlop, Lauren Fabian, Cherie Harlow, Whitney Hildebrandt, Jane Jacobsen Townsend, Geeta Khashav Lloyd, Martin Ledigo, Danielle Lux, Nina Malyshev, Jess Marvel, Alex McLester, Caroline Munro, Joanne Panteloukas, Shaheen Safdar Sutton, Fay Schopen, Blanca Valencia and Sarah Wood.

Justin, taster-in-chief, soulmate, and source of so much Joy and Power in my life, thank you, and boundless love always.

Heartfelt thanks to the Childwickbury guinea pigs for your ebullient appetites and dutiful tasting of my recipes in progress, and for your invaluable love and support: Christiane, Tracy, Paula, Jane, Jan, Alex, Joe, Jack, Polly, Camilla, Penny, Tony, Jonathan, and Sam.

Thanks to chef Luke Hawkins for the salt-baked celeriac inspiration and coaching.

Thank you Alli Godbold for your hard work casting my text through your expert nutritionist prism and helping me make it solid.

Infinite thanks to Lindy Wiffen at Ceramica Blue, 10 Blenheim Crescent, Notting Hill, London W11 1NN, for the loan of the incredible dishes and props that bring such beauty and style to the photographs.

Thanks to the following for supplying the most gorgeous vegetables imaginable: Ben's Fruit & Veg in Westbourne Park, Elsey & Bent at Borough Market, and Turnips at Borough Market.

To my diamond-studded photo/styling team: thank you to the moon and back. Photographer Jean Cazals, you are a magician. Marie-Ange Lapierre, thank you for your expertise and patience in the kitchen, and Penelope Parker, thanks for choosing and materialising so many amazing props and toys for the shoot.

Thank you Kay Halsey Delves for lending your generous support, talent and meticulousness.

Vivien Valk, I am so fortunate to have had your talents enriching this volume. Thank you so much. Katie Bosher and the Murdoch team, I'm immensely grateful for your dedication and enthusiasm. Thanks all!

Diana Hill, you steered me on my path and made this happen. Thanks for championing *SuperVeg* and fighting my corner. I'm eternally grateful and I simply can't thank you enough. You are absolutely wonderful!

Celia Brooks moved to London from Colorado in 1989 and forged a career as a chef, food writer and businesswoman. Starting as a private chef for film director Stanley Kubrick, she moved on to TV presenting, consulting and writing about food for several UK publications. In 2002 Celia founded her highly successful food tour business, 'Gastrotours'. When not working on her next book, she spends most of her time creating and conducting unique food experiences in London, in particular around Borough Market – she is the only person licensed by the market to run tours. *SuperVeg* is her ninth cookbook. See more at celiabrooks.com

Published in 2018 by Murdoch Books, an imprint of Allen & Unwin

Murdoch Books Australia
83 Alexander Street
Crows Nest NSW 2065
Phone: +61 (0) 2 8425 0100
Fax: +61 (0) 2 9906 2218
murdochbooks.com.au
info@murdochbooks.com.au

Murdoch Books UK
Ormond House
26–27 Boswell Street
London WC1N 3JZ
Phone: +44 (0) 20 8785 5995
murdochbooks.co.uk
info@murdochbooks.co.uk

For Corporate Orders & Custom Publishing, contact our Business Development Team at
salesenquiries@murdochbooks.com.au.

Publisher: Diana Hill
Editorial Manager: Katie Bosher
Design: Vivien Valk
Project Editor: Kay Halsey
Photographer: Jean Cazals
Props Stylist: Penelope Parker
Home Economist and Food Stylist: Marie-Ange Lapierre
Production Manager: Lou Playfair

A cataloguing-in-publication entry is available from the catalogue of the National
Library of Australia at nla.gov.au.

ISBN 978 1 76052 268 1 Australia
ISBN 978 1 76052 770 9 UK

A catalogue record for this book is available from the British Library.

Colour reproduction by Splitting Image Colour Studio Pty Ltd, Clayton, Victoria
Printed by Hang Tai Printing Company Limited, China

IMPORTANT: Those who might be at risk from the effects of salmonella poisoning (the
elderly, pregnant women, young children and those suffering from immune deficiency
diseases) should consult their doctor with any concerns about eating raw eggs.

OVEN GUIDE: You may find cooking times vary depending on the oven you are using.
For fan-forced ovens, as a general rule, set the oven temperature to 20°C (70°F) lower
than indicated in the recipe.

MEASURES GUIDE: We have used 20 ml (4 teaspoon) tablespoon measures. If you are
using a 15 ml (3 teaspoon) tablespoon add an extra teaspoon of the ingredient for each
tablespoon specified.